The Sunday Telegraph

A–Z GUIDE TO
FAMILY FINANCE

Niki Chesworth has many years' experience writing about personal finance for the national press as well as contributing to magazines, television and radio programmes. She writes regularly for a number of national newspapers including the *Daily Telegraph* and *Sunday Telegraph* and is the author of more than a dozen books including *The Young Professional's Guide to Personal Finance* and *Your First Home* in the *Telegraph* Lifeplanner series.

The Sunday Telegraph

A–Z GUIDE TO
FAMILY FINANCE

NIKI CHESWORTH

PAN BOOKS

First published 2001 by Macmillan
This edition published 2013 by Pan Books
an imprint of Pan Macmillan, a division of Macmillan Publishers Limited
Pan Macmillan, 20 New Wharf Road, London N1 9RR
Basingstoke and Oxford
Associated companies throughout the world
www.panmacmillan.com

ISBN 978-1-4472-6159-9

A CIP catalogue record for this book is available from
the British Library.

Typeset by SetSystems Ltd, Saffron Walden, Essex
Printed and bound by CPI Group (UK) Ltd, Croydon, CR0 4YY

To Katerina
for her perfect timing
and Guy
for his patience

Contents

Acknowledgements

My thanks go to Tessa Kendall, who helped to research this guide, and Liz Dolan, personal finance editor of the *Sunday Telegraph*, for ensuring the accuracy of its content.

My thanks also goes to Damien Reece, who, when deputy personal finance editor of the *Sunday Telegraph*, wrote the first edition of this book. Without his excellent groundwork and in-depth research, this edition would have been far harder to compile.

Introduction

I was amazed how much has changed in the world of family finance since the first edition of this book was written just four years ago. Some products no longer exist, new schemes have been introduced, tax laws have changed and so has the economic and regulatory environment, which in turn affects what personal finance products we are sold and how we are sold them.

No wonder one aspect of family finances has remained little changed – lack of consumer understanding. Most of us want to make the most of our money and are aware of what we need to do, but simply don't know how to start, where to go and who to trust. Even if we do manage to master an aspect of finance, as soon as we do the rules seem to change. Jargon, small print, acronyms and lack of consumer education also play their part in making the world of money seem confusing and often impenetrable.

This guide explains the complex terms used by the financial industry so that lack of understanding need not be a barrier to making the most of your money. Written in plain English it covers all aspects of family finance from the simplest savings schemes and insurance products to government bonds and financial futures and options.

A

ACCIDENT INSURANCE

It may be a cliché but accidents *do* happen and when they do they can have a major impact on your finances. As with most disasters that could affect your pocket, you can insure yourself against a serious injury caused by an accident. The cash can then be used to help finance specialist equipment, such as a stair lift, or specialist care, or even tide you over until you can work again.

Accident insurance pays out a lump sum in certain circumstances, for example, if you break a bone or have to have your leg amputated. It will not cover you against: injuries sustained at work which should be covered under your employers' policy; long-term sickness such as a bad back which can be covered by permanent health insurance, or against a serious life-threatening illness which can be covered by critical illness cover.

It sounds a bit ghoulish, but you need to know how severe an injury you need to suffer before the policy pays out. Some policies will pay out for a broken bone, others require permanent disability.

Policies pay out different amounts for different injuries, but as a rough guide you could get £1,000 for a broken leg, £2,000 for a broken hip or pelvis or £1,000 for a broken arm or collarbone. Losing a finger could pay £10,000, losing an eye £50,000 and total disablement £100,000. Some companies will also pay out double if the injury is as a result of being assaulted and will also pay out a bigger lump sum for accidental death. Accident insurance is generally a low-cost form of insurance and there are several ways to buy it – either as an add-on to another insurance policy such as a sickness or unemployment policy or as a stand-alone policy. As a stand-alone policy it will cost in the region of £100 a year.

If you have credit or a loan you may be offered payment protection insurance which will pay out sufficient money to cover your monthly repayments and usually includes protection against accident, sickness and unemployment (ASU). In some cases, you may be able to get it free; for example, some gold and platinum credit cards have travel accident insurance as a free perk. So you may already have some accident cover without realizing it.

It is automatically included in most travel insurance policies although you should check exactly how much you are covered for, what injuries are included and which are excluded.

However, not all companies will cover you automatically for sports-related injuries although you can purchase separate sports insurance policies.

There's no need to have a medical check-up before taking out accident insurance as you're not being covered against a future illness or other medical condition. There will be exclusions though such as winter sports, or injuries caused by existing medical conditions, for example, osteoporosis.

Men are much more likely than women to have an accident – 651,000 men under sixty-five have an accident at home every year which needs hospital treatment, most commonly because of a fall.

Children are also vulnerable. Some 2,500,000 are taken to hospital each year after an accident and of those 10,000 will be permanently disabled. Check that the policy covers them for all kinds of sport and physical activity, both in and out of school. Policies pay out a lump sum if the child is disabled in an accident and should also cover the cost of dental treatment if teeth are damaged. The cost for one child should be around £30 a year. Schools may be able to advise on policies available for children travelling on school trips.

If you want advice on accident cover contact a local insurance broker, who should be a member of the British Insurance and Investment Brokers' Association (for details see the **Useful Addresses** section).

(See also **Critical Illness Cover**, **Holiday Insurance**, **Payment Protection Insurance**, **Permanent Health Insurance** and **Sports Insurance**.)

ACTIVE MANAGEMENT

This means that the fund manager of an investment fund – usually a unit trust – actively (rather than passively) manages the investments in that fund. Tracker funds, which aim to track or follow the rises and falls in a particular stock-market index such as the FTSE 100, are passively managed in the sense that a computer model picks the shares so that the portfolio can mirror the performance of the index. As a result shares only need to be bought and sold if the composition of that index changes.

Active fund management, on the other hand, involves stock selection with the aim of beating or out-performing an index or a peer group of similar funds. Shares tend to be traded more frequently with the aim of boosting performance, but this can also lead to increased costs.

There has been an ongoing debate among fund management companies as to whether active or passive fund management is best, particularly as many active fund managers fail to match, let alone beat, the overall performance of the stock market or their particular stock-market sector. As a general rule, active trusts have a much greater range of returns than passive trusts. Passive trusts, however, tend to produce slightly below index performance due to costs. Even so, passive trusts generally have far lower charges than actively managed funds. Actively managed funds have initial charges of around 5 per cent and annual charges of between 0.75 and 1.5 per cent compared to initial charges of 1 per cent or less for many passively managed funds with annual management charges of 0.5 per cent or less.

In any five-year annualized period, investors in an active trust have around a one in four chance of out-performing a tracker according to the WM Company. These figures take management charges into account but not the bid-offer spread (the difference between the buying and selling price of units in a fund). So opting for an actively managed fund is riskier than opting for a tracker fund – the investor could make significantly higher returns in the right actively managed fund, but there are no guarantees.

(See also **Tracker Funds** and **Unit Trusts**.)

ACTUARIES

Considering they are the financial world's equivalent of a bookmaker, actuaries get a poor press for being boring people doing one of the world's most boring jobs.

Although most investors never need the services of an actuary, the work they do behind the scenes is vital. Actuaries basically make financial sense of the future. They are skilled mathematicians who analyse past events, assess present risks and model what could happen in the future.

So, for example, an actuary may be required to look at life expectancy so that the risks of a policyholder making a claim on a life insurance policy can be assessed and therefore the premiums calculated. They are basically calculating the odds against something occurring, just like a bookmaker.

They are also employed by pension funds to assess future funding requirements of the fund and under the Pensions Act 1995 trustees of a pension scheme have a statutory requirement to appoint an actuary. Actuaries are also increasingly involved in wider areas of finance such as corporate finance, asset management and major capital projects, as well as in helping to design new forms of insurance such as mortgage payment protection policies and permanent health insurance.

Private investors may need the services of a consultant actuary if they are planning to leave an employer's or occupational pension scheme and want an independent and qualified expert to assess whether or not they could be better off leaving their pension behind in the occupational scheme (where it will continue to grow) or transferring it to a new company scheme or personal pension.

Although some financial advisers are specialists in pensions, the pensions mis-selling scandal in which more than a million members of company schemes were misled into moving to personal pensions has left many investors concerned that the advice they are being given is driven by the desire of the adviser to earn commission. Actuaries work on a fee basis, and therefore have no incentive to recommend that a scheme member transfers a pension entitlement built up in an occupational scheme into a personal pension.

Often when larger companies make staff redundant, they offer them the services of a consultant actuary to help in making the decision as to what to do with monies invested in the company scheme.

To find an actuary if you have left your employer's scheme and want advice as to what to do with your pension fund, ask the trustees of your existing scheme if they can recommend an actuary (this will probably be the firm of actuaries appointed to advise the trustees). If you are being made redundant, your employer may even offer the services of a consultant actuary at no cost. Alternatively contact the Institute of Actuaries or the Association of Consulting Actuaries (see **Useful Addresses**) for details of members. If you employ an actuary yourself, you will usually pay an hourly fee of around £125 to £200. Although this may seem expensive, the potential losses from failing to make the right decision can cost you thousands of pounds. An alternative is to use a financial adviser that specializes in pensions.

(See also **Occupational Pension Schemes**.)

ADDITIONAL VOLUNTARY CONTRIBUTIONS (AVCs)

Additional voluntary contributions are top-up pension plans linked to occupational (company) pension schemes. All pension schemes must give members the opportunity to improve the benefits they receive at retirement by making additional contributions. However, scheme members do not have to opt for a top-up plan from their employers' scheme – they can shop around and buy a private policy from a life insurance company. These are known as free-standing AVCs or FSAVCs. The charges for FSAVCs tend to be higher than for AVCs as when an employer runs a scheme it tends to meet the administration costs. Also employees do not incur the costs of advice with an AVC. Often all of the first six months' or year's contributions into an FSAVC can be eaten up in costs with much of this being paid in commission to the salesperson or adviser.

In some cases employers will add extra cash to contributions that individuals put into their AVC making AVCs even better value. Often any enhanced employer contribution will not apply to an FSAVC.

The main incidents where an FSAVC may offer a better option is if the employee plans to move jobs or wishes to take their pension at an early age. With an AVC the benefits are only paid out when the scheme member retires and takes his or her company pension. With a FSAVC, on the other hand, payments can start at a different time to when the main scheme pays out. Another drawback is that contributions built up in an AVC scheme cannot be transferred to a new pension scheme. As average employees have seven jobs in their working lives, they may have to leave behind contributions in an AVC even though they can transfer money built up in the main scheme to their new employer's scheme or a personal pension. As an FSAVC is free-standing employees can continue to pay into that scheme and have no transfer problems.

(See also **Free-standing AVCs**.)

NOTE: although scheme members can take up to 25 per cent of their pension fund as a tax-free lump sum upon retirement, this does not apply to AVCs or FSAVCs. All the monies in the fund must be used to provide an income in retirement and none of the money can be taken as a tax-free lump sum.

The same tax relief rules apply to AVCs and FSAVCs as apply to all pension schemes. The scheme member cannot exceed the investment limits set down by the Inland Revenue, which are a maximum of 15 per cent of pensionable earnings, and tax relief (at the time of writing) is given at the top rate on all contributions.

ADVICE/ADVISERS

'Where can I go to get good, sound, independent financial advice I can trust?' is one of the most common questions asked of financial journalists. Despite numerous attempts to clean up the image of the financial services sector, scandal after scandal has left many investors wondering just who they can trust.

Even so, many make the classic mistake of taking advice from whoever offers it – usually their bank or a company that sends them a mailshot – rather than shopping around to find someone they feel will give them impartial advice. They may not even realize that the adviser can sell the products of only one company or only a limited range of products and that there may be better value alternatives available.

With so many sources of advice available – from banks, building societies, insurance companies and their salesmen, financial advisers, solicitors, accountants and even estate agents – finding an adviser is not a problem. Finding the right one is. Ideally you should look for someone with whom you can build an on-going relationship, who will get to know you and understand your needs and goals and who can shop around to get you the best deal.

There are two basic types of financial adviser. Tied agents (also known as direct salesmen or appointed agents) who work for and sell the products of only one insurance or investment company. Most bank staff work on this basis selling the products of only one company, usually the bank's own insurance company.

Independent financial advisers are not linked to any single company and have to shop around a number of companies before recommending a particular product to a client.

The strict definition between the two types of adviser – known as polarization – was introduced in the Financial Services Act, which took effect in 1988. As a result financial advisers were required by law to identify whether or not they worked independently or could recommend only the products of one financial institution. There are plans to dilute the polarization rules that required financial advisers to either be tied or independent and in future there could be a new breed of financial advisers who will be multi-tied – selling the stakeholder pensions and CAT-standard ISAs of a limited range of companies. When advising about regulated investment products such as life insurance policies, pensions and unit trusts, advisers must by law tell clients whether they are independent or tied. Make sure you are clear about the status of your adviser so there is no confusion.

Both types of adviser earn their living in the same way, by earning commission from selling products to clients. However, a few investment and insurance companies do not pay commission (their staff usually do, however, earn bonuses for selling more products) and some independent financial advisers charge a fee and give the client back the commission.

So how do you go about finding a financial adviser?

The first step is to ask those you trust if they can recommend a financial adviser. This could be a relative, friend or colleague. However, don't rely on a recommendation alone. Bear in mind that if friends have been seduced by the silver tongue of a slick salesman, they may not realize they have received poor or inappropriate advice. Some investors believe that because an adviser takes an interest in them and spends a couple of hours talking to them, that they are getting a good service. However, remember the adviser is a salesman and could be earning upwards of £1,000 in commission for just a couple of hours work. You can also contact IFA Promotion (see **Useful Addresses**) for details of independent financial advisers in your area.

It is recommended that you shop around and do not just opt for the first adviser with whom you have contact, so compile a shortlist of advisers (at least three) to interview before deciding which you wish to use.

These are the questions you should ask before making up your mind:

- Are you an independent financial adviser or are you tied to a single insurance company?

- For how long have you been an adviser? For how long have you worked for your present employer/company?

- Do you specialize in certain areas of advice – pensions, investments, life insurance, etc.?

- Are there any products that you do not advise upon? If so, is there someone else in your company/bank/firm of financial advisers who is an expert in these areas?

- What qualifications do you have? All advisers must pass the Financial Planning Certificate exam or its equivalent, but this is only a minimum qualification. The initials MSFA, ACII or FCII signal higher qualifications. Some other initials are less meaningful. Member of the Institute of Financial Planning merely means the adviser has paid a subscription.

- How big is the company you work for? How long has it been in business? A small firm of financial advisers may not be in business in a few years time so you may not be able to build an on-going relationship. However, small can mean a more personal service.

- Will they make money out of commission or will you pay a fee for advice? Do you have a choice? The telephone number of a list of fee-charging IFAs is listed at the back of the book.

Although you may be happy with your choice of adviser, for more complex problems or investments you may want to seek the advice of a specialist such as an accountant for tax issues or an actuary or pensions consultant for pension problems. Consider your financial adviser as a GP from whom you would be happy to receive general advice but would prefer to be treated by a specialist or surgeon for more serious problems.

Once you have picked your adviser, if things then turn

sour – perhaps because of their poor administration or bad advice – there are compensation and complaints procedures to obtain redress. These are covered more fully under the **Financial Services Authority** later in this book.

(See also **Commission, Fee-based Advice** and **Independent Financial Advice**.)

AFFINITY CARDS

Affinity cards, also known as charity or donation cards, are credit cards which donate money to charity when the card is taken out (typical donations are between £5 and £10 when the card is first used) and then make a small donation every time it is used – usually around 25p.

The card can either be linked to one good cause, either a charity such as Comic Relief or even a football team, or the card holder may be able to choose which charity receives the donation. Well over 1,000 affinity groups receive donations in this way.

Although the idea may appeal, bear in mind that the cards tend to charge much higher interest rates than the best value cards. So, those who pay interest on their card balances may find it more efficient to choose a low interest card and donate some of the money saved to charity. However, those who clear their credit card balance in full each month and therefore do not incur any interest, can donate money to a charity of their choice without it costing them a penny.

Affinity cards are promoted by charities and other good causes, although they are managed by credit card issuers. So to take one out you should contact the relevant organization to find out if they have a credit card.

(See also **Charitable Giving**.)

ALL SHARE INDEX

The FTSE Actuaries All Share Index is the broadest measure of the UK stock market and gives investors a picture of how well shares are performing. Despite its name, the index does not include all companies that are listed on the stock market, only those worth more than £67 million.

(See also **Indices**.)

ALTERNATIVE INVESTMENTS

Shares and houses are the most popular investments with the British, but our innate eccentricity means that we find lots of other weird and wonderful things to invest in from race horses and pop memorabilia to vintage wines and theatre productions. These so-called alternative investments tend to go in fashions. Classic cars were very popular until the bottom fell out of that market in the recession of the early 90s when prices plummeted. Ostrich farming then became a bizarre fad, but once again many investors lost money.

There is nothing new in the concept. In the sixteenth century there was a fashion for buying tulip bulbs in Amsterdam that sent the price soaring before it crashed. The golden rule is – if something looks too good to be true it generally is.

Not all alternative investments turn out to be failures. Those who have invested in the best – and most fashionable – modern art have made a killing. However, the general rule is that there are no guarantees. Investors are just as likely to pick a winner as a loser unless they know their markets well, and even then they can lose their shirts.

Many alternative investment schemes are promoted as serious investments with full and complex prospectuses. But there are rarely any safety nets as the plans are not covered by the protective cloak of the Financial Services Act. Therefore, it is worth asking yourself a few general questions before parting with any cash.

- Are the assets you are buying limited in supply?
  A vintage wine, for example, of which there are only a limited number of cases is more likely to hold its value.

- Is ownership expensive because of special insurance requirements or storage and maintenance? Buying part of a greyhound with some friends may seem like a good idea but if it never wins any races it can quickly be a drain on your pocket.

- Can you sell your investment easily to realize any gains?

- Is there a reputable and objective way of valuing the assets? If you are relying on the seller to tell you the value, then you could be paying over-the-odds. Look at any recent auction or sales catalogues to get an idea of an objective price.

- Are there any tax benefits to the investment?

Alternative investments should only be tried once safer, more orthodox investment and savings routes have been exhausted. Investors are also advised to take a keen interest in their investments. In fact, a hobby – such as philately or antique collecting – often turns into an investment.

Enjoyment should also be a big feature of any alternative investment. Theatre angels, for example, who back West End shows often invest not only in the hope that the show will turn out to be the next *Cats*, but also so that they can attend the first night and mix with the stars.

ALTERNATIVE INVESTMENT MARKET (AIM)

The Alternative Investment Market has replaced the now defunct Unlisted Securities Market (USM), which was established by the Stock Exchange in 1980 to attract small and medium-sized companies to seek a stock-market listing. However, in 1990 the Stock Exchange made it easier for companies to gain a main market listing hitting the popularity of the USM.

So in 1993 the Stock Exchange announced that the USM would be closing and it was finally shut at the end of 1996. In the meantime, in June 1995 the Alternative Investment Market was launched as a replacement for the USM, with even less onerous demands. Instead of applying to the exchange for membership, companies are nominated by an adviser, a firm that is supposed to act as a gatekeeper and ensure that the company adheres to the AIM rules.

Companies listed on this 'junior' stock market are considered far more risky than those listed on the Official List or main stock market and there have been some failures. However, the AIM has also attracted smaller, young and growing companies that have or will go on to join the main stock market. The typical AIM fundraising is between £3 million and £5 million.

Investors can buy shares in AIM listed companies through stockbrokers, but they could find that they are less easy to trade as buyers and sellers have to be matched and the shares themselves are far more volatile. Also known as penny shares, investors have the potential to make vast returns – and losses.

ANALYSTS/ANALYSIS

These are employed by stockbroking firms to analyse and thoroughly research all the relevant facts pertaining to a company or market and then pronounce on its future prospects. Stock analysts usually work within a specific sector – banking, for example – and their recommendations are then used to encourage institutional investment clients to buy or sell shares in a particular company. Some analysts do not predict future prospects of a particular company, instead they analyse share price movements and using historical data predict future trends – these are known as technical analysts. Fundamental analysis looks at the major influences on markets such as economic and political policies, liquidity and market structures. Quantative analysis looks at the risk and return profile of a particular investment on a mathematical basis.

Analysts' reports and recommendations are normally only available to institutional investors; however, private investors who use the advisory services of a stockbroker will be given analysts' recommendations. For investors who use execution-only dealing services, and therefore receive no advice, analysts' recommendations are regularly printed in newspapers and are available on many web sites. Simply type 'share dealing' into your search engine and it will list sites that offer stockbroking services. Many of these also list details of analysts' reports under lists of shares to buy or sell. A limited amount of information is usually available free.

ANNUITIES

These are the investment policies purchased on or after retirement, to provide you with an income for the rest of your life. You pay a lump sum from your pension fund to an insurer and in return are promised a set monthly, quarterly or annual income.

Those with personal pension plans and those who are members of money-purchase occupational pension schemes (where the pension is dependent upon how much has been paid into the plan) are required to purchase annuities. The same rules do not apply to those who are members of final salary schemes as their pensions are dependent on pay at or near retirement.

When you retire you can take up to 25 per cent of the pension fund you have built up as a tax-free lump sum to spend or invest as you wish. The rest must be used to buy an annuity, which will pay you an annual income for the rest of your life with this income dependent on a number of factors such as your age, sex, medical history and projected investment returns. Men, for example, receive higher annuities than women as they have a shorter life expectancy and therefore the insurance company who sells the annuity can expect to pay an income out over a fewer number of years.

Heavy smokers or those who have suffered ill-health can also expect to receive a higher income to reflect their lower life expectancy. These are known as impaired life annuities.

However, the biggest factor affecting the level of income is the gilts market as annuities invest in gilt-edged securities with the rate of these dependent on interest rates. In the current low inflation, low interest rate economic environment annuity rates are at an historical low.

Despite the fact that the choice of annuity will affect the rest of your life and once purchased it cannot be changed, only one in three people shop around for the best one. Newspapers including the *Sunday Telegraph* regularly publish articles and produce league tables showing which annuities are best buys. In addition, investors can contact an Independent Financial Adviser (see IFA Promotion in **Useful Addresses**) who should be able to shop around to find the best deal. Some IFAs, such as the Annuity Bureau, specialize only in annuities so are experts in this field.

There are different types of annuity. Some are flat-rate and although they may appear to pay out a higher amount than other annuities, retirees should remember that this amount will be worn away by inflation year on year until its purchasing power is much reduced.

Other annuities guarantee to rise by a set amount each year, usually by inflation (index-linked) or a set percentage. The amount paid initially will be less to reflect this guarantee. With an escalating annuity, the greater the escalation, the lower the initial income. A 5 per cent escalation, for example, on an annuity taken out by a sixty-year-old male would reduce the starting income by around 40 per cent.

Although inflation is currently at an historical low, even

a low rate of inflation has a dramatic effect over time. Even fifteen years (the average retirement period of a male retiring age sixty-five who could be expected to live into his eighties) of inflation at a rate of 2.5 per cent, will reduce the buying power of £1,000 to just £684.

You can buy an annuity that continues paying an income to your spouse or dependants should you die known as spouses, dependants or joint-life annuities. These are more expensive but mean that your annuity does not die with you. One of the major drawbacks of an annuity is that if you buy one and then die the next day all that money is lost, unless you pay extra to protect your investment. Ensuring that your annuity goes to your dependants can cut your income by as much as 25 per cent. Alternatively you can buy a guaranteed annuity that will make payments for the guarantee period – five or ten years – so that even if you die within that period your dependants will continue to receive the income. With some company pension schemes a spouse's pension must automatically be included along with a five-year guarantee period.

There is another option – to defer buying the annuity until the age of seventy or seventy-five. If the retiree requires an income in the meantime he or she can choose an income drawdown option.

With this scheme, the pension fund is invested until you buy the annuity. In the meantime you can drawdown an income equivalent to that which you would have earned should you have purchased an annuity. However, the drawdown option may not work for everyone and does have its risks. Retirees must gamble on the investment performing better than the return on the annuity, and investing comes at a price, with charges and commissions eating into returns. Also there is the added risk that annuity rates will deteriorate further by the time the retiree comes to purchasing an annuity.

However, the older you are when you buy the annuity, the higher the income will be, so you will have more money to live on each year. Also deferring purchasing an annuity means that, if you should die, the money will go to your dependants according to your will instead of your pension proceeds dying with you or only going to your spouse or dependants had you purchased an annuity.

When choosing an annuity it is important to exercise your open market option. This is your right to buy the annuity from a provider of your choice not the company pension scheme or the insurer from whom you purchased your personal pension plan.

The difference between the best and worst annuity rates can vary by as much as 30 per cent and although the annual income may not appear to be that different, over twenty years of retirement you could end up £30,000 worse off.

In the early 1990s annuity rates peaked at almost 11 per cent which meant that someone retiring with £100,000 to invest in their annuity would have purchased an annual income of around £11,000 for life. Rates have since plummeted and a decade later that same £100,000 would purchase an income of around £5,500.

There is an alternative option – purchasing an investment-linked annuity instead of a standard annuity. These are usually only available to retirees with a personal pension plan and are not often accessible to retirees from company schemes. There are two types of investment-linked annuities, with-profits annuities and unit-linked annuities. These link the income to an investment and as such carry a degree of risk, with unit-linked annuities the riskiest variety.

It is also possible to buy a purchased life annuity or temporary annuity with your own cash rather than the proceeds of a pension fund. Many retirees purchase this type of annuity to boost their retirement income. There are certain tax benefits.

While income from a pension annuity is considered earned income and therefore taxed as such, part of the income from a purchased life or temporary annuity is treated as return of your own capital and is not taxed. This has led to the development of long-term care annuity products designed to give the elderly cash to pay for nursing care. In some instances a long-term care annuity can be paid gross with no tax deducted.

(See also **Gilts, Index-linked, Inflation, Long-term Care, Occupational Pension Schemes, Personal Pensions**.)

APR

This stands for the Annual Percentage Rate. This is the interest rate charged on credit cards, loans and other forms of borrowing. Basically, the higher the APR the more the loan will cost you.

In theory, the APR is supposed to be the true cost of borrowing and should be standard and transparent to make it easy to compare products. However, how it is calculated varies between products.

The APR is not always the only charge you have to pay. With most overdrafts as well as interest there could also be an arrangement fee, a monthly or quarterly fee and trans-action charges. All of these costs could be rolled up into one APR but this would then mean making assumptions about the amount borrowed and for how long, for example. So the regulators have decided that the equiva-lent annual rate (EAR) may be quoted.

With credit cards, the rate is based on an assumed amount borrowed so to find out how much borrowing will cost you, you may be better off looking at the monthly interest rates plus any charges rather than the APR.

When you take out a loan, the APR takes into account when and how often you pay the interest and charges. Also, check that the APR is the same for the life of the loan – if there is a discount at the beginning, this can make it look cheaper than it is. If you have to take out credit insurance as a condition of the loan, the premiums must be included in the APR so be careful when comparing products to ask exactly what is included and what is not.

New regulations are being set up to simplify mortgage APRs – at the moment there are three different ways of calculating them. Lenders will have to include in the APR any premiums for life cover and payment protection insurance where these are required as a condition of the mortgage. This would apply on repayment mortgages where lenders impose a specific condition that life cover be taken out by the borrower. However, endowment mortgages will not be included in this regulation so it will still not be easy to compare the two types of mortgage. Also if someone does take out insurance but not with the lender, this will complicate matters even further. Generally, ask for a list of everything included in the APR and whether this will change over the life of the mortgage to help you calculate the cost.

(See also **EAR**.)

ARREARS

Arrears are when a borrower falls behind on their repayments of a loan or other debt such as a mortgage. Falling one month behind on payments does not usually have major repercussions provided you make up the shortfall in payments quickly and give a valid reason, for example, you were on holiday and unaware you had insufficient funds in your bank account. However, if you fall more than a few months into arrears you are likely to be issued with a county court summons and be taken to court for the recovery of the debt. If you fail to pay by the time of the hearing you will probably have a county court judgement awarded against you. Falling behind on payments can also lead to an adverse credit rating even if you are not taken to court.

(See also **Credit Scoring**.)

ASSET ALLOCATION

Asset Allocation is how the assets of an investment fund are split. For example, a life insurance fund may split its investments between equities, property and fixed-interest investments. The asset allocation generally shows the percentage invested in each area.

ASSET VALUE

The asset value of a company to its shareholders is the total assets of the company minus all its liabilities in the balance sheet and minus the combined value of any prior capital charges (these can include preference shares and debentures). The net asset value is the asset value divided by the number of ordinary shares and is expressed as a figure per share.

ATM

This stands for Automated Telling Machine – more commonly known as a cash point.

B

BANCASSURANCE

Long gone are the days when your bank was just interested in your current account. Today banks are one-stop financial centres that own their own insurance subsidiaries, hence the term bancassurance.

BANKRUPTCY

Those in financial difficulties can either declare themselves bankrupt or may be forced into it. Although most of those declared bankrupt used to be businessmen, around 20 per cent of cases are now individuals who have run into difficulty with credit. Anybody can be made bankrupt by a creditor if they owe more than £750. Every year there are some 20,000 bankruptcies.

However, bankruptcy is not inevitable if you run into debt. There are alternatives that those faced with the prospect of bankruptcy can consider. Individual voluntary arrangements (IVAs) give those in financial difficulty more say in how their assets are dealt with and how payments are made to creditors. An IVA is a formal proposal to creditors to pay off all or part of the debts. Those wishing to take this option need to employ the services of an insolvency practitioner who will present their case to the courts. If accepted it will then be put to the creditors for approval. For advice on alternatives either talk to your accountant, if you have one, or contact the Society of Practitioners of Insolvency (see **Useful Addresses**).

Individuals often escape being forced into bankruptcy as there is little point in seizing assets if there are none. As a result those running into financial difficulties often face years of monthly payments to pay off debts they have accumulated. Some are tempted to declare themselves bankrupt to shake off these debts. To declare yourself bankrupt you need to contact your local county court, which will tell you where to present your bankruptcy petition. However, this is not an easy way out. Bankrupts are required to hand over all their assets, including any interest in their home, life-insurance policies and some-times even their pension fund. Although clothing, furni-ture, household equipment and other basic home essentials will have to be declared too, bankrupts usually keep these items unless they are particularly valuable.

The official receiver contacts the creditors to inform them of the bankruptcy and acts as – or appoints – a trustee to dispose of all the bankrupt's assets and to use the money to pay the fees, costs and expenses of the bankruptcy as well as to pay creditors.

Bankruptcy lasts for three years. It is virtually imposs-ible to get a bank account and illegal to apply for credit of more than £250 for the period of the bankruptcy. Even after the insolvency period is up, credit files will be marked for the next fifteen years. Bankrupts, even after they have been discharged, are not allowed to hold particular jobs such as certain public offices or work in the financial services industry. They are also not allowed to promote, form or manage a company without court permission.

BANKS

The major high-street banks provide the cornerstone of most households' – and businesses' – finances, which is why it is vital that they offer a competitive, reliable, trustworthy and fast service. Consumer champions claim they do not which is why the government appointed Don Cruickshank to review banking services in the UK. His now famous report, published in March 2000, concluded that neither personal or small business customers are getting a fair deal from banks and that they are paying up to £3 billion to £5 billion a year too much for their banking services.

The closure of hundreds of local bank branches, a now failed attempt to charge more customers to withdraw money from hole-in-the-wall cash machines, and the issue of financial exclusion have done little to help the image of the banks.

The root of many of these problems is that the banks are for ever trying to boost profits by cutting costs. They want customers to stay away from branches and use online banking via the Internet or even television, which has far lower overheads than traditional branch-based account management.

Despite the introduction of this new technology, some aspects of the banking system still appear to be in the dark ages. Although Barclays now offers instant access to cash before cheques have cleared, the bank clearing system is barely unchanged from the 1950s and it can still take up to seven days for a cheque to clear into your account.

This works in the banks' interest as they make an estimated £1 million a day on the £4 billion stuck in the clearing system. They pocket another £20 million a year by raking in a day's interest on payments made by standing order. Those who want their cheques to clear through the system more quickly usually have to pay a fee of around £15 for express cheque clearance.

The government's response to the Cruickshank Report included the introduction of CAT standards for credit cards (and possibly also for other financial services products), a review of self-regulatory mechanisms such as the Banking Code to ensure that banks deliver sufficient consumer benefits and the encouragement of comparative tables of banking products and complaints against financial firms. The setting up of a payments regulator to open up the payments system and the opening up of the ATM network to non-bank providers, banning double charging for withdrawals, were other proposals following the report.

The existing Banking Code was published in September 1998 and came into effect on 31 March 1999. It sets the minimum standards of service that personal customers can

expect from all banks and building societies in connection
with:

- information about your accounts, changes affecting
  your accounts and choosing products and services;

- how your accounts operate, your cards, PINs, and any
  lending and foreign exchange transactions;

- protection for all your personal information, your
  accounts, your cheque book, cards, electronic purses,
  PINs and passwords;

- difficulties and what can be done if you find yourself in
  financial difficulties, or you wish to complain to your
  bank or building society or to the independent
  Ombudsmen.

Copies of the Banking Code should be available at all
branches. If they are not on display, ask for a copy. The
Code tells you what to do if you have a complaint and also
what you can expect from your bank.

If you have a complaint against your bank, you should
make it promptly. For example, if a cheque has gone astray
or money has been debited from your account wrongly,
your bank can then take action to find out why and ensure
that this does not happen again.

If complaining in person or by telephone, keep a record
of your conversation. If you get no response, put your
complaint in writing (always keep copies of any correspondence). If you are not satisfied with the way this is dealt

with, you can then take your complaint to the Banking Ombudsman or, when this is replaced by the Financial Services Ombudsman, to that organization. These Ombudsmen make no charge for investigating your complaint and can award compensation.

Although there is tough competition among banks and new competition from Internet and telephone banking services, it is generally true that most services, charges and interest rates are broadly similar between the banks. So how do you choose between one bank and another? Points to consider are more than just the costs of banking.

What should I look for in my bank?

- Does the bank have the accounts and services to meet your needs? Some offer personal banking services for a fee, which appeal to those on high incomes but with little time to manage their finances, while other banks have accounts with no fees and low overdraft interest rates that appeal to those looking for value for money.

- Does the bank have branches and cash machines (ATMs) that are convenient to your work/home? Are these likely to remain open?

- Does the bank offer you alternative ways to bank – via the Internet or telephone?

- Does the bank have longer opening hours so that you can visit your bank before work, later in the afternoon or on Saturdays?

- Will you be given a cheque guarantee card for a higher amount than the standard £50? – it may not be sufficient to meet your needs.

- If you require an overdraft, is this fee free?

In addition to the high-street or retail banks, the banking sector also covers investment banks, which deal with the banking needs of companies and governments as well as local authorities and other large institutions. Investment banks raise share and loan capital for their customers and advise on matters such as takeovers and mergers. They also have big fund management operations managing money for individuals, charities and pension funds. As with the retail banks they are currently authorized and monitored by the Bank of England, nicknamed the Old Lady of Threadneedle Street, with depositors protected against the collapse of a bank by the Deposit Protection Scheme which is being brought under the Financial Services Compensation Scheme.

As well as the high-street chains, the world of banks includes the very posh and the very obscure. People who feel like paying for a bit of cosseting and impressively embossed note paper can go to the private banks such as Coutts or C. Hoare & Co. Private banks can serve a useful purpose for wealthy individuals whose affairs are unusually complex and who need individual and time-consuming attention. This kind of business is more lucrative for the bank than standard current accounts, which are generally free for those who remain in credit, and as a result the high-street banks are increasingly offering personal banking services to their more wealthy customers – but at a price.

(See also **CAT Standards, Current Accounts** and **Online Banking**.)

BASE RATE

Set by the Bank of England this is the general level of interest rates in the UK. Savings and mortgage interest rates are linked to this base rate.

The base rate used to be controlled by the Chancellor of the Exchequer and implemented by the Bank of England and was a crucial weapon in the government's economic armoury. However, the New Labour government gave control of interest rate decisions to the Bank of England, which makes decisions independently of political interference.

The Bank of England's Monetary Policy Committee meets once a month to determine whether or not the base rate needs to rise or fall.

One of the prime aims of the Bank of England is to control inflation so that it remains near or below the 2.5 per cent target set by the government. Raising the base interest rate puts a damper on the economy by increasing borrowing costs and therefore rate rises are implemented when the committee believes there is a danger of inflation rising. A base rate fall, on the other hand, makes borrowing cheaper and is therefore designed to stimulate economic activity.

The official name for the base rate is the Minimum Lending Rate. This is the rate at which the Bank of England will lend money to the big high-street and investment banks.

The property market is particularly sensitive to base rate rises and falls and also has a major impact on inflation. How confident homebuyers feel about the value of their property and its prospects for rising in future, affects spending habits and therefore inflation. In addition to this psychological effect on spending patterns, when prices are rising and the number of property sales is at a high (generally as a result of low interest rates and therefore low mortgage rates), this generates extra expenditure in the form of spending on furniture and furnishings as well as home improvements.

Although the base rate affects all other borrowing and savings rates, these do not necessarily move in line with the base rate or at the same time. Often banks and building societies pass on increases far more quickly than they pass on base rate cuts. Also, if the base rate moves by say 0.25 per cent, interest rates set and offered by banks and building societies may not necessarily move by the same amount. However, if the mortgage or savings account is a base-rate tracker the full rise or fall in interest rates will be passed on to the borrower or saver.

BED AND BREAKFASTING

No, this does not refer to a weekend in a room above the village pub. This was the term given to a very popular capital gains tax avoidance scheme – the selling of shares to realize a capital gain or loss in a tax year and then buying back the same shares the next day or shortly afterwards. That way an individual could make the most of his or her capital gains tax exemption and still own the same assets. Sadly, it was so effective that the loophole was closed in the March 1998 Budget. However, it is still possible to sell an asset to realize a gain in a particular tax year and thus use up your capital gains tax allowance. Investors do however need to be careful if they buy back the same class of share in the same company within a thirty-day period.

If you do buy back shares within the thirty days, you will not escape capital gains tax. The capital gain will be calculated as though you had held the shares from the original date of purchase.

BENEFITS IN KIND

These are perks of the job given to employees by their employer, and include benefits such as a company car, private medical insurance and luncheon vouchers. Some benefits are taxable and some are not. The taxable value of the benefit is usually the cost to the employer apart from in the case of company cars when it is based on the list price when new.

If a perk has a taxable value of £1,000 employees will pay tax on this amount in the same way they would be taxed on pay. So although the perk may appear on their tax coding notice as having a value of £1,000, it will only cost the employee the tax on this amount. So for a higher rate taxpayer paying tax at 40 per cent, the cost will be £400. The fact that the cost of the perk to the employee is so much lower than the actual value of the perk, generally makes employee benefits worthwhile. Employees would need a far higher wage packet to buy the equivalent benefit – for example, a car – for themselves and they would not have the luxury of their employer paying for maintenance, road tax, servicing and insurance.

Tax on benefits in kind is usually deducted through pay packets by an adjustment in the employee's tax code.

BONDS

Bonds are interest-paying investments. They therefore appeal to people trying to generate income from their capital, for example, those in retirement. Bonds pay investors a fixed rate of interest called a coupon, once or twice per year. Most bonds have fixed lives and at the end of a bond's life it matures and an investor's original capital is repaid, or at least that is the theory.

Bonds can take many forms – savings bonds offered by banks and building societies, investment bonds offered by life insurance companies, government bonds known as gilt-edged securities, or gilts and corporate bonds issued by companies.

Although each type of bond pays the investor interest – and therefore an income – not all protect the capital or initial investment.

Savings bonds are safe. In exchange for investing a lump sum (usually a minimum of £1,000) for a set period (usually a minimum of one year), the bank, building society or other savings institution such as National Savings will pay the investor an agreed rate of interest. At the end of the bond's life the capital will be returned in full. There can be interest penalties for those who wish to cash in their bond before the term is up.

Investment bonds from life insurance companies take the form of broker bonds, guaranteed income bonds, with-profits bonds and guaranteed growth bonds. They work in a similar way except that the initial capital is invested in a life insurance fund which pays out an income. The capital, although relatively secure, may not be returned in full.

Bonds traded in the City are those issued by the government, local authorities and companies as a way of borrowing without needing to issue shares or raise bank finance. The bond is issued at a set price (for example, £10,000) with a set coupon, say 10 per cent, and for a set period, say ten years. So the investor earns a 10 per cent income of £1,000 for ten years and at the end of that period their capital is returned in full.

However, as the bonds are traded (just like shares) the price of the bond can rise and fall. If it rises to £15,000 and is sold for that price, the £1,000 a year income represents a rate of just under 7 per cent – so the yield drops for the new investor. However, the original investor has made a substantial capital gain on the initial investment. Of course, if the value of the bond drops the yield increases but there is a loss of capital. Only if the investor keeps the bond for the full term is the capital protected – that is, providing the company issuing the bond does not default.

It is not unknown for companies that issue bonds to go bust leaving bondholders with no capital and no income. To help investors decide which bonds are the most risky they are credit rated. But this higher element of risk has its attractions. Corporate bonds tend to offer better returns than much safer gilts. How investors can go about investing in these is explained later in this book under **Corporate Bonds**.

To get a balanced portfolio of investments, investors are usually advised to have a mix of shares and bonds. If share prices are volatile and there are fears of falls, bonds tend to be more attractive to investors.

One way to spread the risks is to invest in a bond fund, the general choice for the private investor. These funds, run by unit trust fund managers, work in a similar way to share-based unit trusts. Investors need to look at the yield to assess the income from the fund. The yield shown alongside the unit price in newspapers and in advertising should be net of all charges and expenses, which makes these yields easier to compare. There are several different types of bond fund – UK Gilt, UK Corporate Bond, UK Other Bond and Global Bond.

(See also **Corporate Bonds**, **Credit Ratings Agencies**, **Gilts** and **Unit Trusts**.)

BONUSES

In the City when dealers talk of bonuses they may be referring to their six-figure annual bonuses which top up their already inflated pay packets, but in the world of personal finance a bonus is far more modest. It is the share of profits of a with-profits life insurance fund given to investors each year and upon maturity of the policy.

(See also **With-profits**.)

BROKERS

The term 'broker' is a general term incorporating stockbrokers, investment brokers and insurance brokers. What they have in common is that they are there to broker deals for you. The role of stockbrokers is dealt with later in this book and investment brokers are covered under **Advice**, **Discount Brokers** and **Independent Financial Advisers**.

To call him- or herself an insurance broker, the broker must be registered and regulated under an Act of Parliament. However, not all firms selling general insurance as intermediaries are regulated because only the title is protected by current legislation not the function. Many firms selling insurance are not in fact regulated at all.

Insurance brokers are regulated by the Insurance Brokers Registration Council which was set up under the Insurance Brokers Registration Act 1977. The IBRC will be wound-up once the Financial Services and Markets Act replaces existing financial regulators with one chief city watchdog. This is expected to happen during 2001. Insurance brokers often deal with all aspects of general insurance such as car, motor and household cover as well as life and income protection insurance. Buying general insurance through a broker is one of the cheapest ways to get cover and easiest as they do the shopping around to find the best deal for you and can compare a much wider range of products than customers have the time or generally the knowledge to do.

However, if you are using an Internet broker to buy insurance, you would be advised to go to a traditional one as well to compare costs. Many online broker sites have a very limited range of products to choose from so they cannot offer such good deals. In some cases, the same insurance product from the same broker can cost more online.

(See also **Advice, Broker Bonds, Fee-based Advice, Independent Financial Advice, Stockbrokers**.)

BROKER BONDS

These are investment bond funds managed by an investment broker – usually a financial adviser (not to be confused with a stockbroker). As investments these schemes have come under fire in recent years as they allow advisers to earn large amounts of commission by buying and then selling investments in a portfolio of bond funds.

Broker bonds or broker-managed funds are usually lump-sum insurance policies with the broker actively managing the underlying investment. This in theory means that the performance will be better than if left to an insurers' fund managers alone. But this 'added performance' comes at a price – usually 1 per cent or more on top of the insurance company's charges, which can mean that instead of outperforming a range of less actively managed bond funds, broker bonds often underperform.

THE BUDGET

The Budget (as opposed to a budget) is presented by the Chancellor of the Exchequer each year and sets out how much the government spends, how much it earns and how much it needs to borrow – or in the case of the current Labour government how much government borrowing it plans to repay. New tax rates and allowances are set affecting how much income tax individuals pay and the level of duty on tobacco, petrol and alcohol.

The government uses the Budgets to change not only its own finances but also those of industry as well as private individuals. It is the time when the economic tool box is opened up to the Chancellor. He can turn whatever economic handles or wheels are needed to achieve his party's political objectives, which is why the Budget is so significant.

As far as the economy as a whole is concerned, the Chancellor will reveal the public sector borrowing requirement (PSBR) – the level of government borrowing. He can also use the budget to reveal the government's current thinking on general economic policy and he will comment on the rate of inflation and set targets for this and for economic growth.

Following the Budget speech, which is currently given before the end of the tax year in March, the proposals are officially put forward in the Finance Bill, which is debated by MPs. Once it passes through Parliament it then becomes a Finance Act and the proposals become a reality – although some announcements take immediate effect from the day of the Budget.

Gone are the days when the Budget was eagerly awaited and its contents kept a tight secret. The current government publishes much of its proposals in a pre-Budget report published the preceding November. Even so, the Chancellor likes to keep a few headline-grabbing measures up his sleeve to attract the right kind of post-Budget publicity.

(See also **Income Tax.**)

BUILDING SOCIETIES

Building societies are mutual organizations owned by their members (these are certain classes of savers and borrowers). However, they are more than just savings and mortgage providers today and instead are increasingly one-stop financial centres offering everything from current accounts and credit cards to insurance and stock-market based investments. This expansion into new markets followed the 1986 Building Societies Act, which gave them wider powers but also led to a wave of mergers and takeovers.

The number of building societies has shrunk dramatically in the past few decades with large numbers either being taken over by banks, merging with other societies or converting into banks, known as demutualization. This has led to a number of so-called windfalls – free shares or cash payments for members. As a result members of societies that have yet to convert have pushed boards to put resolutions to members so that they can vote on whether or not the society should convert. These windfall seekers are known as carpetbaggers.

At the time of writing there were just sixty-eight building societies left in the UK down from 167 in the mid 1980s. Even so they still represent a major force in the mortgages and savings market with total assets of around £160 billion.

The reason why windfalls are paid out is that societies have built up large financial reserves over many years – a requirement to ensure that they have enough assets to meet any liabilities. When they convert into stock-market quoted banks, they can put these often huge sums to work in a variety of ways.

However, as stock-market quoted banks, the former building societies have different priorities with their share-holders coming first. Profits have to be diverted to pay for shareholder dividends rather than being used to benefit savers and borrowers.

As a result the banks tend to have a bigger margin between rates charged and rates paid – which means it costs more to borrow from them and savers do not always get such good rates. Even so savers and borrowers have been tempted to push for demutualization to get an instant windfall. Many societies now have measures in place to deter these carpetbaggers and insist that new members sign any potential windfalls away to charity.

Despite the rapid decline in the number of building societies, about 17 million adults have building society savings accounts and about 3 million adults are currently buying their own homes with the help of building society mortgages.

Although the major building societies such as the Nationwide account for a large slice of this market, smaller building societies are increasingly courting business on a nationwide scale. Smaller building societies used to be just for local people but now they are open to everyone regard-less of geographical area thanks to postal accounts. The smaller building societies often have a much smaller mar-gin – the difference between the borrowing and the savings rate. Some of these societies have member-only accounts and bonds which pay even better rates, so it could be worth opening a regular savings account with a small amount to become a member. Members who do not live anywhere near a branch can open and operate savings and mortgages by phone or post and, in an increasing number of cases, via the Internet.

(See also **Windfalls**.)

BUY-TO-LET

Buying property for investing rather than nesting took off in the mid 1990s as the property market recovered from a slump and private investors realized that there were potential profits to be made from capital appreciation of property as well as rental incomes. The introduction of mortgages to make purchasing a property for let far easier helped fuel the demand from private landlords. One scheme in particular, buy-to-let, launched by the Association of Residential Letting Agents in 1996, helped investors get access to funds.

Since the buy-to-let mortgage scheme was launched in September 1996, over 60,000 properties have been bought. Before that it was almost impossible to get a mortgage for this purpose. Today investors no longer need to be in a position where they have already paid off their original mortgage. Second mortgages taken out to cover an investment in a second property are widely available. Most of the major lenders offer further advances to enable homeowners to release capital from their existing property (this cash can be used to fund a second property purchase) but not all offer buy-to-let mortgages. However, as some sixty different lenders offer these types of loans there is plenty of choice.

Some lenders base their decision on rental income, some on rental income plus earned income and some will consider either rental or earned income. The level of rental income required also varies. Some lenders insist that the rent must cover at least 75 per cent of the mortgage repayments while others require more than 150 per cent. A more usual requirement is 125 per cent. As a general rule, investors need to have a deposit of at least 20 per cent of the value of the property and in some cases as much as 30 per cent.

Unlike traditional residential mortgages, the size of the loan a lender will agree to advance is usually linked to the expected rental income from the property rather than the salary of the borrower. To help assess whether or not the rental income assumptions are realistic, lenders will often ask that an independent letting agent confirms your potential rental income and verifies that there is a demand for the type of property.

Buy-to-let is by no means a risk-free investment. Landlords may find that there are times when they have no tenants – or tenants do not pay the rent – and during these periods they will still have to pay the mortgage interest and other costs of running the property. There are also maintenance costs to take into account as well as the cost of advertising for new tenants and possibly paying for a letting agent to manage the property. Rental income should be viewed as covering costs only and, according to industry experts, anyone who does buy should plan to keep the property for between ten and fifteen years.

You should also consider how the mortgage will be paid in times when the property is empty – between tenants, for example. When calculating rent the experts recommend charging between 130 and 150 per cent of the mortgage.

A newer way to cash in on property appreciation is let-to-buy where you rent out your own home and use the income to buy another one. Once the cost of moving, stamp duty, mortgage deposit and contingencies are added in, moving may not be so viable unless you have a substantial income and a deposit to put down on the new property.

When looking for tenants, it is advisable to use an agency to find them but make sure that the agent is reputable so that any money taken in deposits or rents does not go astray. Look for members of the Association of Residential Letting Agents (see **Useful Addresses**). You should also consult an agency about the possible rental value of the property as well as the rights and responsibility of the landlord before buying.

Once you have bought the property, agents will charge about 10 per cent of the rent for basics and up to 16 per cent for full management – this is tax deductible along with other legitimate expenses like insurance, maintenance, servicing and furnishing. The other alternative is to use an agent to vet tenants for a fee but not to manage the property. The Council of Mortgage Lenders (see **Useful Addresses**) also has a free booklet with advice for would-be buy-to-let landlords.

C

CAPITAL GAINS TAX

This is a tax paid on profits (or gains) from the sale of most financial and physical assets. Everyone can make a certain amount of capital gains each year tax free but any gains over this tax threshold are taxable at a rate depending on the individual's top rate of income tax. These rates are 10 per cent for those paying less than the basic rate of income tax, 20 per cent for basic rate taxpayers and 40 per cent for higher rate taxpayers.

The capital gains tax allowance usually rises each tax year following the Budget (for the 2001/2002 tax year the annual exempt amount is £7,500) and few individuals make sufficient gains each year to pay the tax. This is mainly because our biggest assets – our homes (your principal private residence), private cars, pension funds and life insurance policies are generally exempt from the tax as are tax-free savings schemes such as Individual Savings Accounts (ISAs), Personal Equity Plans (PEPs) and Tax Exempt Special Savings Accounts (TESSAs). Other exempt assets include National Savings Certificates, Premium Bonds, UK government stocks (gilts) and betting, lottery or pools winnings.

The gain is calculated by taking the selling price and subtracting the cost of purchase and any other related costs such as auction fees, dealing charges or restoration costs. The Inland Revenue allows people to reduce their capital gains tax bill each year by subtracting losses from profits and it applies the tax to the net gain. However, investors can no longer deduct the effects of inflation to reduce the gain they declare for assets purchased after 1998. The Budget of that year reformed the already complex capital gains tax system and replaced indexation (deducting the effects of inflation) with a new taper system which reduces the rate at which gains are taxed depending on how long the asset has been held. The new system is designed to encourage long-term investment.

Taper relief reduces the amount of gain chargeable to tax, according to the number of whole years the asset has been held after 5 April 1998. The greater the number of years an investor has held the asset the smaller the percentage of gain which is chargeable to tax. The total gain is taxable if the asset is sold within the first two years; however, the amount taxed then starts to drop with 90 per cent of the gain chargeable to tax if it was held for four years before being sold and then to 80 per cent after six years gradually dropping to 60 per cent if held for ten years or more.

Investors can, however, still deduct the indexation allowance if the asset was owned before April 1998. This adjusts gains for the effects of inflation by giving an allowance equal to the amount by which the cost of the asset would have risen if its value had kept pace with inflation, as measured by increases in the retail prices index (RPI), since the asset was acquired.

There are different rules for business assets with the

current maximum rate of capital gains tax set at just 10 per cent for all business assets after just four years. In the March 2000 Budget the holding period for CGT taper relief for business assets was reduced from ten years to four years. This change in the tax treatment of business assets was designed to encourage business investment by making it more tax efficient to invest in the shares of unquoted trading companies.

CAR FINANCE

'Most people spend six months deciding which car to buy and less than fifteen minutes deciding how to finance it,' according to the AA.

You will probably be offered a finance package in the showroom but should consider the other options first. Interest-free credit is the cheapest deal but you do have to put down a big deposit – usually around 50 per cent.

Unsecured personal loans are another option and often the cheapest way to finance the purchase of a car if you do not qualify for interest-free credit. Some car dealers offer special car loans but the rates on these are almost always beaten by the cheapest unsecured personal loans from banks and building societies.

Another option is a personal contract plan – PCP offered by the dealer. A minimum guaranteed future value (MGFV) is deducted from the purchase price – this is what the car is expected to be worth in two or three years' time when the deal ends. Then you pay a deposit, which is smaller than that required for o per cent finance, and a monthly amount for two or three years. You are committed to an annual mileage allowance and will pay a charge for every mile you go over it. You also have to keep the car in good condition and have it serviced regularly. At the end of the agreement there are three choices: Firstly, you can keep the car and pay the MGFV – the amount deducted from the purchase price. Or, alternatively, you can hand back the car and make no more payments. Or, finally, you can hand back the car and use any profit over the MGFV towards a new car from the same dealer.

With all finance packages bear in mind negative equity. If it takes five years to pay off the loan, you could end up owing more than the car is worth.

CAR INSURANCE

It is illegal to drive without insurance even though cover can often cost more than the value of the car, particularly for young, inexperienced drivers who own second-hand vehicles and live in high-risk inner-city areas.

The cost of cover depends on the type of insurance.

There are three main types:

- Third party is the most basic and only covers any injuries or damage that you may do to other people or

their property – not any damage done to your vehicle
or yourself. It is not widely available.

- Third party fire and theft covers you against damage
done to other vehicles, people or property and also
compensates you if the car is stolen or destroyed by
fire. This is the type of cover taken out by those who
cannot afford fully comprehensive cover. These types of
policies are recommended for cheaper or older cars and
for younger drivers who have yet to build up a no
claims discount.

- Fully comprehensive covers you for all of the above
plus any damage done to your own car. As it gives the
most cover, it is the most expensive. However, there are
still exclusions – don't be misled by the term fully
comprehensive – so always read the small print. The
best policies offer free hire cars when an insured car is
being repaired and have approved repair outlets so you
can get minor repairs such as smashed windscreens
repaired without having to go through a lengthy claims
procedure or having to find a suitable garage.

Insurers reward careful drivers who do not make any
claims by giving them no claims discounts of up to 70 per
cent on premiums.

Although you can lose your no claims discount even if
you claim for something which is not your fault, you can
insure your bonus so that making the occasional claim will
not affect your insurance premiums. These bonuses can be
transferred from one insurer to another.

The easiest way to cut the cost of cover is to shop around – you may discover that one insurer charges half that of another for broadly the same, and sometimes better, cover. Different companies offer better deals for different types of car and also rate your risk differently depending on your post code, age, sex and driving history. As no two insurers may assess your risk the same – and therefore will charge different premiums – it is best to use an insurance broker who will do the shopping around and find the cheapest cover for you. Increasingly brokers offer online Internet services to help you to shop around yourself. Telephone services, which tend to be open at times that suit you rather than the insurance company, can also offer competitive rates.

Some insurers have developed policies to cater for specific groups – for example, for the over fifties or for members of a trade organization or union – which can offer better value for those who meet the criteria.

Direct insurers usually sell via the telephone or Internet but do not shop around for the best rates – they only offer their own policies. Most are highly selective about who they insure, which is known as cherry picking. They keep their premiums low by restricting low-cost cover to those least likely to claim whilst charging much higher rates or even refusing to cover those aged under twenty-five, those with high-performance cars and those with a poor driving record.

Other ways to reduce premiums include:

- Limiting your mileage – most companies offer up to 10 per cent discounts

- Limiting the named drivers – up to 30 per cent discounts

- Fitting security, immobilizers, tracking devices – up to 20 per cent off

- Opting for a higher excess – this is the amount you pay towards each claim

- Parking the car in a garage or driveway

Although your car insurance will cover you for items stolen from a locked car, there is often a very low limit even if everything is locked in the boot – typically about £100. Do not rely on the car insurance to cover valuable items you take out of the house regularly; consider insuring them separately as an add-on to your household insurance policy.

Do not be tempted to lie when buying a policy, even if it means you have to pay a higher premium. Drivers paying reduced premiums after saying they do not use their cars for work may find insurers refusing to pay claims for cars stolen or damaged in their office car parks.

CAT STANDARDS

CAT stands for low Charges, easy Access and fair Terms. The standard was introduced to provide a minimum level of protection for those buying financial products so that they know they are getting a fair deal.

First introduced as a standard for ISAs, the individual savings accounts, which were launched in April 1999, the standard has since been extended to mortgages and credit cards and may soon apply to all financial products.

But there is one major drawback – the standard is voluntary. As a result many ISAs and mortgages still fail to meet the CAT standard. (Details of the CAT standard requirements for ISAs are covered later in this book.)

The CAT standards for mortgages were announced in January 2000 as a means to ensure consumers get 'clear, comprehensive and comparable information to drive up standards, cut costs, improve competition, and above all improve consumers' ability to make informed choices'.

With more than 4,000 different mortgage deals on offer at any one time, comparing mortgages can be difficult, particularly as each can have a different interest rate, additional charges and hidden penalties.

However, the new benchmark standards for variable and fixed-rate or capped mortgages are voluntary – so not all lenders offer CAT standard loans, and of those that do, not all of their mortgages meet the standard. Also they only cover the mortgage products not advice. The Financial

Services Authority (FSA) has responsibility for regulating key aspects of mortgage selling (see **Useful Addresses**).

The CAT standards for credit cards have yet to be decided in detail and were announced in August 2000 following the publication of the Cruickshank Report into banks.

(See also **Mortgage Regulation**.)

CHARGE CARDS

These work in the same way as credit cards except that the balance must be paid off in full every month, usually by direct debit from your current account. The advantages are much higher credit limits than for credit cards and good perks that can include free travel insurance, medical insurance and free card and purchase protection as well as loyalty schemes such as air miles.

Some charge cards do require a minimum income, others are 'at the manager's discretion' or 'by invitation only' which means that if you're a big shopper you may get an application form through the post without having to request it. Other cards are available only to the particular banks' own current account customers.

Although you do not borrow on a charge card some are linked to current accounts that give the cardholder an automatic or negotiable overdraft at a low rate of interest.

CHARITABLE GIVING

On average we may give very little to charity – just £230 a year – but we could be giving far more by making the most of the tax breaks on offer. A package of measures to boost charitable giving, introduced in 2000, is expected to boost giving by £1 billion a year over the next five years. Rather than putting a few pounds in a collection box, individuals can increase the amount they donate by getting the government to join in the giving by using one of the following schemes.

- With **deeds of covenant** donors make monthly, quarterly or annual donations for at least four years. The government tops up the donation through basic tax relief so the charity effectively gets a bigger donation from you. If the tax rate is 22 per cent, for example, basic rate taxpayers need give only £78 to give £100. The charity claims £22 from the taxman to make up the difference. Higher rate taxpayers can also claim further tax relief for themselves when they fill in their tax return.

- **Gift Aid** was set up by the Inland Revenue to help people make lump sum donations rather than regular payments. There used to be a minimum donation of £250 but this was scrapped in 2000 and new rules were introduced to allow donors to join the scheme by telephone or Internet so it now has a much broader appeal. The advantage to the charity is that it can reclaim tax relief on these donations. For further information on gift aid contact the relevant charity.

- **Payroll giving** involves making regular donations through your company's payroll scheme. The main advantage of this is that the donations are taken out of gross income before tax is deducted, so you can give far more than if you made a donation out of taxable pay. There used to be a maximum limit on the amount that could be donated to charity each year but this was abolished in 2000 when a 10 per cent supplement was introduced on donations for three years.

- **Charity accounts** are run by the Charities Aid Foundation. People pay money into the account and have donations grossed up by the taxman as the charity can reclaim tax deducted from your earned income. Donors receive a cheque book and charity card which can be used only to give money to recognized charities – even via the Internet – and it is also possible to set up standing orders for regular donations.

In addition, legacies to charities made in a will are free of inheritance tax. A less tax efficient but still effective way to donate, is to take out an affinity card – a credit card that donates a small proportion of everything spent to a good cause.

For details about setting up a deed of covenant, leaving a legacy or joining the Gift Aid scheme either contact the charity you wish to benefit or the Charities Aid Foundation

(CAF). This organization is a charity that helps people to make more of their giving (see **Useful Addresses**).

(See also **Affinity Cards**, **Wills**.)

CHARTISTS

These people try to predict future share-price movement by looking at historical data. Their crystal balls are charts which show trends in the prices of shares, bonds, commodities or market indices such as the FTSE 100 Index.

Share-price movements often seem to bear little resemblance to the state of the economy or to a company's financial prospects. Chartists say these swings are caused by changes in sentiment and result in investors trading en masse. Chartists try to predict these movements and buy before a bull market, one where prices are rising, and sell before a bear market, one where share prices fall. The charts contain and process price data in different combinations.

The main tools of a chartist's trade are as follows:

- Recent and longer-term moving averages. These are plotted by totalling a company's share price over a certain period – say, fifty days – and dividing the result by the number of days involved.

- Relative performance against the stock market. This is calculated by dividing the share price by an index such as the Footsie, the FTSE 100 share index, and shows whether the share has outperformed, underperformed or performed in line with the index.

- Long-term trends in a share price. Trend lines are plotted by joining points on a share-price chart forming a straight line.

- Head and shoulders – an indicator intended to show the turning point of a market. If a share price graph resembles the outline of a human head and shoulders, this suggests shares are about to fall. Conversely if a reverse head and shoulders formation develops (a head and shoulders upside down), this suggests shares could rise.

CHILDREN'S SAVINGS

Children are learning the value of money at an ever younger age. One recent survey of six to nine year olds found that two-thirds save most of their pocket money and by the time it comes to leaving school, between two-thirds and three-quarters will have done some paid work. In addition to earning and saving their own money, children are increasingly likely to be given cash as a present. For the thrifty there is no lack of choice in how to invest this money.

Children's savings accounts can be opened by anyone under the age of eighteen. The advantage is that while adults have to pay tax on savings, children don't. There are also current accounts for sixteen to eighteen year olds.

As with adults, children have their own tax allowance, which in the 2001/2002 tax year is £4,535. As most children will earn less than this tax threshold in savings interest, this income can be paid gross (without tax deducted). However, parents or guardians will need to sign form R85 when they open the account to make sure tax is not deducted.

Parents should be wary of giving children money which will earn more than £100 in interest in a year as parents may have to pay tax themselves on any interest over this amount. This rule is to prevent parents from putting savings in their children's names to avoid paying tax. Gifts from grandparents and other relatives and friends do not suffer this restriction.

Most children's savings accounts can be opened with either £1 or £10. Some offer rewards like magazines, books, toys and discount vouchers, but often these are little more than a gimmick as the accounts with the best gifts generally have the worst rates of interest. Other accounts are offered to young supporters of certain football teams, although if the rates are good any child could be tempted.

Although any adult can open an account for a child, the parent, grandparent or guardian has to provide some ID and proof of address. Accounts work in two ways. Some have a passbook for withdrawals and deposits, some have a card so that the child can withdraw money from a cash machine. The card can't be used for anything else –

children under eighteen cannot be given credit so there is no risk of them getting into debt.

Children's bonds are offered by a few banks and building societies. In most cases, money cannot be withdrawn before the end of the bond's term – four or five years. The bond has to be started by an adult and managed by them until the child is at least twelve. Rates vary and even the best do not always match the best savings accounts so think twice before tying money up for this period.

The National Savings Children's Bond is for up to sixteen year olds and runs for five years with a maximum investment of £1,000. At the end of the five years, the bond is either cashed in or rolled over for another five years.

An alternative to a savings account is to start an investment scheme. As shares tend to outperform savings over the longer term, investing in a stock-market based investment will usually produce significantly higher returns.

Friendly societies offer tax-free children's bonds, also known as baby bonds, which have low investment limits and often have relatively high charges but can produce good returns. The maximum that can be invested in a children's bond is just £25 a month or £270 a year, so many parents may not miss this cash. However, you have to keep the plan going for a minimum of ten years and plans can only be taken out for children under sixteen. Cashing in the investment early will usually lead to financial penalties.

An alternative that can often provide higher returns is to take out a stock-market based investment such as a unit trust or investment trust. As with savings accounts the returns will be tax free provided the child does not exceed income tax or capital gains tax allowances. Some investment management companies accept savers as young as fourteen; however, for most the age limit is eighteen. For younger children, any adult can buy units in his or her own name and add the child's initials to indicate who owns the units. This is known as a designated account.

COHABITATION

Firstly, there is no such thing as common law marriage. No matter how long a couple is together, when they split up the house belongs to whoever's name is on the deeds. If there is only one name, the other partner can claim part of the value only if he or she can prove substantial contribution either to the mortgage or the upkeep – paying the bills is not enough. Also be aware of whose name is on the bills. Each partner is liable for their own debts plus any in joint names. Other expensive items such as a car or computer should also be put in both names if they are for joint use.

Men who are not married to their child's mother have no automatic legal right to look after the children or even in some cases to sign consent for surgery forms in hospital as next of kin. However, they are legally required to pay maintenance if the couple splits. A Parental Responsibility Agreement will give the father rights and this can be obtained from the local court.

The easiest way to avoid complications later is a cohabitation agreement. This may sound calculating but, like a marriage certificate, it is a legal document. The agreement sets out who gets what if the relationship fails and costs around £500.

Couples living together should also look to the long-term future. If one partner dies without making a will, the other will not automatically inherit. If there are children from a previous marriage, they would be the inheritors and your partner could find themselves evicted from your home. If you were married and never finalized a divorce, your ex will still inherit however long it is since you have had any contact with him or her.

(See also **Wills**.)

COMMISSION

There is no such thing as free financial advice. Even though investors may not have to 'pay' for advice in hard cash, they pay for it through charges with the adviser usually earning a commission.

There is however an alternative. Investors can pay a fee instead – usually a set amount per hour. The commission that the adviser would have earned is then rebated to the investor – either in cash or with the rebate invested in the life policy, pension, ISA or other investment. The effect of paying a fee instead of the adviser earning commission can be dramatic on the value of an investment. Fees also appeal to investors who want to know that they will be obtaining truly independent financial advice and that there is no temptation for the adviser to recommend a product that pays a higher commission than one that earns them a lower income.

Commissions are not only paid to financial advisers, they are also charged by stockbrokers (a dealing commission) and on foreign exchange transactions.

(See also **Advice/Advisers, Fee-based Advice, Independent Financial Advice**.)

COMMODITIES

Coffee, copper, gold, grain and oil are among commodities traded in London's financial markets. Brave investors can bet on whether prices are going to rise or fall but, although the actual commodities themselves can be bought and sold, in many cases investors are merely gambling on price movements and buy and sell contracts rather than actual goods.

Producers use the exchanges to sell future production at pre-agreed prices, to reduce the risk of producing commodities when prices are healthy but selling them when prices have fallen. This is done through futures and options contracts. A futures contract allows a commodity producer to sell a commodity at a fixed price on a specified date. Buyers enter the market to satisfy raw material requirements if prices look like rising.

Speculators trade futures and options contracts before their expiry date and brave small investors can join them by becoming clients of a commodities broker. But novices should be wary: commodities are volatile and futures can massively magnify the risks involved. Private investors do not have to play the commodities markets – they can simply buy the shares of companies involved in or connected to these markets such as BP.

Commodities including cocoa, coffee, white sugar, wheat, barley and potatoes are traded on the London International Financial Futures and Options Exchange (LIFFE). The London Metal Exchange is where copper, aluminium, lead, nickel, tin and zinc are traded, and oil is traded on the International Petroleum Exchange.

In addition to providing a market where participants can protect against risks arising from movements in prices – known as hedging – these exchanges also provide reference prices for the worldwide pricing of commodities.

COMPLAINTS

The first step in making a complaint against a financial institution is to go through the official procedure offered by the company itself – this can be anything from complaining to the manager to contacting the Customer Services department. Keep a dated record of all correspondence and conversations as well as copies of any other relevant documents – send photocopies if evidence is needed.

If this fails, turn to the relevant watchdog, regulator or ombudsman who can help you get the cash compensation you are due. Most of these schemes will not touch your complaint until you have exhausted a company's in-house procedures first.

(See also **Financial Services Ombudsman Scheme** and **Ombudsmen**.)

CONTRACTS FOR DIFFERENCES

Known as CFDs, these are a comparatively new way to gamble on the movements of share prices. You speculate on whether a share will be higher or lower than a price quoted for that share in the future. If you think it will be higher you 'buy' it and if you think it will be lower you 'sell' at the price quoted by a market maker. If, for example, you decide to buy shares quoted at 400p and two months later they are quoted at 440p you will then 'sell' the shares making a 40p per share profit once you close your position. However, you do not actually own the shares you 'buy'. You borrow the money to pay for them and pay interest on the amount owed. But you do receive the value of any dividends. You can also go short on a share 'selling' it at a high price and then 'buying' it back when it has fallen in price. In many respects CFDs are similar to actually buying the share – what you make or lose is the difference between what you buy and sell them for. However, you do not need to actually buy the shares or have sufficient capital to

do so. As such you can gamble using a larger amount –
buying for example £10,000 of shares even though you
only have £1,000 of capital. So any profits are magnified. A
10 per cent rise in the value of the shares would earn you
£1,000 of profits, doubling your money. However, a fall in
the value of the shares by 20 per cent would mean you lost
more than your original investment. As such there is
significant risk to your capital. With a share you are
unlikely to lose all your original investment. With CFD
trading you could.

CFD trading incurs no UK stamp duty.

CONSOLIDATION

The term given when an individual's finances – usually
debts – are combined together or consolidated, usually
with the aim of cutting borrowing costs.

CONVERTIBLES

Nothing to do with cars, convertibles are fixed-income
stocks that can be converted into ordinary shares at a
particular date. Their price follows the movements in the
price of the ordinary shares but they tend to be less volatile
because they have a fixed rate of return. Not only do they
offer a fixed income but they also have the potential of

capital growth from the equity into which they can be converted.

CORPORATE BONDS

These are bonds issued by companies to raise finance. The company agrees to pay a set income on the bond and will then pay off the debt – in other words, buy back the bond – at an agreed price usually on an agreed date. In this sense they are essentially IOUs.

So corporate bonds are similar to government bonds or gilts. However, whereas government bonds have the security of the state behind them, corporate bonds are only as good as the company issuing them. As a result of this additional risk the rates of interest – which are fixed – are generally higher than the rate offered by gilts. The higher the perceived risk of the corporate bond, the higher the yield (or rate of interest) has to be to attract investors.

An added element of risk comes from the fact that the value of a corporate bond can rise and fall. This in turn affects the yield. A bond issued at £100 with a rate of interest of 10 per cent over ten years will pay the investor 10 per cent interest or £10 each year and then give the investor back the £100 original investment after ten years. However, that bond can be traded on the stock market. If it is traded (sold) for £125, the yield of £10 drops to just 8 per cent and the new investor has to pay more to get a lower interest rate while the original investor has made a capital gain.

A number of factors affect the price or value of a bond. Generally, if investors can get higher rates of interest elsewhere – say, from savings accounts – than they can from corporate bonds then the value will fall.

Individual corporate bonds cost tens of thousands of pounds and as such are out of the reach of private investors. The most cost-effective and easiest way to invest in them is through a corporate bond fund – either a unit trust or an open-ended investment company (OEIC). This not only cuts the cost of investing but also spreads the risk. If one company defaults, it will only have a small impact on a fund that owns a number of corporate bonds.

In addition to paying an income from the interest paid on corporate bonds, fund managers buy and sell bonds to make capital gains. There is, however, a risk that not all of an investor's initial investment will be returned when the investment is cashed in. Often there can be capital erosion if some of the capital is used to keep the yield high. Investors also need to check whether annual charges are taken from capital rather than income.

What attracts investors to corporate bonds is the prospect of a high income, some capital growth and a low risk of default. To identify which corporate bond funds are most likely to meet these requirements investors can look at the running yield. This measures the annual income received from the capital invested. Generally, the higher the risk the higher the yield.

Investors also need to look at the redemption yield. This

is the projected yield if any particular bond matured. As the bonds held by the fund are traded regularly this figure will keep changing. However, it can give an indication of future prospects. If the redemption yield is higher than the running yield there is a greater chance that there will be capital appreciation.

Very high yields may make a bond fund appear to offer a better rate of return than a deposit account; however, if the redemption yield is far lower this could indicate a capital loss. Generally, high yield bond funds also mean higher risk.

As a result, investors are advised to be prepared to invest for at least five years, to cover the costs of investing and so that any fluctuations in the value of the bonds can be ironed out. This is particularly true of higher risk, higher yielding funds.

Higher risk corporate bonds – also known as junk bonds – are generally sub-credit rated. Credit ratings are usually given by Standard & Poor's and indicate the risks attached to each investment. Investment grade bonds are rated above BBB, with the most secure rated AAA, where a company's capacity to meet its financial commitments is 'extremely strong'. Bonds rated below BBB – non-investment grade or junk bonds – are considered to have a greater chance of defaulting. The lowest grade is D, where the fund or company is already in payment default.

However, investors should not be deterred by the term junk bonds – they can be medium rather than high-risk investments and include major companies such as mobile phone giant Orange. The higher risk bonds are those that invest in foreign bonds as they are also subject to a currency risk.

THE COUPON

This has nothing to do with money-off vouchers that can be redeemed at supermarkets. The coupon is the rate of interest that a government or company promises to pay the holder of a particular bond. The coupon is fixed and is calculated on the nominal value of the bond. So a bond with a nominal or face value of £100 with a 10 per cent coupon will earn the investor £10 per year in income. Even if the value of the bond rises and falls, which it can do as it is a tradeable security, the £10 income remains the same.

CREDIT CARDS

A credit card allows you to pay for goods now but you do not get the bill until later and have longer still to pay off this credit. When you take out a credit card you will be advised as to your credit limit, the maximum amount you can borrow. If you exceed this limit you will often suffer a financial penalty and could have your card taken away from you.

With more than a hundred different credit cards to choose from, the credit card market is highly competitive.

So competitive, in fact, that card issuers offer special low rates to those prepared to move their outstanding credit card debts to a new card. However, competition has its drawbacks. With so many cards in issue it is not always easy to spot which card offers the best deal. Also, what may appear to be a good deal today might turn out to be comparatively expensive in a few months' time. As a result of this – and customer apathy – an estimated £1.4 billion is wasted by people paying too much for their credit card – enough to cancel the debt of a small African country.

Of course, this is of little consequence to those half of all cardholders who pay off their credit card balance in full each month because they do not pay interest at all.

However, for everyone else, competition in the market means that shopping around can provide good deals. Annual fees are now very rare and there is no good reason to pick a card which has one. Some cards still charge around 20 per cent interest while others charge less than a quarter of this; the high charging cards rely on customers being too busy or not having enough information to switch. A higher rate card usually has no extra benefits or services so the customer has nothing to lose by switching to a cheaper rate piece of plastic.

Many cards offer an introductory rate for around the first six months before the card reverts to the standard rate. It is important to compare both rates before selecting a card. What may appear to be a very good deal in the short-term could turn out more expensive if the standard rate is not so competitive.

It is also possible to transfer the balance owed on another

card over on to the new one to pay off the debt at a much lower rate of interest. The new card company will arrange for the balance to be transferred from the old card for you. Check whether new purchases will also be charged at this lower rate or at the standard rate and also how long any cheap rate applies to the balance transfer.

Check how long the interest-free period is on the card. Some cards give up to fifty-six days to pay. This means that if you buy something the day after the last bill you have a full month until the next bill plus another twenty-five days to pay. However, if you buy something the day before the next bill is due, you have only the twenty-five days to pay. Some cards give only forty-five days leeway so it is easy to be caught out. Generally, cardholders must repay at least 3 per cent or 5 per cent of the outstanding balance each month. However, to escape the interest charges the entire balance must be cleared in full by the payment date.

Remember that it can take up to seven working days for a cheque to clear and even if you go to the branch to pay in cash, it will not be cleared for five working days. Failure to make a payment on time increasingly results in penalties with some card issuers charging up to £25 if a payment is missed. So paying late every month would cost you up to £300 a year. And if these fines are not paid straight away, interest will be charged on them too.

Gold cards and platinum cards usually have higher credit limits and offer perks like travel insurance, free extended warranties on household appliances bought with them, medical insurance and travel discounts. However, check the small print; with travel insurance for example, only the card holder and their family are covered; if you buy a ticket for someone else on the card, they will not be covered.

Also weigh up whether you want the card for the higher credit limit or the perks; if you are not going to use the perks there is no point choosing a card which has them but also charges a higher interest rate or an annual fee.

Long gone are the days when gold cards were only offered to a high-earning elite. The minimum salary requirements are now generally around £20,000 – around the level of the average male wage.

Although credit cards are generally thought to be free if the cardholder pays off the balance in full each month, there can be hidden charges. When using a credit card abroad, for example, there will be a foreign exchange loading which means you will be charged around 2.5 per cent on top of the exchange rate. Those withdrawing cash from ATMs at home or abroad are also usually charged a fee, which is generally 1.5 per cent of the withdrawal or a minimum of £1.50.

(See also **Charge Cards** and **Store Cards**.)

CREDIT RATINGS AGENCIES

In addition to individuals being given a credit rating or credit score which shows how creditworthy they are, companies are also credit rated.

Each corporate bond issued by a company to raise money is usually given a credit rating by an independent ratings agency – Standard & Poor's and Moody's are the two best known. Standard & Poor's ratings start at AAA for top-rated bonds and go down the scale through AA, A, BBB, BB, B and CCC. The further down the scale the more risky the strength of the company is deemed to be and therefore these companies will pay a higher yield to attract investors.

To find out the credit rating of a bond fund or a particular bond ask your financial adviser or stockbroker.

Any bond that has been rated BBB or above is considered to be investment grade and therefore a secure bond with little chance of the issuer defaulting on the interest payments. That is why government bonds – gilts – are AAA rated because the government guarantees repayment and is therefore considered the most secure bond issuer there is. Bonds that have been rated BB or below are described as non-investment grade. Low ratings can be given for a number of reasons. The ratings agency may feel that the company has poor prospects and the agencies also tend to prefer large companies with long histories. So small, young companies at an early stage of their development, but with good prospects for growth, may be given a low rating even though the risks may appear to be low. This may be because they do not have strong cash reserves.

CREDIT REFERENCE

See **Credit Scoring**.

CREDIT REPAIR AGENCIES

These services claim to be able to clean an individual's credit reference files – for a fee. However, in most cases if you have an adverse credit history, perhaps because you have defaulted on a loan or been taken to the county court for non-payment of a debt, there is nothing that can be done to improve your credit rating.

Credit repair agencies may also offer debt management services. They offer to take charge of your debts so instead of struggling to pay off a lot of different bills each month (or failing to pay them) you pay the agency one amount every month which they then use to pay the people you owe. But they charge you for this – usually all of the first month's payment as the arrangement fee and then about 15 per cent of the following payments. Effectively, they are adding to the debt.

The National Debtline, the Consumers' Association and the Citizens' Advice Bureau strongly advise people against using these agencies. One of their main criticisms is that the agencies rarely tell people what their options are and just present themselves as the only solution. They may not tell you that there is nothing to stop you taking charge yourself. You can call up your creditors and come to an arrangement with them. For example, they may well agree to freeze the interest so the debt does not get any bigger or they will allow you to come to an arrangement about how much you can afford to pay off every month. It may take much longer to pay off a debt this way but at least the people you owe know they will get their money and will view you more favourably because you are showing a responsible attitude. The bailiffs only come round if you refuse to deal with debt and ignore letters or phone calls.

Advice is available free from your local Citizens' Advice Bureau or from the National Debtline (see **Useful Addresses**).

CREDIT SCORING

Information on your credit status is used by banks, building societies, loan companies and retailers to help them decide about an application for credit. They have a scoring system which determines whether applicants have enough points and the information they use is supplied by credit reference agencies as well as information you supply on the application form. The credit reference agencies do not have a credit black list, they just supply information about existing and past credit agreements and how these have been managed by the individual concerned. They have files on nearly everyone in the country. There are two main credit reference agencies – Equifax and Experian (see **Useful Addresses**).

There are certain criteria that all companies use when rating or scoring an applicant. They prefer someone who has been resident at the same address for some years, has bills in their name, a regular job and has paid off past debts. Someone who has never borrowed money may be seen as a bad risk just because they have no track record of being able to repay debts. This means that the fact that you don't have lots of credit cards and loans could work against you.

There is nothing you can do if you are refused credit because you failed to pass a lender's credit scoring system. However, you can check that the information used by the lender is correct by asking to see a copy of your credit reference file from the credit reference agency the lender used. It costs £2 to get a copy of your credit file. Whoever has turned you down for credit must say which agency they used. The agency has seven days to reply. If there is a mistake on the file, write to the agency and ask them to remove or amend it.

Some people turn to credit repair agencies when they are turned down. The agencies claim to be able to make County Court Judgements or Scottish Decrees vanish from your record but any such judgement will stay on your record for six years even after it is repaid. When it comes to correcting mistakes on the credit file, they charge for a service which you can do yourself for just £2.

CREDIT UNIONS

Credit unions are mutually owned financial co-operatives (established under the Credit Unions Act 1979). They enable members to borrow money when other forms of finance are unavailable – often because of a poor credit history – or to borrow at competitive rates. They are often run by groups of workers or those with a common interest, for example, self-employed taxi drivers or staff associations. They work by encouraging members to save. This money is then loaned to other members at reasonable rates of interest. There are 686 credit unions registered in Great Britain with a membership of 293,000 and assets of £180 million.

CREST

This is the name of the electronic share settlement system which was introduced by CRESTCo in July 1996. If, as a shareholder, you want to trade shares electronically without the need for share certificates your stockbroker will, for a fee of around £10, make you a sponsored member of Crest. This will enable you to buy and sell shares far more quickly as you will not have to wait for share certificates to be issued when you buy them or sign transfers when you want to sell them. As a result you can meet the tighter settlement times – the period in which you must pay for shares you have purchased.

Even after you open a Crest Personal Account and your shares are held electronically, your name will stay on the companies' share register so you will still receive company information such as the annual report and accounts. Dividends can either be posted or sent to your bank account.

CRITICAL ILLNESS COVER (CIC)

Critical illness cover insures you against exactly that – a critical illness. A lump sum is paid out if you are diagnosed with a serious, life-threatening illness such as a heart attack, cancer, kidney failure and multiple sclerosis. Over a million people in the UK have this type of insurance which is designed to help them cover the costs of care, modifying their home or even a trip of a lifetime if they have only months left to live.

A man aged between twenty and forty has a one-in-four chance of developing a serious illness before retirement age, so if he is the only breadwinner in the family cover could be essential. The cost of taking out a first time CIC policy rises sharply after the age of forty so it is a good idea to buy it early if you need it. However, it can be expensive which is why it is now often sold packaged with life insurance. The policy then pays out either upon death or diagnosis of one of the insured illnesses. These policies are usually term assurance policies in that they only cover the insured for a set period or term – usually up to the point when the mortgage is repaid or retirement. The only drawback with these combined policies is that if there is a claim for a critical illness then the policyholder is left without life cover.

Critical illness cover is becoming more widespread partly because, due to medical advances, it is now much more likely people will survive a serious illness rather than it proving fatal.

CURRENT ACCOUNTS

A current account should be the cornerstone of everyone's finances, but an estimated one in ten of the population does not have access to one either because they prefer to use a savings account or are financially excluded because of poverty or a poor credit history.

Current accounts used to be fairly straightforward financial products. Each bank offered an account and there was little difference between them. However, the deregulation of the building societies in the 1980s opened up banking to new competition which has since been followed by the launch of Internet or online banks.

The bricks and mortar banks have responded with telephone and Internet banking services of their own, driven by a desire to cut costs.

Instead of just one current account, some of the larger banks now offer two, three or even four. Some are interest-bearing accounts that pay interest – usually a minimal amount – on credit balances.

Current account customers usually pay no charges provided they are in credit. However, more recently banks have started to introduce packaged accounts that offer a range of additional services, but for a monthly fee which is payable even if the customer is in credit.

It is when current account customers borrow money using an overdraft that the charges mount up. Agreed overdrafts usually have two costs: a monthly or quarterly fee, plus interest. Unauthorized overdrafts (borrowing without the agreement of your bank) have penal rates of interest and much higher fees which can mean that it costs £100 to borrow £100 over a short period of time. Overdraft rates are given as monthly rates as well as annual rates which are expressed as an EAR or effective annual rate (see entry on **EAR**). In addition banks have a range of other charges for services such as duplicate statements, bounced cheques (cheques which the customer has written out but cannot be honoured because there are insufficient funds) and letters informing them they have exceeded their overdraft.

Increasingly banks offer buffer zones. These are charge free and/or interest-free overdrafts up to a certain limit which can range from £50 to £250.

Most current account customers are given a three-in-one card that acts as an ATM card, a debit card and a cheque guarantee card, which guarantees that cheques will be honoured up to a certain limit, usually £50 or £100, as well as a cheque book. Other banking facilities include direct debits and standing orders.

D

DAILY RESTS

When interest on a mortgage is calculated on the outstanding balance each day – rather than at the end of the month or end of the year – this is known as daily rests. Traditional repayment mortgages calculate the repayments due over the year on the balance outstanding at the start of the year. So no account is taken of the repayments of capital made during the year. In effect, borrowers are therefore paying interest on money they no longer owe.

By calculating interest on a daily basis, every time the borrower makes a payment to reduce the mortgage debt the amount of interest he or she is charged is reduced automatically. With overpayments the effects can be dramatic which has led to the introduction of current account and flexible mortgages. Daily interest calculations are a requirement of the new CAT standards for mortgages.

(See also **Flexible Mortgages** and **Mortgages**.)

DAY TRADING

Day traders are a relatively new phenomenon. They are private investors who make the most of new technology – generally online share trading – to buy and sell shares or even futures contracts. The reason why they are called day traders is that they usually close their position at the end of the trading day, which means they do not hold any shares overnight when markets can move against them.

More gamblers than investors, day traders are tempted by the prospect of quick profits. Most trade the US markets which are more volatile and therefore offer the prospect of quick rises – and falls – in share prices. A day trader's tools are state-of-the-art technology and information feeds so that shares can be traded instantly and the trader has the most up-to-date inside information available. One recent study in the US found that seven in ten lose money.

(See also **Online Share Dealing**.)

DEBENTURE

Debentures are another way for companies to raise money – along with issuing shares and raising bank finance. Debentures are loans raised by the company and they pay a fixed rate of interest, which is secured on the assets of the company. They usually have a redemption date of between ten and forty years ahead of the date of issue. They may be secured by a floating charge on the company's assets or they may be tied to specific, named assets. As a result debenture holders have more security than ordinary shareholders and debenture interest has to be paid by a company whether it makes a profit or not or else debenture holders can legally force the company into liquidation to realize their claims on the company's assets.

DEBIT CARDS

A debit card is in effect an 'electronic cheque' but these cards are also increasingly a replacement for cash as even the smallest purchases (some retailers impose a minimum transaction level of £10) can now be paid for using a debit card, negating the need to carry large amounts of money. Debit cards are also being used as cash cards by customers frustrated by the fact that local bank branches have closed and there may no longer be a convenient – or free – ATM in their area. Supermarkets are now dispensing vast amounts of cash to customers at tills in addition to accepting debit cards to pay for groceries.

Debit cards work differently from credit cards because the money is taken out of your current account in two or three days, sometimes sooner, rather than you borrowing this money to repay it when your credit card statement arrives or at a later date. The card is linked to your current account and is usually a three-in-one card combining a debit, cash machine and cheque guarantee card on one piece of plastic.

The main debit card systems are Switch and Delta. These cards can now also be used abroad both to buy things and to withdraw cash from machines in the same way credit cards can. The Cirrus symbol on the card is the cash withdrawal service and the Maestro one is for making purchases.

DENTAL INSURANCE

Three in four dentists in the UK are no longer taking on new NHS patients. Even if you do manage to find one who will, you may have to pay 80 per cent of the costs yourself unless you are entitled to free dental care.

Dental insurance will cover things like check-ups, scale and polish, x-rays and fillings, extractions, root canals, bridgework and surgical treatment. Some will also cover you for emergency work, facial injuries and oral cancer. Make sure that if you accidentally chip a tooth, you will be covered.

Prices and the level of cover do vary greatly so compare exactly what you will be getting and how much it will cost. Some companies will insist on a check-up before you take out the policy so they can assess how much of a liability you are.

Not every policy will refund the full cost of private

treatment – some pay out for only 75 per cent and expect you to meet the rest of the cost yourself unless the treatment is urgent following an accident.

There may also be a qualification period which means that you will not be able to claim for check-ups and routine treatment for the first three months after taking out the policy. However, emergency treatment should be covered from the start.

To find out more about the dental insurance policies available, ask your dentist. If you have private health insurance also check with your insurer as to what dental treatments are covered by your policy.

DEPOSIT ACCOUNTS

These are savings accounts run by banks and building societies. Rates vary greatly but generally, the longer the period of notice you have to give before withdrawing the money, the higher the interest.

Giving 30, 60 or 90 days notice of withdrawal will push up the interest rate and so will opting for an account which limits the number of withdrawals you can make a year. It is possible to withdraw money from notice accounts without waiting the required period, but there will be a penalty – on a 30-day notice account for example, you would lose 30 days interest. However, instant access accounts whereby customers have access to their cash without having to give any notice are increasingly competitive, particularly from the newer savings institutions – the supermarkets and online banks.

The best rates on deposit accounts are mostly offered on telephone and postal accounts or on the Internet. With these, the account must be opened either on the telephone, by post or online. Cheques can be deposited by sending them in the post or in the case of online savings accounts cash can be moved electronically. The reason why savings institutions can offer such better rates is that they do not have the expense of running a branch network to deal with your business. These accounts are managed from a central location and the cost savings that result are passed on to savers.

In addition, term accounts, which are also called savings bonds, tend to offer highly competitive rates. With these the saver's cash is tied up for a set period, or term, with bonds usually paying a fixed rate of interest.

Some accounts have ridiculously low rates – as little as 0.1 per cent – so be very careful which one you choose and do not automatically go for a deposit account with your own bank when others may pay much higher interest. Despite the fact that banks and building societies give their deposit accounts names that imply they pay a high rate of interest, generally any account with gold in its name does not offer a glittering rate of interest.

Bear in mind that all interest earned in these accounts is paid net, which means it is taxed, so although it may be useful to keep a certain amount in these accounts for easy access, there are better ways to make your money work tax free such as investing in a tax-exempt individual savings account, i.e. an ISA (see entry on **ISAs**). If, however, you are a non-taxpayer you can register to receive interest gross, without tax deducted, by filling in form R85 available from your bank or building society.

When opening a deposit account, check if there is a flat rate of interest for all amounts or if interest is tiered. With tiered interest, the amount earned rises as more money is put into the account. However, if you make a withdrawal the amount remaining may drop into a lower tier and so earn less interest.

Interest rates change frequently so keep an eye on them and move to a better paying account if the rate drops. Some accounts pay a bonus for the first six months or so which will give savings a boost.

DEPOSIT PROTECTION BOARD/SCHEME

The Deposit Protection Board operates the Deposit Protection Scheme, which was established under the Banking Act 1979. The purpose of the scheme is to establish and maintain a standing fund, the Deposit Protection Fund, to give a measure of protection to depositors in the event of a bank failure.

The scheme covers 90 per cent of a bank's total liability to a depositor subject to a maximum payment to any one individual of £18,000 (or 20,000 Euro if greater).

The Financial Services Authority was, at the time of writing, establishing a single compensation scheme to replace the six existing compensation schemes operating in the financial services sector. It is proposed that the new scheme will be divided into three sub-schemes, one of which will cover deposits taken by banks and building societies. The new scheme is expected to be in place during the course of 2001.

(See also **Financial Services Compensation Scheme**.)

DERIVATIVES

Nick Leeson is perhaps the most infamous of derivatives traders over recent years. As his story revealed, derivatives are high-risk investments promising roller-coaster rides of big potential returns and magnified losses. The collapse of Barings Bank proved that derivatives can make fortunes and lose them. But they are not just for wealthy risk takers, and plenty of modest private investors use derivatives to reduce or hedge risks in their investment portfolio. In fact, many may indirectly own derivatives through other types of investment such as a pension fund or unit trust without even realizing it.

Derivatives are securities whose value depends on some other security or commodity. The basic ingredients are futures and options and the latter are more suited to private investors. Warrants are also a form of derivative similar to options.

Options are bets on the future price of anything from a commodity to a stock-market index to an ordinary share. Investors buy an option which gives them the right (or option) to purchase at a future date at a future price. Investors do not have to exercise this option but can let it lapse, for example, if the option price is higher than the actual price. Options are traded – bought and sold – on the London International Financial Futures and Options Exchange (LIFFE).

An investor may look at shares trading at 100p and feel they may rise quickly. Instead of buying the shares on the stock market and selling at a profit if they do rise, an investor could take out an option to buy at the exercise price of 100p at any time in the next three months. If the share price rises he or she can exercise the option and buy at 100p, which will be below the market price. If it falls, the investor can allow the option to lapse, do nothing and lose just the premium, or price of the option, probably at about 15p a share.

The example above is of a call option where the investor has the right to buy in the set time period. On the other hand, investors who think shares might fall can take out a put option, which bestows the right to sell if the market moves as they predict. In effect options give investors the right to buy or sell shares at a fraction of the market price.

When considering whether it is worth exercising an option investors have to look at the exercise price in comparison to the market price, but also add on the price paid for the option. If an option is worth exercising it is said to be in-the-money. An option which would cost an investor the same to exercise as buying the shares in the market is said to be at-the-money, and an option which if exercised would result in a loss is said to be out-of-the-money.

Buying options is a low-risk way into the stock market; at worst, people stand to lose the price they paid for the option. The opposite of buying options is to sell them, or 'write options' as it is known in the market, and this can be extremely risky. Selling options imposes obligations but no rights, whereas buying options bestows rights but no obligations.

A person who sells or writes a call must sell shares to the person who has bought the call option when it is exercised. This is bound to involve losing money for the option writer on what could be had from selling the shares into the stock market. Even worse is in store for people who write call options without owning the underlying shares. If the option is exercised they must go out and buy the shares in the stock market and then sell them for a lower price to the option holder.

Writing put options involves buying back shares from the put option holder who wants to sell the underlying shares. They must pay the put option holder the exercise price even though the market price of the underlying shares is sinking rapidly.

Futures contracts are riskier because the investor has to exercise the option to buy or sell even if the market goes against him. Losses can be unlimited.

(See also **Commodities**, **Futures** and **Warrants**.)

DIRECT DEBITS

The number of people paying by direct debit has soared in recent years rising fourfold in the ten years to 2000 with almost 32 million people in Great Britain now making at least one payment by direct debit. On average we pay six bills each by direct debit.

A direct debit is a mandate to a third party to take money from your bank account, for example, the gas or electricity company. You authorize your bank to pay an amount on instruction from a specified person or organization on a set date.

There are two reasons to pay by direct debit, one is convenience and the other is the discounts some companies offer. However, it can be more expensive to pay this way.

Direct debit works in two ways. When a customer receives a bill, it can be paid off in full, for example, renewing an annual subscription to a club or magazine. The other alternative is monthly payments. If you want to set up a monthly direct debit, forms will be supplied by the company you wish to pay. When setting up direct debits over the Internet, you should still be sent a form to sign for confirmation.

Some companies give discounts because it means they have the money on time each month, others charge extra because they would rather have the money up front. So when you are asked if you want to set up a direct debit, check if there are any savings or if it will cost you more to pay this way.

The most popular bills paid in this way are for mort-gages and cable or satellite TV. Internet and mobile phone bills are also rapidly catching up. These are the regular bills it is easier to pay this way so you don't have to worry about paying every month.

Direct debit is reliable. The DD Scheme offers a money back guarantee which ensures a full refund if an incorrect amount is taken or if the money goes out of an account before the agreed date. If the company you are paying wishes to change the amount of the direct debit or the date, it must give the customer written notice – usually around ten working days.

Some store cards offer a lower rate of interest for direct debit customers but their interest rates are so high anyway that this makes little difference.

Paying power bills by direct debit means the company works out how much you have used over the past year and assumes this year will be roughly the same. The cost of that much gas or electricity will be divided into twelve equal monthly payments. This may make the amount paid during the summer months look high but will be used to pay the extra used during the winter. Check if the amount does even out over the year; if you are paying too much each month you are effectively giving the company an interest-free loan. If payments are too low, then you will receive an extra bill at the end of the year.

A new type of direct debit system was introduced in 1999. Paperless direct debits were introduced to make the most of the convenience of technology over form filling. In its first year alone, these new paperless direct debits accounted for 10 per cent of all new direct debits set up. Instead of filling in a direct debit form, the debit can be set up via the telephone or Internet so that they can benefit from products and services earlier. Insurance, for example, can be purchased instantly without the customer having to wait for forms to be sent in the post. Paperless direct debit originators are subject to rigorous vetting procedures and must give customers written confirmation of a new instruction before any money is debited from their account.

(See also **Standing Orders**.)

DISCLOSURE

Hollywood made disclosure interesting when it made the movie of the same name starring Michael Douglas and Demi Moore. In the world of family finance disclosure is a little more mundane than the sexual politics, harassment and intrigue of the box office hit. It simply means that people selling insurance or pension policies must tell – disclose – how much of their premiums will be eaten up in charges and fees. The information must be presented in clear language and in a form that people can understand.

In addition to being given details of the commission in cash terms, investors will also get information on charges deducted from their investment or policy in a key features document which outlines what the product is, its costs, risks and other vital information. The effect of charges on the performance of the policy will also be given as a reduction-in-yield – how much the costs of the policy will reduce the investment returns.

The aim of the disclosure rules was to help consumers to shop around for the best-value policies before they buy. However, as they will only be given details of the commission the adviser will earn on products they are being recommended it is still difficult to compare how much a salesman will earn from different products.

If an investor is sold a life-insurance based investment such as a with-profits bond the commission paid to the adviser will be significantly higher than for a tax-free ISA, but the investor will probably not be given this information. So investors have no means of checking that they are not being recommended products because they earn the adviser more commission.

There are also disclosure rules for stockbrokers, who are required to tell you if they hold any shares in a company they are recommending you invest in. In other words, brokers must disclose any financial interest in shares they're making recommendations about. If the broker actually holds shares in the company or is acting as an adviser to that company it could influence his investment advice.

(See also **Advice** and **Commission**.)

DISCOUNT BROKERS

When you buy an investment – an ISA, a pension or an investment bond – the adviser selling it to you usually earns a commission. This money is taken out of the amount you invest. There is generally a commission charge up front and a smaller annual or renewal commission.

However, investors who do not need advice and who know the product they want, still have to pay this commission as the same charges are deducted from their investment or policy as are deducted from those who need advice. So in effect more informed investors are paying for a service they are not getting.

This has led to the rise and rise of the discount broker: a firm of financial advisers who give no advice (known as an execution-only service) – although they will often do the paperwork – and in exchange for keeping their costs low they rebate some or all of the commission they would have earned. Some discount brokers offer a slightly more sophisticated service listing their recommended products in brochures or offering investors the chance to assess their own needs by using interactive software on their Internet web service.

For example, if you invest in a stocks and shares ISA you will get an average of 3 per cent commission back and the broker keeps the 0.5 per cent annual commission. So if you have done the research and know exactly which ISA you want, you could significantly boost your investment returns. On the full ISA investment of £7,000 (per tax year), not paying an average 5 per cent commission would save £350.

Some brokers now even return half the annual fee as well. Although 0.25 per cent doesn't sound very much, if you have a lot of different investments then getting half of the annual fee back can add up considerably.

Not paying commission on bonds could save you £500 on a £10,000 investment, for example. This money could then be reinvested. Some brokers do not charge commissions on pensions either, just a flat fee. They must always tell you up front what their charges are so you can compare costs. If the fee is lower than the commission you would get back, then it will be worthwhile opting for the fee-based service.

Investors should weigh up the need for guidance with costs – taking a risk of going without any advice to save money may end up costing more in the end.

(See also **Advice**, **Commissions** and **Disclosure**.)

DISCRETIONARY

There are three types of fund management service offered by stockbrokers. Execution only – where your transactions are executed according to your wishes but no advice is given. Advisory – whereby you are advised and recommended to make certain investment decisions, but the ultimate decision is up to you. And, finally, discretionary whereby you give your manager the authority to buy and sell investments for you without obtaining your prior approval on each and every occasion. One of the major advantages of a discretionary service is that your fund manager will be able to take immediate action in response to changing market conditions without having to wait while he tracks you down to find out your wishes. Even though you hand over management to a professional you will, of course, be given details of any transactions so you can keep track of what you are investing in and how well your investments are performing. Generally, to employ a private client stockbroker on a discretionary basis you will need investments of at least £50,000 to £100,000.

DISTRIBUTION BONDS

Offered by some life insurance companies the objective of these is to provide security, income and capital growth with the investment structured so that capital growth and income can be separated from each other.

A significant part of the portfolio is invested in fixed interest stocks such as corporate bonds and gilts to provide the underlying income. The other main investment is usually income-bearing equities. However, note that some bonds that are called distribution bonds do invest up to 100 per cent in fixed interest areas or even up to 100 per cent in equities, although the general split should be nearer 40 to 60 per cent in each.

The returns on distribution bonds are paid net of basic

rate tax so only those who pay higher rate tax have any tax liability on encashment or regular withdrawals. Note that on encashment, the gain is divided by the number of years that the bond has been in operation to ascertain if the investor is pushed into a higher rate of tax.

These bonds are similar to with-profits bonds in many ways. However, with-profits bonds only move in one direction – upwards. The value of a distribution bond, on the other hand, can fall as well as rise. The fixed-interest element of the distribution bond should, however, limit any falls. However, on the upside, there is additional growth potential with a distribution bond if equities perform well.

DIVIDENDS

When you buy an ordinary share in a company, you become a shareholder and this gives you the right to receive dividend payments as set by the board of directors and approved by the shareholders. The dividend is a cut of the profits earned by the business for the year and is the income you earn as a shareholder. This pay-out is not guaranteed and the amount paid out will vary from company to company and year to year.

The dividend is usually expressed as the dividend per share in cash terms with investors usually receiving an interim (half-yearly) and final (end of year) dividend. So shareholders may be informed that they will earn a 10 pence dividend per share.

The dividend yield shows the current dividend as a percentage of the share price. A £1 share paying a 10 pence dividend has a yield of 10 per cent. If the share price falls to 50 pence the yield will rise to 20 per cent. Investors may also be given a dividend yield forecast which gives a good indication of whether or not brokers believe the company will increase its dividend. However, a very high dividend yield may indicate that the share price has fallen and not that brokers expect a dramatically increased dividend.

Dividends are subject to tax which is deducted before the dividend is paid. When calculating your tax liability dividends are treated as the top slice of total income, savings (interest) as the next slice and other income including wages and salaries as the lowest slice. However, dividends are currently taxed at a different rate to savings and other income. A rate of 10 per cent is paid up to the higher rate tax threshold and then the tax is 32.5 per cent. Non-taxpayers can, however, reclaim the 10 per cent tax deducted.

Smaller, younger and growing companies often pay smaller dividends as they want to hold back most of their profits to invest in the future of the company. Larger companies, however, tend to pay out steadily increasing dividends.

To find out how much of the profits are distributed to shareholders, investors need to look at the dividend cover. If a company makes £50 million of profits and allocates just £5 million for paying dividends it has a dividend cover of 10, which means the dividend payment is covered 10 times by the pre-tax profit. If the profits are just twice the amount of the dividends the cover will be 2. The dividend cover gives an indication of how safe future dividends will be. Obviously, a high level of cover means it is less likely that dividends will be reduced or dropped altogether if future profits fall.

Even if a company suffers a dramatic drop in profits or makes a loss, it can still continue to pay dividends showing that it expects this downturn in its fortunes to be only temporary. If dividends are paid during a year of losses, they will be paid out from reserves.

Shareholders should also look at the price earnings ratio or P/E ratio of a share and the earnings per share (EPS) when evaluating the investment potential of a share.

(See also **Earnings Per Share**.)

E

EAR

This is yet another way of expressing the cost of borrowing. It is the effective annual rate borrowers pay on an overdraft. As with the APR – or annual percentage rate – it is designed to make it easier for borrowers to compare the cost of borrowing. The reason why overdraft interest rates are expressed differently to other forms of borrowing is that overdrafts usually incur charges as well as interest. If the bank or building society charges no monthly or quarterly account fee for those who are overdrawn, the APR may be quoted.

Borrowers should not rely solely on the EAR as an indication of the cost of their overdraft. Fee-free (and sometimes interest-free) buffer zones will be cheaper than borrowing above the buffer zone limit.

EARLY REDEMPTION CHARGE/PENALTY

Mortgage lenders may charge a redemption penalty on certain types of mortgages, usually those with cheap introductory, discounted or fixed rates. Borrowers may have to pay a penalty if they pay off or redeem their mortgage during the low-rate period which is usually up to five years. However, some lenders charge borrowers beyond the low-rate period – these are known as extended redemption penalties. Redemption penalties are designed to lock borrowers in so they cannot take advantage of a low rate and then switch to another low rate from another lender within the first few years of the loan. The penalties can either be equivalent to the discount received or as much as three or even six months monthly interest payments. CAT standard mortgages cannot have extended redemption penalties.

EARNINGS CAP

This is the maximum earnings on which you can make contributions to a personal pension or occupational pension scheme. As pension contributions offer such generous tax breaks, there are limits on how much you can pay into a scheme and take out upon retirement. For example, members of employer's or occupational pension schemes are only allowed to pay in a total of their net relevant earnings each tax year into the scheme. However, they can only pay in this percentage up to the earnings cap which was set at £95,400 for the 2001–2002 tax year and is usually increased at the start of each tax year following the Budget.

EARNINGS PER SHARE (EPS)

Perhaps the single most important measure of how well (or otherwise) the board of directors are doing for the shareholders, the earnings per share measure shows how many pence the company is earning for every share held. Calculated by dividing the pre-tax profit by the number of shares in issue it is expressed in pence. So if a company makes £100 million of profits and has 500 million shares in issue, the earnings per share will be 20 pence.

Finding out the EPS of a company is vital as it shows the value given to shareholders. After all, if a company boosts its profits by 100 per cent but also doubles the number of shareholders then there is less value for shareholders than if the number of shares in issue remained the same.

EASDAQ

This Brussels-based Pan-European stock market was set up in November 1996 along similar lines to NASDAQ in the USA.

EMERGING MARKETS

These are the economies of Latin America, Eastern Europe and Asia which are expected to grow faster than their more mature counterparts and therefore offer the prospect – but not the promise – of higher returns to investors prepared to gamble on their future growth. Characterized by cheap, flexible labour forces and a willingness to embrace new technology, the emerging markets have had a roller-coaster ride in recent years.

The fact is that these economies are highly vulnerable to market sentiment – a jitter about debt repayments in one country can lead to stock markets crashing around the world – as well as political and economic factors. So they should be viewed as a high-risk investment for a small proportion of an investor's portfolio, not a guaranteed get-rich-quick scheme.

Investing in overseas markets directly is difficult. That is why fund managers have set up unit trust funds to make it easier for private investors to tap into these markets. Not only do these funds provide a spread of risk by investing in a number of companies and markets they also provide expertise. The best performing funds have analysts in each country spotting investing opportunities for investors. Pension and life insurance policies may also offer investors the chance to put some of their contributions into emerging markets.

Investors can either invest in a global emerging market trust that invests in a range of markets round the world with the mix of these markets changing as the fund managers see fit. Or they can opt for a regional trust that does the same, but only for specific areas such as Latin America or the Far East.

EMPLOYEE SHARE OWNERSHIP

For many years employees have enjoyed tax breaks to encourage them to buy shares in the company for which they work. Even more are expected to take the opportunity to buy shares following the introduction of a new all-employee share plan introduced in July 1999.

Under the new scheme employers can give up to £3,000 of free shares to employees, employees can subscribe up to £1,500 for shares from tax-free income and employers can match the employee's ownership of these shares 2:1. So if the employee buys the maximum allowed, the employer can give a further £3,000 worth. In addition, any shares held for five years will be exempt from income tax, capital gains tax and National Insurance contributions and up to

£1,500 worth of dividends can be reinvested in shares free of tax each year.

These tax savings are substantial. Being given up to £3,000 of shares free of income tax can give a saving of up to £1,200, buying £1,500 of shares from pre-tax salary can give a maximum tax saving of £600 a year and, for workers who do purchase shares, employers will be able to award an additional £3,000 of shares, another saving of up to £1,200.

The more established employee share schemes – save as you earn (SAYE), Sharesave and company share option plans (CSOPs) – which between them have around two million participants continue to run despite the introduction of the new scheme. However, when the all-employee share plan was introduced, it was announced that approved profit-sharing schemes – which are very similar to the new plans – will be gradually phased out by 2002.

Under the new scheme employers are obliged to make their schemes open to all employees, whether full-time or part-time. In return for running these schemes, companies will get corporation tax relief for the costs incurred in providing the shares to employees.

The aims of the scheme are to increase the level of share ownership in employees' own companies and to improve long-term company performance – something that can be achieved by linking the awarding of free shares to employment performance.

Save-as-you-earn schemes are set up by your employer, under which you get share options. These give you a right to buy a certain number of shares at a fixed price on a set date. But you can only buy shares using amounts you have saved under a special savings contract – the save-as-you-earn account. Employees are in a win-win situation as the option is usually granted at a discount of up to 20 per cent of the current market price – so the shares would have to fall by this much for employees to lose out. Even if they do fall, employees cannot lose. They can simply take the money they have saved and not buy the shares. You can save a fixed amount – between £5 and £250 – a month for a fixed period of three, five or seven years with a building society or bank into the save as you earn scheme. You can normally only join the scheme if you are a UK employee with five years' service. But a company can take people into the scheme with less than five years' service.

Company share option plans give the option to buy shares at a fixed price on a set date. The option price (the price you will pay for the shares) must not be less than the market value of the shares at the time you are given them. As the name implies, you only have an option to buy the shares – if you don't want to buy them you don't have to. The total value of shares which can be held as options cannot exceed £30,000.

ENDOWMENTS

Few financial products have had as bad a press in recent years as endowments, particularly since it emerged that millions of homebuyers may be paying into policies that will not pay off their mortgage debt, let alone provide a promised tax-free lump sum in addition.

Inflexible, expensive and poorly performing, these investment plans have been criticized for benefiting the people selling them more than the buyers. Endowments are now no longer widely sold as policies to repay mortgages. In the late 1980s as many as nine in ten mortgages were sold on an interest-only basis which meant that the borrower paid only the interest on the loan. The capital was to be repaid using an endowment policy, an investment scheme that also offered some life insurance cover.

However, today fewer than three in ten mortgages taken out are backed by endowment policies with many of the major lenders now no longer selling these policies.

Even so, those who have long-standing policies are still finding that when their policy matures, usually after twenty-five years, they have sufficient capital to not only repay their mortgages but also have a lump sum in addition. It is those who have taken out policies in more recent years that are likely to suffer as investment returns are unlikely to provide sufficient growth to produce the projected amount when these policies were first taken out. Many life companies have been forced to write to policyholders warning them that there could be a shortfall and asking for them to increase their monthly contributions to their policies if they want to be sure that their mortgage will be repaid in full at the end of the policy term.

Homeowners who receive the bad news that their endowment may not repay their mortgage have several choices. The first option – the one life insurance companies ask policyholders to choose – is to increase monthly premiums to make up the shortfall. This option will ensure that the endowment will produce sufficient returns to pay off the mortgage debt based on current investment performance assumptions. However, there are no guarantees that further premium increases will not be required in future.

An alternative is to ignore the request for a premium increase and instead invest the extra cash in a different investment such as a tax-efficient ISA, where the money could grow faster and the charges will be lower. However, the life company will no longer guarantee that your endowment will produce sufficient returns to repay the mortgage debt. A third option is to leave the endowment policy 'paid up', which means you pay no more money into it, although the existing investment will continue to grow, and instead start an alternative investment. This could be an option if the endowment has been taken out in the last few years. Starting an alternative investment could give the homebuyer a chance to produce a higher return or even pay off their mortgage early.

The pessimistic forecasts of investment performance which have led to thousands of endowment policyholders being warned of an investment shortfall, actually paint a rosy picture. High charges mean that investors often get very little back if they need to cash in their plans early. These surrender values can even be less than the amount paid in if the policyholder cashes in their endowment in the first few years. An alternative is to leave the endowment paid up which means that the policy continues to grow – although at a slower rate – until maturity. Another option is to sell or auction the endowment on the traded endowments market. Several firms act as intermediaries between buyers and sellers of policies with sellers getting up to 30 per cent more than the surrender value of their policies. Only with-profits endowments can be sold in this way. If you want to sell an endowment policy the Association of Policy Market Makers can supply lists of companies that offer this service. (See **Useful Addresses**.)

With-profits policies are designed to smooth out the peaks and troughs of stock-market movements. Investors start with a basic sum assured and have this increased each year by a series of annual or reversionary bonuses. Once added, these bonuses cannot be removed even if markets crash. But fund managers do not pass on all the benefits of a market rise straight away. Some growth is held in reserve so that they can still pay bonuses in years when the stock market is flat or falling. Investors who stick with the endowment to its maturity are paid a final or terminal bonus which can comprise up to half the total payment.

Unit-linked endowment policies do not work on this basis. They are much more straightforward in that the investor buys units in an investment fund or funds and the value of these units rises and falls in line with the underlying trend in the stock market. As such these funds are more risky – there is no ironing out of stock-market movements using the bonus system. However, performance tends to be higher than for with-profit type policies.

A newer type of policy is the unitized with-profits endowment which is a combination of the two types of policy. Investors buy units in a fund but also receive bonuses.

Many of the larger lenders no longer sell endowment mortgages. So, if a mortgage broker or lender does recommend one, ask why they are selling you this policy – there are cheaper and more flexible alternatives available. Also bear in mind that many lenders and financial advisers are tied to one insurance company, so even if you are convinced that an endowment policy is the best option, you also need to ensure that you are buying the best policy available. Performance varies widely. Over twenty-five years, a £500 annual investment in an endowment policy could have produced a return in excess of £100,000 if invested with a top performing company. In a poor performing company that return would be nearer £70,000 – i.e. £30,000 less.

Endowments are also offered as investments, particularly for school fees planning. Once again, there are cheaper and more flexible alternatives available that can produce better returns.

Generally, endowments are only a wise investment for those prepared to commit to regular investments over a long period of time, who know for sure that they will not have to cash in their policy early and who are prepared to accept that their investment returns may be lower in exchange for additional security and lower risk.

ENTERPRISE INVESTMENT SCHEME (EIS)

Tax breaks to encourage investors to back small, higher risk companies that are seeking funding have been a main part of government policy to help boost the enterprise economy.

The enterprise investment scheme is one of these and allows individuals to invest up to £150,000 a year in an unquoted company and enjoy the benefit of some juicy looking tax breaks.

The tax breaks are:

- Income tax relief available at a rate of 20 per cent. In other words, invest £1,000 and the taxman gives you back £200.

- No capital gains tax relief.

- Relief against losses which you may suffer on disposal. If the investment falls in value the losses you have suffered can be set against any other profits you have made to reduce any other capital gains tax liabilities.

To claim the above tax benefits you must invest for a minimum of three years – this was reduced from five years in the 2000 Budget.

EIS schemes have similar reliefs to venture capital trusts

(VCTs). However, the EIS tend to invest in individual companies and VCTs spread your investment between a number of companies, thereby spreading the risk.

(See also **Venture Capital Trusts**.)

EQUITIES

Equities – the risk-sharing part of a company's capital – are usually referred to as ordinary shares. Companies have a number of ways of raising finance. They can raise bank finance (debt), issue bonds (these are like loans) or issue shares. These equities give investors the potential for an income from dividends and a capital gain, but if the company fails shareholders suffer most and therefore they take the biggest risk.

Equities tend to outperform savings (deposits). Over the ten years from April 1990 to April 2000, a £1,000 investment in the average UK All Companies fund would have grown to £3,316, a healthy 230 per cent return. The average deposit account would have returned £1,491 for the same ten-year period according to the Association of Unit Trusts and Investment Funds.

ETHICAL INVESTMENTS

Investors have been 'going green' for years and putting their money where their morals are. Ethical and environmentally friendly funds do not invest in companies that pollute or produce products such as arms or tobacco or are involved in animal testing, nuclear power, arms trading, GM food or human rights abuse.

Increasingly popular among investors, some £2.8 billion is now being invested in these so-called green funds.

However, not all ethical funds are the same. The dark-green funds have the strictest policy while lighter green funds will invest in companies which are making good progress in improving their ethical performance.

Choosing only dark-green funds will limit the shares you can choose from. Try to match your main priorities with the funds and go for a good spread of small, medium and large international companies to even out the risk and returns. So if human rights abuse is more important to you than alcohol or tobacco investments, tailor your investments accordingly.

However, if top returns are the investor's main priority, ethical funds are not the best bet. On the whole, they do not perform as well as non-ethical investments and in the medium term are higher risk. For example, with the top performing ethical fund you could double your money in three years whereas with the top non-ethical one, it could quadruple. Doubling your money is still pretty good compared with bank and building society rates so these funds should not be dismissed entirely.

For anyone who doesn't have investments but who would like to make an ethical effort, the Co-op is the leading bank with a policy of not investing or lending money to companies involved in the activities shunned by the ethical fund managers. The Ecology Building Society also has an ethical policy targeting its mortgage lending to environmentally friendly homes.

The Ethical Investment Research Information Service (EIRIS) keeps an eye on how UK companies respond to ethical, environmental or social issues and advises many ethical fund managers how to check their portfolios conform to their investment charters. The UK Social Investment Forum (UKSIF), is the body responsible for the promotion of all aspects of ethical investment and provides a guide to who's who and what's what including ethical independent financial advisers.

(See **Useful Addresses** for contact details for EIRIS and UKSIF.)

EUROS

The euro, Europe's single currency, officially came into being on 1 January 1999 in eleven countries in the European Union. The new currency zone excludes Britain which has yet to decide whether it will adopt the single European currency and ditch the pound.

Countries that adopted the euro now have their currencies pegged to it at set exchange rates so there are no longer any currency fluctuations within the eurozone. However, the euro itself does fluctuate and has consistently fallen in value since it was adopted.

Actual hard currency – notes and coins – did not become legal tender until 1 January 2000 when each member country's existing currencies stopped being circulated in order that they can be replaced by euros. After 1 July 2002 local currencies will cease to be legal tender. Until then euros are mainly used for commerce – it is possible to have euro bank accounts and shares and other financial securities are traded in euros. In the meantime each member country is also operating a dual currency system where goods and services are priced in both the local currency and euros. Euro coins are denominated in cents.

EXCESS

When making an insurance claim, policyholders are expected to pay the first part of this claim themselves. This is known as the excess and is usually around £50, but for something like subsidence can be as much as £2,500.

One way to reduce premiums is to opt to pay a larger excess on any claim. But opting for a higher excess could exclude you from some claims entirely. For example, if your house is broken into, claims for a lock replacement may have a built-in maximum of around £250, so if you had opted to pay that much as an excess there would be no point claiming. However, if you made a claim for several thousands, the £250 excess would not make much difference.

Excess on car insurance does not reduce the cost of policies significantly – an average of £43 a year – and one small dent which the excess excluded you from claiming for could cost more than you save.

Home building and contents insurance excesses also save very little on the premiums. With one company, an excess of £250 would save only £7 a year on the premium.

So, with such little savings, it may not be worthwhile to opt for a higher excess. However, it is always worthwhile asking how a higher excess will affect premiums as in some cases you may find that the reduction in premiums is significant. Only opt for a higher excess, however, if you are sure that you could afford to pay for any claim below the excess limit out of your own pocket and that your chances of making a claim are very slim.

EXECUTION ONLY

Nothing to do with death sentences, this term simply means that a deal is merely executed or transacted on an investor's behalf – no advice is given.

Execution-only services appeal to more sophisticated investors who know what they want to buy but do not want to pay for advice – or to have commission deducted from their investment to pay for advice they do not need or want.

In general, stockbrokers are referred to as execution-only brokers if they do not give advice. Financial advisers who offer execution-only services are often called discount brokers.

The rise in private share ownership has seen execution-only dealing increase rapidly and it now accounts for almost half of all private investor activity with much of this through telephone and Internet broking services.

Convenience, speed and the low cost of these services – with minimum share dealing charges starting at around £10 to £15 – make execution-only services ideal for those who simply want to buy or sell a particular share.

The costs of a full investment management service from a stockbroker would make buying small amounts of shares uneconomical hence the fact that stockbroking companies in the City require minimum portfolios of £25,000 upwards. Rather than a full discretionary service (where investment decisions are at the discretion of the stockbroker) a cheaper alternative is dealing-with-advice.

F

FEE-BASED ADVICE

Most financial advisers earn their living by taking a commission from the life insurance or investment companies whose products they sell. So although they advise an individual they are paid by a financial institution, which has led to concerns that they may not always have the investor's best interests at heart particularly if the most suitable product does not earn them a commission. Even though the commission has to be disclosed some investors fear that they are being recommended a particular product because it pays the adviser a higher commission than a different one.

This has led to the rise of fee-based advice services from some independent financial advisers, who usually work for either a set or hourly fee in the same way as an accountant or solicitor. Any commission that would have been paid on an investment is then rebated to the investor. Fee-based advice can therefore work out to be cheaper than what appears to be 'free' advice, if the fee is less than the commission. The added advantage of fee-based advice is that investors will be recommended products of companies that do not pay a commission to advisers.

(See also **Commissions** and **Discount Brokers**.)

FINAL SALARY SCHEMES

These are occupational or company pension schemes that pay out a pension to scheme members (employees) based on a fraction of their pensionable earnings (those taken into account by your scheme) at or near retirement for each year they have been a member of the scheme. The most commonly used fraction is one-sixtieth, so if you are a member from age twenty-five to sixty-five, your pension would be forty-sixtieths, or two-thirds, of your final earnings. Fewer years in the scheme means a smaller pension. The pension usually gets regular increases, there's nearly always a pension for your wife or husband if you die first and, if you die before retirement, most schemes include life cover of up to four times the employee's annual salary. Retiring early generally means a reduced pension (unless ill health is the cause) and upon retirement you will be able to take part of your pension as a tax-free lump sum.

The guaranteed nature of these pensions (you know what you will get on retirement) makes them a valuable perk for employees, but also expensive to run and many employers now no longer allow new employees to join final salary schemes. Instead they must join a money purchase pension scheme that pays a pension based on the level of contributions into the pension, how well these are invested and the annuity rates prevailing at the time of retirement.

FINANCIAL EXCLUSION

Lone parents, those on low wages, ethnic minorities, people with disabilities and the unemployed are more likely to be without personal finance services. The government and the Financial Services Authority have been looking at ways to tackle financial exclusion. This has led to the proposed launch of Universal Banking services by the Post Office which will enable those with no bank account to receive benefits. In addition the banks have also rolled out no-frills current accounts aimed at customers with no credit history in response to government pressure. These accounts usually require no minimum monthly credit, offer a debit or cash card but no cheque guarantee card and have no overdraft facilities.

Until the government's proposals are finalized and implemented, those who find that they are financially excluded have very few options. A few banks have current accounts which have no overdraft facilities and sometimes no cheque guarantee card which are targeted at those with a poor credit history or no credit history. Provided the account holder maintains the account in credit and shows that they can manage their finances, they may then be able to progress to a more mainstream current account.

THE FINANCIAL OMBUDSMAN SERVICE (FOS)

Although this new single financial dispute resolution scheme was set up in February 1999, it did not receive its statutory powers until the Financial Services and Markets Act became law.

The scheme largely mirrors the coverage of the eight previously existing dispute resolution schemes it replaced, but extends access to small businesses (as complainants) in the insurance sector for the first time. The dispute resolution schemes being replaced were: the Banking Ombudsman, the Building Society Ombudsman, the Investment Ombudsman, the Insurance Ombudsman Bureau, the Personal Investment Authority Ombudsman Bureau, the Personal Insurance Arbitration Service, the Securities and Futures Authority Complaints Bureau and Arbitration Service and the FSA Complaints Unit.

Said to be the largest ombudsman scheme in the world, at least 10,000 firms are subject to the scheme's compulsory jurisdiction, which applies to FSA authorized firms only. Based on the experience of the existing schemes the FOS expects to receive each year a minimum of 30,000 written complaints requiring conciliation and/or formal awards, 30,000 written enquiries and 150,000 telephone enquiries.

Although the aim of the FOS is to provide consumers with access to speedy and effective dispute resolution, just as with the Ombudsmen schemes it replaced, there is a requirement for complaints to be made to the financial firm involved in the first place. Each firm must have appropriate procedures for resolving complaints and only after these procedures have been exhausted will the FOS investigate the matter.

The new ombudsman service will be available to private individuals, small businesses with a turnover of less than £1 million and third parties (i.e. not direct customers) in specified circumstances. The limit on individual awards that the new Financial Ombudsman Service can make is £100,000.

All authorized firms – banks and building societies, insurance companies and investment firms, etc – are covered by the Financial Ombudsman Service on a compulsory basis for regulated activities, plus those previously unregulated activities – such as mortgage lending – which were not covered by the previous ombudsman schemes. In the long term, the aim of the new Financial Ombudsman Service is to cover as many areas of financial services as possible.

FINANCIAL SERVICES AND MARKETS ACT

The original Financial Services Act of 1986 was a monumental piece of legislation which spawned a huge bureaucracy, a complex network of self-regulatory bodies and introduced regulations designed to ensure that investors would be given greater consumer protection than ever before. When the Act came into effect in April 1988 all those carrying out investment business in the UK had to be authorized, adequately trained and regulated.

However, there were flaws in the regulatory system and it was plagued by a series of scandals, including widespread mis-selling of personal pension plans even though the Act was supposed to ensure that investors were given best advice.

When New Labour came to power it immediately went about reforming the system. In May 1997 the new government announced plans for a single statutory authority to regulate the financial markets and by July 1998 a draft financial services and markets bill was published. Finally, after some political wrangling and changes to the bill after it was claimed it would breach the European Convention on Human Rights, the Financial Services and Markets Act was given Royal Assent in June 2000, giving sole responsibility for financial regulation to the Financial Services Authority. However, as so many firms are to be brought under the new regulatory umbrella and rulebooks need to be written and new complaints and compensation schemes set up, it will not be until mid to late 2001 that the new FSA regime is fully operational.

The main purpose of the Financial Services and Markets Act, is to provide a single legal framework for the Financial Services Authority in place of the different frameworks under which the various regulators currently operate. As a result, most of its provisions represent consolidation of existing law or self-regulatory requirements.

In this category are:

- arrangements for authorization of firms, currently operated in all three sectors (insurance, investment business and banking);

- arrangements for approval of individuals, currently operated in different ways in all three sectors;

- rulemaking powers, currently available in the insurance and investment business sectors;

- information gathering and investigation powers, currently available in relation to all three sectors;

- intervention powers, for example, to require a firm to stop taking on new business, currently available in all three sectors;

- powers to impose financial penalties on authorized firms and approved individuals, currently available to self-regulating organizations in the investment business sector, which the Bill now puts on a statutory basis with a right to a full hearing before an independent tribunal established by the Lord Chancellor's Department.

The main new powers provided by the Act are:

- powers to impose financial penalties on those who abuse investment markets, for example by insider dealing or market manipulation;

- the role of the United Kingdom Listing Authority, which will be undertaken under substantially the same powers as previously exercised by the London Stock Exchange.

As with the previous regulatory system every individual and firm that carries out financial business in the UK must be authorized by the FSA. The authorization is a bit like a driving licence in that there is one licence but it has a list of permissions on it – all the things which the regulator allows a financial firm or individual to do. Some 10,000 firms are being brought into FSA authorization and as such the new regime is not expected to be fully operational until the end of 2001.

The regulatory net extends to cover banks, building societies, life insurance companies, financial advisers, friendly societies, the Lloyd's insurance market, stockbrokers, fund managers, derivatives traders and even professional firms such as solicitors, accountants and actuaries carrying on investment business. Firms are required to meet certain solvency requirements to ensure that individuals are trained and competent.

THE FINANCIAL SERVICES AUTHORITY

The Financial Services Authority (FSA) – until October 1997 known as the Securities and Investments Board (SIB) – is an independent non-governmental body with statutory powers. It became the sole regulator of the financial services sector under the Financial Services and Markets Act 2000.

The Securities and Investments Board (SIB), which it replaced, was established in 1985 and acquired its powers under the Financial Services Act 1986, which established what was then a new and wide-ranging system of regulation. The SIB was given the main responsibility for ensuring that this system operated effectively with a number of self-regulatory organizations (SROs) including the Personal Investment Authority (PIA) having responsibility for various market sectors. These SROs – the PIA, the Investment Managers Regulatory Organization and the Securities and Futures Association – are now being merged into the FSA.

The SIB then formally changed its name to the Financial Services Authority in October 1997. It then became the sole regulator in 2000 and took on a number of extra responsibilities including regulation of Lloyd's of London, credit unions, mortgages and professional firms. It also took over from the London Stock Exchange the role of the UK Listing Authority.

The four main aims of the FSA are to:

- maintain confidence in the UK financial system;

- promote public understanding of the financial system;

- secure an appropriate degree of protection for consumers; and

- contribute to reducing financial crime.

The FSA has pledged to adopt a 'proactive and preventative' approach to regulation aiming to head off problems in advance by identifying and addressing the most important risks to firms, markets and consumers. The FSA is also responsible for the new complaints handling system, the Financial Ombudsman Service.

It has already introduced a number of initiatives to help educate consumers including publishing a range of booklets and announcing plans to provide impartial comparative data on personal pensions, endowments, investment bonds, unit trust ISAs and mortgages on the Internet. These comparative tables will help consumers understand the factors they need to take into account when thinking about buying a financial product.

THE FINANCIAL SERVICES COMPENSATION SCHEME

Just as the Financial Services and Markets Act set up a single regulator, it also set up a single Financial Services

Compensation Scheme, which came into operation in February 2001 and provides compensation for consumers when a financial services firm is unable to meet certain claims against it.

Six existing compensation schemes are being merged into a single 'one stop shop': the Deposit Protection Scheme, the Building Society Investor Protection Scheme, the Policyholders Protection Scheme, the Friendly Societies Protection Scheme, the Investors Compensation Scheme and Section 43 Scheme.

As a result the varying levels of compensation offered by these former schemes are being unified to provide a reasonable level of compensation to individual consumers and small businesses that have lost money through the collapse of a bank, building society, insurer or investment firm. The current proposals for levels of compensation in the event that a financial firm ceases to trade and cannot repay money it owes are:

- claims relating to non-compulsory general and life insurance to be met in full;

- increase in the maximum amount payable on claims relating to deposits from £18,000 to £31,700;

- for claims relating to investment firms the first £30,000 of any claim in full and then 90 per cent of the next £20,000 up to a maximum of £48,000 for each investor;

- large companies will be excluded from deposit protection;

- large partnerships are to be excluded from protection for claims on non-compulsory general insurance policies, but small companies will be included for the first time;

- deposit protection to be extended to deposits in all currencies.

FLEXIBLE MORTGAGES

Flexible mortgages are one of the fastest growing financial products on offer. In 1999 they accounted for 11 per cent of total gross mortgage lending and by 2004 this is predicted to rise to 50 per cent. They were first introduced in the UK in the mid 1990s from Australia where flexible mortgages are the norm.

However, like many financial terms, this one can be misleading. In theory flexible mortgages are what they seem – flexible to meet a borrower's needs and changing circumstances by allowing the borrower to vary monthly repayments and allowing overpayments, underpayments, payment holidays. However, some so-called flexible mortgages are less flexible than others.

Although almost 18 per cent of borrowers think they hold a flexible mortgage only 5 per cent do, according to a survey in 2000 by flexible mortgage lender First Active.

Flexible mortgages should charge interest on a daily basis known as daily rests so that any additional payments are used immediately to reduce the amount of interest a borrower is charged. However, not all of them do. With traditional mortgages overpayments under a certain amount (often £500) will not be credited to the account until the end of the calendar year – so borrowers are effectively paying interest on money they have already repaid. This is because the mortgage interest and level of repayments is calculated on the outstanding balance at the start of the year. Some flexible mortgages recalculate the interest monthly and can still make borrowers savings provided they only want to make monthly overpayments.

As a result of daily rests and the ability to make additional payments, flexible mortgages can save the borrower vast amounts of interest and enable homebuyers to pay off their mortgage earlier than otherwise.

For example, a homebuyer with a £70,000 mortgage over twenty-five years who pays off an extra £50 a month would save over £20,000 in interest and clear their mortgage off in less than twenty instead of twenty-five assuming a mortgage rate of 7 per cent.

Although flexible mortgages allow overpayments, not all allow for reduced monthly payments or payment holidays – where you make no payments at all. Underpayments are usually restricted by the maximum loan to value – which can range from 75 to 90 per cent of the value of the property. When borrowers take advantage of underpayments or payment holidays, the interest mounts up and the amount owed will rise.

This is why many lenders insist borrowers build up a reserve through prior overpayments before they can underpay or take a payment holiday. In some cases there is a qualifying period and there might be a maximum period during which borrowers can underpay.

Another facility offered by many – but not all – flexible mortgages is loan drawdown. With a traditional mortgage, borrowers have to apply for a further advance if they want to take out equity built up in their home or increase the size of their mortgage. This is expensive as it usually involves a new property valuation and an application fee. There is usually a minimum amount that can be borrowed and it usually has to be borrowed over a long period – usually the same period as the original mortgage. Also many lenders will only agree to further advances if they are to pay for home improvements.

The loan drawdown facility offered by flexible mortgages is far more convenient – there are no delays while an application for a further advance is made, small amounts can be withdrawn and the borrowing can be repaid at any time subject to equity in the property. However, with some flexible mortgages the drawdown facility is restricted to a reserve built up through previous overpayments.

The most flexible of all flexible mortgages and the ones that potentially offer the biggest interest savings are current account mortgages which are also known as all-in-one mortgages.

These link all the borrower's personal finances – current account, mortgage, savings, loans and credit cards – to one account. One flat rate of interest is paid on all borrowings – so overdrafts and loans are at the much lower mortgage rate. Any credits – such as money in the current account or in savings – are used to offset the amount owed on a daily basis and therefore reduce the amount of interest borrowers have to pay. It means that the day the borrower gets paid and their salary is paid into their current account, their interest charge drops. So if a borrower owes £60,000, has £5,000 in savings and has just been paid £2,000 then interest is only charged on £53,000 of mortgage debt.

Some mortgages are not all-in-one accounts but do offer an offsetting facility so that the cash held on deposit or in a current account can be used to reduce the borrowing costs on any debts. However, each pot of money is kept in a separate account rather than all-in-one.

So should you opt for a flexible mortgage? Flexible mortgages mainly benefit those who are prepared to pay off more than the minimum required each month. Borrowers who only want to make standard monthly repayments with no flexibility, will not make savings unless their existing mortgage does not calculate interest on a daily basis. However, most borrowers can benefit from an all-in-one account. This is because all of their money works for them all of the time including any money in their current account.

(See also **Mortgages**.)

THE FOOTSIE

The FTSE 100, the index of the top 100 shares by market capitalization, is the most popular index for tracking the movements of the London stock market. Devised by the *Financial Times*, the London Stock Exchange and the Faculty of Actuaries, this is just one index used to monitor the performance of shares. It is the average of the share price of the biggest 100 companies with larger companies given more importance by a system of weighting to take into account their size. It is recalculated every minute. When first launched on 3 January 1984 the index began at a base level of 1,000. It now stands at around 6,000. Shares enter and leave the index every quarter.

(See also **Indices**.)

FOREIGN CURRENCY

The world of foreign currency has two very different faces. One is the side holidaymakers see: small amounts of foreign currency bought and sold over the counter at travel agents, banks, building societies, post offices, bureaux de change offices, airports and ports before they leave home. Then there is the international foreign exchange markets where currencies are bought and sold by governments and institutions such as banks, insurers, pension and investment funds to the tune of hundreds of billions of pounds a day around the world.

For the humble holidaymaker the price of foreign money differs depending on where it is bought. Buyers should check both the exchange rate charged, which can change daily, and the commission or fee. There will be a difference between the buying and selling price of the currency so check which rate is being quoted or whether it is a mid rate that is advertised. The exchange rate is often different for cash than it is for travellers' cheques.

Most high-street currency sellers have stocks of the main European coins and notes on hand at all times. Less common currencies normally have to be ordered at least twenty-four hours in advance.

Although these same currency changers will accept returned foreign currency to change it back into sterling, most will not exchange foreign coins and will only accept notes. Even if they do accept the currency there may then be a second charge for converting the currency back into sterling and the holidaymaker will be given a poorer rate of exchange than if they were purchasing the currency.

Some companies offer a buy-back promise offering to exchange foreign currency back into sterling with no commission and at the rate it was originally bought, provided the holidaymaker produces a receipt proving that the currency was purchased at that outlet in the first place. Some banks and building societies offer commission-free currency and travellers' cheques to gold credit card customers.

It is also possible to use cash machines and bank branches to get local currency while abroad as most cash-point cards are now part of international groups and can be used around the world. As these are not credit cards, users can only withdraw as much as their home accounts can stand and there are usually limits on how much can be withdrawn on any particular day.

What is the best way to buy foreign currency?

- Using a debit card to withdraw cash from an overseas cash machine is one of the most convenient ways to buy foreign currency. You can withdraw enough to meet your needs and have access to more if you need it. There are no additional fees and the exchange rates tend to be good.

- Travellers do need to take some foreign currency with them to pay for incidentals, taxis or meals when they first arrive at their destination. Travel agents tend to offer a poorer deal than banks. Costs tend to include a £3 or more minimum commission with the commission rate varying from 1 to 2 per cent. In addition, exchange rates vary widely.

- Exchanging sterling for foreign currency can be good value at a foreign bank, however, avoid bureaux de change in holiday destinations as the exchange rate can be poor and the minimum commission high.

- Spending using a credit card abroad is also good value as there are no commission charges. However, the

exchange rate you are given may not be the best rate
available.

- Try to avoid using your credit card in a cash machine
  as you will generally be charged a 1.5 per cent cash
  advance handling fee and may get a poor rate of
  exchange.

- Travellers' cheques offer security (they will be replaced
  within twenty-four hours if lost or stolen), can be
  cashed at most places including restaurants and shops
  and usually come with a commission-free buy back if
  you fail to spend the full amount. However, if you do
  not get a commission-free buy back guarantee you
  could find you pay a commission to buy the travellers'
  cheques and one to sell them.

FREEHOLD

This is the legal right to hold land/property as the absolute
outright owner, free of payment or any other duty owed
to another party. Generally when you purchase a house it
is on a freehold basis. You not only own the house but also
the land upon which it stands. When you purchase a flat it
is generally on a leasehold basis which means you must
pay a ground rent to the freeholder who owns the building
and grants you a lease.

(See also **Leasehold**.)

FREE-STANDING ADDITIONAL VOLUNTARY CONTRIBUTIONS (FSAVCs)

Free-standing Additional Voluntary Contributions (FSAVCs) are top-up pension plans for those who are members of company pension schemes, but, as their name suggests, they are free-standing from that scheme. All company (or occupational) schemes offer members the option of boosting their pension by paying in additional contributions to an AVC scheme. However, scheme members do not have to opt for the AVC offered by their scheme – they are free to shop around to buy one from a life insurance company.

FSAVC s have been widely mis-sold in recent years and financial watchdogs are now forcing life companies to review their selling practices and give investors compensation where mis-selling has been identified. An estimated one in ten of the one million people sold policies between 1988 and 1999 may have been given bad advice.

The cases where scheme members would have been better off using an AVC rather than an FSAVC include matched AVC schemes – where the employer is willing to match an employee's AVC contributions either in total or in part – and subsidized AVC schemes – where the employer offers some other form of subsidy such as guaranteed annuities or added years of contributions.

The deadline for firms for completing the review of the selling of FSAVCs is 30 June 2002.

FRIENDLY SOCIETIES

The Friendly Society movement dates back to the sixteenth century. These mutual organizations were set up to benefit their members by offering savings vehicles to pay for funeral costs. They were the forerunners of modern building societies and insurance companies.

Today there are around 350 Friendly Societies in the UK – the biggest one is Liverpool Victoria – and some of the older societies are still in existence (including ones with strange names like the Ancient Order of Druids).

Although they still operate on the same principles as when they were founded, are still effectively owned by their customers and offer affordable investments to ordinary working people, the products and services on offer today are far more sophisticated.

Some of the larger societies offer a wide range of financial products including credit cards and loans, but the most popular is a regular tax-free savings bond. Investors pay a maximum of £25 a month or £270 a year for a minimum of ten years to qualify for the tax break. The society then invests this money and returns are free both of income and capital gains tax.

However, investors lose out if they have to cash in plans

before the ten years is up and may not even get back the full premiums they have paid in. Some societies allow investors to pay in the full ten years' worth of savings up front; the money is then put on deposit and fed into the tax-exempt bond over the ten years.

While Friendly Societies can be a way of saving for anyone on a low income or who already has reached the investment limits on an individual savings account (ISA) or other tax-free savings, there are disadvantages. Charges are high and performance has not always been very good. In the past, up to 60 per cent of the first year's premiums were taken in charges, along with high monthly fees. The societies explained this by saying that they needed high charges because the low maximum investment limits meant they were unable to earn much back on their operations.

Some have cut charges since the maximum investment was raised to £25 a month and all are trying to improve their funds' performance. New investors get better deals and existing savers are also slowly seeing their policy terms improve, often in terms of slightly reduced monthly fees.

Since 1991 it has been possible to take out these tax-exempt policies for children, though each child is allowed only one policy and there are better rates for children elsewhere. As children have a yearly tax allowance anyway, unless a lot of money is being invested for them, the tax-free status is not needed.

Some Friendly Societies are trying to broaden their appeal by offering green and ethical funds as well as the normal ones, while others have set up long-term care and nursing home fee insurance policies.

To find out details of Friendly Societies contact the Registry of Friendly Societies (see **Useful Addresses**).

FUND MANAGERS

Fund management companies employ individual fund managers to run pension, investment, insurance, unit or investment trust portfolios. Fund managers also work directly for life insurance companies and other financial institutions such as banks.

Management companies normally offer a range of funds investing in different types of shares and other instruments around the world. Each fund will probably be run by a different manager who is given strict briefs – to concentrate on UK blue-chip shares, European smaller companies shares or Latin American shares, for example. Because of this, fund management groups may not produce great results in every sector and some are famous for, say, Far Eastern investments while others have better track records on European funds.

Individual fund managers run portfolios according to set goals, so some funds aim to achieve capital growth while others aim for high income. Most individual fund managers are big stock-market players and some are in charge of portfolios worth hundreds of millions of pounds. Individual fund managers are backed by teams of researchers and assistants and follow leads from in-house or external stockbrokers. Many managers travel widely to visit the companies they invest in.

Some successful managers have built up strong reputations as leaders in their investment fields and have a large number of fans among private investors. Individual fund managers are sometimes poached between fund management groups and the cult of the personality is such that some investors switch their investments and follow individual managers between companies.

Not all individual fund managers are human. Index-tracking funds more commonly known as tracker funds use computers to replicate various stock-market indices. The computers – rather than highly paid fund managers – say how many shares in each company have to be bought to match the index.

Some banks, building societies and other players do not have in-house fund managers for the own-label investments they offer customers, but instead contract out funds to existing fund management groups. Before starting any investment it is worth checking who will be managing the money and looking at their track records.

To find out information on fund management groups contact the Association of Unit Trusts and Investment Funds, AUTIF (see **Useful Addresses**).

FUNERAL PLANS

It is said that two things in life are certain: one is taxation, and the other is death. Tax is dealt with elsewhere in this book. Apart from the obvious suffering that death causes to families and friends it has one other sting in its tail and that is cost. Inheritance tax or the lack of a will can both prove costly to those left behind, as can a funeral. Prepaid funeral plans are designed to cover this latter cost and were first offered in Britain in the 1980s. The theory behind the plans is simple. People pay a lump sum or a series of monthly payments now, on the understanding that whenever they die their funeral will be paid for in full by the prepaid plan company.

Why bother taking out a plan? Well, the cost of a funeral can be high and they are getting dearer all the time. The cost of a funeral does vary considerably across the country but the average burial costs around £1,675 and a cremation £1,101. Some funeral directors rely on people being too distraught to shop around and so charge higher prices than others. Even in one local area, the cost can vary by as much as several hundred pounds for the same service and the final bill can be almost double the original quotation according to recent research.

Some insurance companies offer small sum policies with monthly or annual premiums to pay for the funeral when someone dies, however much has been put into the scheme. Other organizations will combine planning a funeral and the cost using a funeral plan, and some funeral directors will accept payment in advance.

While planning ahead will bring you some peace of mind, be aware that companies that offer prepaid schemes are doing it to protect their market share rather than out of concern.

If you do opt for a prepaid plan, check the following:

- Whether the cost is all-inclusive or whether there are extras.

- The specifications of the chosen funeral – is it the sort of service you want?

- Is there a choice of funeral director?

- Also, because you could be paying quite a long time in advance, check whether the funds are held in trust, with independent trustees.

NOTE: if you receive any means-tested benefit then you should be aware that buying a funeral plan could affect your entitlement. (See also **Wills.**)

FUTURES

A futures contract is a contract for the purchase or sale of a commodity, financial instrument or index at a fixed price at a fixed date in the future. Futures contracts were originally invented to allow those who regularly buy and sell goods to protect themselves – or hedge – against future changes in the price of those goods. Futures enable producers to lock into a price for goods that they will deliver later and buyers to have certainty over the price they will pay at a later date. However, the futures market is also for speculators who give liquidity to the market by speculating on the future direction of prices by trading futures contracts.

Futures are high-risk investments. Unlike options, the other form of derivatives traded on the London International Financial Futures Exchange, futures commit you to purchasing or selling at a fixed price on a fixed date. Options merely give the investor the option of buying or selling. As such investors in futures could find that they are forced to buy at a particular price when the actual price is much cheaper. As the contract only costs a fraction of the amount an investor has to pay, investors can lose several times their original investment.

(See also **Commodities** and **Derivatives**.)

G

GARDEN INSURANCE

Spending on gardening has reached nearly £3 billion a year but 80 per cent of gardeners do not know the value of their garden contents and six out of ten have no idea what is covered outdoors by their home insurance.

One in ten gardeners has suffered from theft, but in many cases insurance does not completely cover the loss – insurers will not usually cover something which is left in the open and can easily be carried off. Items such as lawn mowers and garden tools will be covered provided they are kept locked up in a garage or shed, but other items are covered only up to a certain limit. Statues, tubs, plants and garden furniture are the most likely to be stolen, along with hanging baskets.

Every company has a different policy when it comes to gardens and the amounts it will cover you for. Some will add on extras like garden gnomes, sundials and hanging baskets at an extra charge, but gardeners who are thinking of investing in koi carp should be aware that it will be almost impossible to find an insurance company which will cover them.

If you do not know how much your garden is worth, price it up by visiting the local DIY or garden centre, then

check on your household policy to see if you are adequately covered.

It is also advisable when planting trees to calculate how
far the roots are likely to spread as they are the major
cause of subsidence (see entry on **Subsidence**).

GAZUMPING

This nasty practice first started in the 1980s housing boom
and then reared its ugly head once again when prices
started to soar in the late 1990s. It happens when someone
selling a house agrees a price with a potential buyer who
then usually pays to get a survey done, instructs a solicitor
and arranges a mortgage. But just as the buyer is ready to
complete the deal, the seller gets a better offer for the
house and accepts it. The first buyer has been gazumped,
which usually leaves him or her several hundred pounds
out of pocket and with nowhere to move to: an expensive
problem if an existing property has already been sold.

There is also gazundering, which is the opposite situation in that it is the buyers who do the dirty. Buyers agree
a price with the seller, proceed with the sale up to the
exchange of contracts and then tell the vendor that they
are going to reduce the price they are prepared to pay for
the house. If the sellers need to move quickly and don't
have time to go through the whole process again, they may
have to accept the lower offer.

In England, Northern Ireland and Wales, the law allows

this behaviour but in Scotland the rules are different. Letters or missives between buyers and sellers form binding contracts. The conclusion of missives, when a price is agreed between two parties, is a written deal which cannot be altered.

However, while gazumping may never be completely eradicated south of the border, there are proposals to make it much harder. Government proposals for the introduction of home sellers' information packs, containing much of the documentation needed to complete a sale, are expected to help speed up the selling process, leaving less leeway for problems. The scheme was piloted in Bristol and cuts the cost of selling by at least half in most cases. The pack includes copies of title documents, guarantees for any work carried out on the property, local authority searches, insurance details and surveys. There is also a proposal for solicitors to do their side of the process online which would also reduce the time it takes, once again reducing the risks of gazumping.

GEARING

This is a term investors may hear when they invest in shares – particularly investment trusts. Gearing is simply borrowing – the percentage of borrowing relative to assets. Anyone can gear. For example, if you own a home worth £100,000 and have an £80,000 mortgage, your gearing will be 80 per cent. However, the term is generally confined to investment trusts, quoted investment companies that pool together shareholders' money to invest in other investments. These investment trusts can be riskier than shares and unit trusts because they can gear up – borrow to invest rather that investing assets or cash.

The gearing ratio is the amount of borrowings a company has compared with shareholders' assets. More heavily borrowed companies should in theory produce a higher return because they have more money to invest. However, the risks will be higher because, if markets move against them, they can lose money they do not have but have borrowed. Therefore they not only have to pay the borrowing costs on that money, but also for the losses. A high gearing ratio (called leverage in the US) can enhance investment returns or increase losses.

(See also **Investment Trusts**.)

GILTS – GILT-EDGED SECURITIES OR GOVERNMENT BONDS

Gilts are issued by the UK government to raise finance. In return investors are given a fixed rate of interest. They are tradeable securities in that they can be bought and sold at any time.

Investors who hold the gilt until the end of its life – until maturity – will repay the face value which is known as the nominal value (usually £100) and in the meantime will earn interest. This predetermined rate of interest, known as the coupon (see entry on **Coupon**), is usually paid twice a year and is based on the nominal or face value.

However, the price at which the gilt is bought and sold in the market will vary, so at any time it can be bought for more or less than the £100 nominal value. As a result the rate of interest will vary. If the value of the gilt falls, the interest rate will appear to be higher. If the value rises, it will be lower. This is why investors need to know not only the coupon but also the current yield, which is the most important indicator of the income investors will receive from the bond. The current yield shows the rate of interest paid on the gilt trading at the current market price.

Gilts are one of the safest forms of investment – after all, the British government is very unlikely to default on its loans. However, just because they are safe does not mean investors' capital is secure. If the gilt falls in value when an investor wants to sell, then not all of the original capital will be returned.

The date on which a gilt will end its life is known as the maturity or redemption date. However, there are a few gilts that are undated. These are known as irredeemables or undated gilts because they have no fixed date for repayment. The redemption date of a new gilt might be a few years or thirty or more. All gilts become shorter with the passage of time. Short-term gilts or shorts have less than five years to run. Medium-term gilts, mediums, five to fifteen years and long-term gilts, longs, fifteen years or more.

A few gilts are issued with variable rates of interest and are known as floating rate gilts. The interest on these falls and rises in line with interest rates in the money markets. Other gilts have their returns linked to inflation. Both interest and capital growth vary with the level of prices and these gilts are called index linked.

The government issues gilts through the Bank of England which holds gilt auctions. These are used mainly by institutional investors to buy gilts for their investment funds. Despite the fact that private investors can purchase gilts at auction, most use a stockbroker to buy them or go through a unit trust that invests in gilts or a range of bonds including gilts. Once the Bank of England has auctioned a new issue of gilts they are then listed on the stock market and can be bought and sold in the normal way.

The rate of interest or coupon is set at the outset and depends upon the level of interest rates in general. However, as gilts are so secure they tend to have lower rates of return than other bonds such as corporate bonds which carry more risk.

Also, at the time of writing, the British government, was paying off government debt rather than needing to raise more finance, so it has little need for gilt auctions or to pay competitive rates of interest.

An important indicator of the total return an investor will receive – assuming the gilt is held to its maturity date – is the redemption yield. It takes into account both the interest and any capital gain or loss when the bond is redeemed. However, those who sell before the redemption date, may make more or less than the redemption yield.

To check the value of gilts investors need to know how they are described. For example, if a gilt is issued with a nominal value of £100, a 4.5 per cent rate of interest and a repayment date in 2005, it will be called Treasury 4.5% 2005. Twice a year the investor will receive half of £4.50 – or £2.25.

Those looking up the gilt price in a newspaper should first look under shorts, mediums or longs and then look for the name of their gilt. Some are referred to as Treas (short for Treasury) and some Exch (short for Exchequer) although the name is not important. This will be followed by the rate or coupon and the date of maturity.

Depending on the newspaper or web site you are looking up the gilt price in you may also see the following information: the current yield which may be listed as Int for interest rate and the Red or redemption yield (the total return you can expect if you hold the bond to redemption). These are gross returns – before tax is deducted. The price at which the gilt was trading at (usually at close of trading the day before) may also be listed along with any price change the day before. In some cases the highest price and lowest price the gilt has traded at in the preceding fifty-two weeks will also be listed.

The main factor affecting the price of gilts is the forecast for interest rates in general which in turn is affected by the prospects of inflation rising or falling. If inflation looks set to rise, then so too do interest rates. Gilts that are index-linked in that they pay a set rate of interest that is linked to – or a set percentage above – the rate of inflation, tend to become more popular when there is a threat of inflation rising. Both the interest rate and the capital repayment on redemption are adjusted in line with inflation.

When base rates or market interest rates rise, gilt and bond prices fall – this is because investors believe they will be able to earn a higher rate of interest than is paid by gilts.

Gilts can be purchased from the Bank of England brokerage service (you pick up a form at a post office and state which stock you wish to buy or sell) or from a stockbroker.

You will be charged the current price plus a commission of 0.7 per cent for the first £5,000 stock and £35 plus 0.375 per cent on anything over that. However, you will not get advice on which gilts to buy. Gilts can also be bought via a stockbroker. Some offer a relatively cheap advisory service. Dealing charges are around 1 per cent on amounts of less than £15,000. Gilts can also be purchased through a unit trust bond fund or another collective investment such as a life or pension fund. In this case the fund manager will select a basket of gilts.

Private investors pay no tax on capital gains from gilts but tax is payable on income – the interest received – at the taxpayer's highest rate.

A newer type of gilt investment is known as strips. The income stream (the interest) is separated out – or stripped – from the capital element of the gilt with each sold as a separate investment. These are sophisticated financial instruments and have yet to take off for the private investor.

(See also **Bonds**.)

GROSS

This is an amount of money before tax is deducted. Your gross salary, for example, is the amount you earn before any deductions. With savings, the gross rate is the rate of interest before tax is deducted and is usually the one advertised. However, only non-tax payers and those investing in tax-free schemes such as individual savings accounts actually get this rate. Everyone else gets the net rate after tax is deducted.

(See also **Net**.)

GUARANTEED INCOME/ GROWTH BONDS

There are two types of investment – guaranteed and risk. A guaranteed investment pays back capital on demand or at the end of a fixed period and a risk investment may not. Cautious investors, therefore, are attracted to the guaranteed variety. However, there is a drawback with many no-risk investments – poor returns. This is why Guaranteed Income Bonds and Guaranteed Growth Bonds were invented. The aim is to provide a level of security whilst also beating the returns offered by traditional safe investments, i.e. savings accounts.

Guaranteed Income or Guaranteed Growth Bonds are

single-premium short-term life assurance contracts issued by insurance companies. They guarantee a fixed income or a fixed level of growth over a fixed term. However, as with much terminology in the financial world, guaranteed may not always mean guaranteed. Some income bonds offer high returns which will be met, but the investor's capital may only be returned in full if certain performance targets are met. If they are not, some of your capital may be used to ensure that the income paid is the level guaranteed.

Bonds usually run for one to ten years and all income and capital growth is free of basic rate income tax and capital gains tax. This is because tax has already been paid – as the life insurance fund that forms the basis of these investments is subject to tax. This means that non-taxpayers cannot reclaim the tax and that higher rate taxpayers may be required to pay additional tax. However, in the case of growth bonds there will be no potential liability to higher rate tax until the investment is cashed in. With guaranteed growth or guaranteed stock-market bonds investors may be guaranteed to get back the higher of two sums – either the original investment or the original investment increased in line with whatever benchmark (usually the FTSE 100) is being used. This protects investors against falling share prices.

GUARANTOR

A guarantor is a third party who will guarantee your debts will be paid if you cannot pay them yourself. A mortgage lender may ask for a guarantor for a young homebuyer or a bank for a business loan.

You can ask anyone to act as a guarantor for a loan or mortgage and they will be accepted provided they have assets – usually property – worth more than the debt that they are prepared to offer as security. The lender will then put a charge on these assets so that they cannot be sold without the lender either being offered another asset as security or the money to repay the debt.

H

HEALTH INSURANCE

There is no such thing as health insurance. Instead there are different types of insurance policies that are commonly referred to as health insurance. Private health or private medical insurance, which pays medical bills up to certain limits of policyholders if they need certain medical treatments and **Permanent Health Insurance** (see entry), which pays an income if the policyholder is unable to work due to ill-health, are often referred to as health insurance. Other policies that pay out in the event of ill-health include **Critical Illness Cover** (see entry) and **Accident Insurance** (see entry). These are covered in detail elsewhere in this book.

HEDGING

If you have ever heard the expression 'hedging your bets' then you probably already know what hedging is. Hedging is the process of managing a risk by offsetting that risk in the futures market. Hedging can vary in complexity from a relatively simple activity through to a highly complex operation.

The ability to hedge means that fund managers or even industry, exposed to price risk and price movements, can decide on the amount of risk they are prepared to accept. If, for example, a fund manager is investing in a particular investment market he or she can bet that the market will fall. That way if the market rises or falls, the fund is covered. So hedging is, in this instance, the opposite of speculation and is often undertaken by producers and purchasers of commodities to eliminate price risks. These contracts are taken out on the futures markets.

However, those who run hedge funds or speculate in this market, are doing the opposite – exposing themselves to risk in the hope of making profits rather than eliminating risk.

Hedge fund managers make bets, not investments, gambling with billions of dollars at a time and using the world's financial markets as their casino. As a result, the activities of a few big hedge funds run by a handful of people can move markets dramatically one way and then another. Hedge fund managers offer clients the prospect of big profits that outperform other investments. To deliver these promises they need to take big risks. One way is to borrow money to boost their exposure to financial markets. This is known as gearing or leverage.

They can also have a dramatic impact on world financial markets as was seen in 1998 when the Long Term Capital Management hedge fund suffered heavy losses following the Russian debt default sparking fears of a broader Wall Street crisis. Fourteen banks, co-ordinated with the New

York branch of the Federal Reserve, had to bail out the distressed fund for US$3.6 billion.

Before that one of the most famous hedge fund gambles was made by George Soros – the man who 'broke the Bank of England'. He made investors in his Quantum hedge fund nearly US$1 billion by selling pounds when sterling crashed out of the ERM in September 1992, despite efforts by the Bank of England to support the currency. He exploited the inefficiencies of the ERM to make profits. His hedge fund went short on sterling. This means he sold pounds on the foreign exchanges with the intention of buying them back at a later date when they were worth less.

Going long means buying an asset with the intention of selling in the future. Going long or short are typical hedge fund bets. This tactic does not require fund managers to physically own the assets involved. Soros sold sterling futures contracts instead. These allowed him to agree a sale but receive payments in three months' time at a fixed price.

When the futures contract matured Soros received the pre-agreed fixed price but was able to make a huge profit by buying back pounds, which had by then fallen in value. While he may have won then, two years later in 1994 he lost $600 million alone in one gamble on the dollar/yen exchange rate.

The vast majority of hedge funds are listed offshore and are not registered for sale in the UK; however, private banks and stockbrokers that target high-net-worth individ-

uals may offer hedge funds as part of a wider portfolio –
but only to those with significant sums to invest and who
understand the risks. These private banks may invest 20 to
25 per cent of an individual's growth portfolio into hedge
funds. They claim that investors can often achieve similar
returns to equities at a much lower risk – which they can,
if the fund manager picks the right funds which have good
downside protection.

Macro funds are riskier, often taking big bets on currencies and interest rates. Less exciting are the market neutral
funds because their performance is less affected by market
movements. Private banks also favour arbitrage funds
which exploit price anomalies in a wide range of instruments and tend to have a lower risk as price anomalies
tend to correct themselves over time. Some funds also
purchase derivative exposure on shares they feel will fall
so they make money when the price goes down and at the
same time buy the shares they feel will rise. These are
known as equity long-short funds. Many hedge funds have
a minimum investment of US$1 million. However, by
investing through a private bank you can purchase a fund
or funds spreading risks. Hedge fund managers take
between 1 and 2 per cent of clients' assets in fees and a 20
per cent or more share of investing profits.

Investors can get some exposure to hedge funds through
investment trusts. Witan, one of the UK's largest, allocated
1 per cent of its investment portfolio to hedge funds in
2000 in a bid to reduce the volatility of future returns. It
has opted for absolute return hedge funds, which aim to
achieve consistent positive returns regardless of what hap-

pens to share prices. Although the hedge investment will increase risks it will also offer downside protection in falling markets. Private investors may also indirectly invest in hedge funds via their company pension scheme.

(See also **Investment Trusts**.)

HOLIDAY INSURANCE

Holidaymakers have had the freedom to shop around for the best deal on travel or holiday insurance since conditional selling – a practice whereby you had to buy travel insurance from the company you bought your holiday from – was banned. Even though the savings can be significant, with those taking more than one trip abroad each year saving up to £130, many travellers fail to exercise their right to buy their cover elsewhere. In addition, one in five people go away without holiday insurance and even those who do buy it do not always read the small print – less than a third know exactly what they have bought.

Buying a more expensive policy does not mean you will get better cover. For regular travellers, annual policies work out cheapest.

When you buy a holiday insurance policy make sure you:

- Tell the insurer about any pre-existing medical conditions. You may have to pay a higher premium if you have received treatment for anything in the last year but if you don't declare it then your policy may well be invalidated.

- If you are taking children, check that they are all covered. Children over sixteen are classed as adults by some companies while others extend the age limit to eighteen. Some companies also limit the number of children covered.

If you need to claim, there is a procedure to follow:

- If anything is stolen, you must make every effort to contact the local police. If this is not possible, get a statement from the travel rep, hotel or other travellers who witnessed the theft.

- Back home, send evidence of purchase of the stolen item with the claim – receipts, camera manuals or photos of items, for example.

- If money is stolen, you will need proof you had it in the first place – foreign exchange receipts, for example.

- Keep proof of when you travelled – plane tickets, booking confirmations or hotel receipts.

Many policy issuers will give you a twenty-four-hour phone number which can be rung from anywhere in the world. But if you don't take it with you the insurer will not be able to provide help or advice on how to make a claim. In some cases, this could jeopardize the chance of getting a full refund when you do make the claim or it could hold up medical treatment. It sounds obvious, but over a quarter of holidaymakers could not confirm whether they had taken this emergency number with them according to one recent survey.

If you have a gold or platinum credit card, you may have free insurance as one of the perks, but will be covered only if the holiday is bought with the card and it may be limited to accident and illness cover rather than theft. Only members of the family travelling with you will be covered – a friend would not be covered even if you paid for their ticket.

If you are planning an action holiday, check your insurance. Most policies do not cover jet skis, parascending, windsurfing, scuba diving or mountaineering. If you are planning to take part in these activities, check out insurance small print carefully and select a policy which will cover you – it will be more expensive. For winter sports holidays, special policies are available.

HOME INCOME PLANS

Older homeowners tend to be asset rich but income poor with most of their capital tied up in their property. A home income plan, also known as an equity release scheme, allows these homeowners to release some of this capital by allowing them to borrow around 30 per cent of their home's value providing it is worth more than a certain amount and they are over a certain age – usually seventy or seventy-five. The loan is repayable when they sell the home, die or go into long-term care.

The scheme works in two ways. You can mortgage part of your property or you can sell all or part of your home to a reversion company while retaining the right to live in it for the rest of your life. Either you get a lump sum which can be invested or you get a monthly payment.

Home income plans that are on sale today are different from the controversial schemes sold in the 1980s. More than 2,000 elderly people were ruined by these and received £30 million compensation as a result of being misled about the prospects for their schemes. How these schemes worked was by mortgaging a property and using the lump sum to buy an investment that would, in theory, pay the interest on the mortgage and provide an income. Rising mortgage rates, falling investment returns and high charges meant that the debt kept rising, incomes fell and the homeowners were left out of pocket with some even losing their homes and their life savings. These investment-backed plans have since been outlawed. However, home income plans retain their tarnished image to some extent.

Today's schemes are far less risky. The most common form of equity release scheme is a home reversion scheme which involves selling your home or a part of your home to a private company called a reversion company. The price you will get will not be the open market value but a percentage of that value depending on your age and sex. In some cases the cash sum can be just 35 per cent of the value and will rarely be more than 60 per cent – the older you are the higher the sum.

Some schemes may pay a higher purchase price but you will be required to pay a rent. In return you receive a cash lump sum or a monthly annuity income. You can remain in the house rent-free or for a nominal monthly rent, for the rest of your life. When the property is sold, usually after your death or if you need to go into long-term care, the reversion company receive the proceeds of the sale, depending on what share of your home you sold. So, if you sold 60 per cent of your home, the reversion company gets 60 per cent of the sale proceeds. The rest is yours or goes to your heirs. Some reversion companies offering lump sums aim to find a buyer for your home. Others may have immediate access to funds with which the purchase can be made.

The other form of scheme, a home income plan that is often called a mortgage annuity scheme, is now less attractive following the March 1999 Budget which scrapped mortgage interest tax relief. You take out a mortgage loan against your home usually up to a maximum of 75 per cent of the property value and the money is used to buy an annuity which pays you a regular income each month for life. The interest payments on the loan are deducted from this monthly income. However, since tax relief, which was available on loans up to £30,000, was scrapped these schemes are less financially attractive although they still may appeal to the over 80s. Those who had existing schemes before the tax change continue to receive tax relief at a fixed rate of 23 per cent. Although the interest is met from the scheme, no payments are made to reduce the outstanding mortgage debt which is repaid from the proceeds of the sale of the property.

You may also be able to raise capital from your home by taking out an interest-only loan, which requires only interest payments to be made with the capital outstanding repaid on death or the sale of the property. Although you receive a lump sum, you will have to make monthly interest payments from the income you receive if you invest this.

Another way of raising capital from your home is the roll-up loan or rolled up interest loan whereby you pay no interest or capital repayments. Instead the interest is rolled up and added to the total loan. These are risky because the amount you owe can grow very quickly and if interest rates rise faster than house prices then they could start to catch up with the property value and you could be forced to sell your home.

Before taking out a home income plan always ask about fees and whether you will be allowed to sell the house if you want to move. If you take out a scheme which provides an annual income, find out if it is a fixed amount which will not increase in line with inflation so it will become worth progressively less. Also check whether the income from the scheme will affect any means-tested social security benefit. You could lose it all together and end up worse off.

Safe Home Income Plans – known as SHIP – were formed after the scandals surrounding these schemes to reassure elderly homeowners that the schemes they were opting for would not leave them homeless or penniless. (See **Useful Addresses** for details on SHIP.) A financial adviser should also be able to advise you on the different schemes available. Age Concern also produces useful guides to home income plans.

HOUSE INSURANCE

House insurance splits into buildings and contents insurance although they can be purchased as a combined policy. Insurers base the premiums on many factors including the amount of insurance cover required, the age and location of the property, how much security there is and how old the customer is.

Traditionally the policies have been purchased together from mortgage lenders with the premiums simply added to the monthly mortgage repayments. However, while this may be an easy option, it is not a cheap one with some surveys estimating that the average householder may be almost £4,000 worse off over the years as a result of not shopping around for a more competitive deal.

As each insurer rates the risk of each homeowner slightly differently, and this is a highly competitive market, there can be significant differences in the cost of policies from different insurers and if bought through different routes. Generally, direct insurers that sell directly to the public over the telephone or via the Internet, and insurance brokers who will shop around a number of insurers to find the best deal, offer the cheapest premiums, whilst buying from a bank or building society can work out far more expensive.

Lenders have been able to retain their stranglehold on this market as they may make it a condition of a mortgage that buildings insurance is in place. This is because the property is security for the loan and, should the building be severely damaged, the insurer needs to know there is insurance to pay for repairs or repay the mortgage. So if the householder does shop around for a better deal, the lender will usually demand proof that insurance is in place and charge a £25 fee to cover the administration costs. Even so, homeowners should not let this fee deter them. Many insurance brokers will refund the £25, and, even if they do not, the savings should far exceed this small charge.

Building insurance covers the structure and any permanent features like baths and fitted kitchens, fitted wardrobes, fireplaces and anything you would not take with you when you moved. Interior decorations are also covered and policies usually extend to include outbuildings such as garages, greenhouses and garden sheds. However, boundary walls, fences, gates, paths, drives and swimming pools may not be covered.

Buildings insurance covers the homeowner against specific risks including flood, fire, theft, lightning, explosions, earthquakes, storms, burst tanks and pipes and heave and subsidence (i.e. movements in the soil, see entry on **Subsidence**) and may also cover accidental damage to the property. You should also be covered for: alternative accommodation if your home is badly damaged and you cannot live in it until repairs are done; liability if, as the owner of your home, you are responsible for any injury to someone or for damage to their property; accidental damage to underground pipes and cables; and breakage of glass, baths, washbasins and WCs. As with all policies there will be exclusions – limits and exceptions to what is covered.

Common exclusions include damage caused by storm or flood to gates or fences and frost damage. You will not be covered for damage caused by wear and tear. So damp caused by a dripping tap will probably not be covered, but damp caused by a flood following a storm will be covered. You will also have a policy excess, which is the amount you must pay towards each claim. For subsidence, heave or landslip this may be £1,000.

The amount of cover that needs to be bought, the sum insured, is the rebuild value of the property. This is different from the market value, the price the property would fetch if sold, and different from the council tax valuation. The rebuild value is how much it would cost to rebuild the home from scratch. It is vital that you are not underinsured. This is when you buy too little cover. If you need to make a claim the insurer may scale down the pay-out accordingly. So if, for example, you should have purchased £100,000 of cover but only bought £50,000, only half your claim may be met by the insurer. To avoid the problem of underinsurance many insurers now offer bedroom-rated policies. So they will base the premiums on an average three-bedroom semi, for example, rather than the actual rebuild value of your home. Householders should also remember that rebuild values will increase each year in line with building costs inflation and that if they undertake any home improvements, such as building an extension, this will affect the amount of insurance they need to purchase.

The cost of premiums is based on the amount of cover, your postcode (some areas are higher risks for insurers because properties in those areas make more claims for things like subsidence) and the age and type of property.

Always contact the insurance company before calling in anyone to start repairs. For example, if there is a flood the insurance company will want to inspect the damage to assess the claim.

Contents insurance covers pretty much everything else – all the moveable items in the property including your furniture, furnishings, clothes and electrical items. Again, make sure you have enough cover. If you undervalue an item which is then stolen, you may not get enough back to replace it. Either make a list of all your possessions, including the contents of kitchen and bathroom cupboards, and work out how much it would cost to buy every item new, or opt for a bedroom rated policy which gives an adequate amount of cover for the type and size of property. Even so, keeping a list of what you own as well as receipts that show the cost of insured items can make claiming easier; it can also be helpful to have photos of irreplaceable items such as jewellery to help the police trace them. If you have any high-value items, such as electrical goods or antiques, you will probably find that there is a limit on the amount that will be covered – either a maximum per item or a maximum for all high-value items – and as such you may have to insure these separately.

The risks householders are insured against include fire, theft and flood and, often for an extra premium, accidental damage. Not every policy offers the same cover so it's important to check the small print. Common exclusions include no cover if a burglary is not as a result of forced entry (you left the door open or the theft was committed by a lodger) and no cover if the property is left empty for a certain period of time, usually more than thirty days.

Policyholders are also required to take precautions to prevent claims and may be required to install a certain minimum amount of security as a condition of the policy. In other cases a discount may be given to those policy-holders who reduce their risks of claiming by fitting greater security such as:

- Window locks with keys stored separately

- 5-lever mortise locks on all external doors

- A National Council of Security Systems approved alarm

- A smoke alarm

- Joining neighbourhood watch

- Having someone at home during the day

- Discounts usually range from 5 per cent to 25 per cent. Some insurers are also offering no claims discounts to policyholders who do not make claims for a certain number of years.

While one company may offer the best deal on buildings insurance, it may not be the best for your contents. However, buying policies separately can lead to difficulties. In many cases claims for theft, flood, fire or storm damage may require a claim on both types of policy. It is more time consuming to deal with two insurers and there may be a dispute as to which policy covers which particular aspect of the claim.

1

INCOME TAX

It was introduced in 1799 and has been heartily disliked ever since. Governments use it as one of their most successful cash generators and its level has changed over the years according to the country's economic needs and political whims. Income tax is charged on most types of income including earnings from employment and self-employment, pensions, savings and investments, property rental and some state benefits.

It is charged as a percentage of earnings, as the basic thinking behind it was that the more people earned, the more they should pay. At its height in the 1960s, wealthy people paid up to 98 per cent of their income to the Inland Revenue. Today's rates are less penal, and they are often changed in the annual budget.

Despite plans to simplify the tax system, there are currently three tax bands. These tax bands usually vary each year. For the 2001–2002 tax year which runs from 6 April to 5 April, the starting rate of tax at 10 per cent was payable on the first £1,880 of taxable income. The basic rate of income tax at 22 per cent was charged on taxable income between £1,881 and £29,400 and the higher rate of tax was payable on taxable earnings over £29,400.

Tax is not paid on every penny earned. Everyone has a personal allowance which is the amount of money they can earn tax-free each tax year. Taxable income is calculated after deducting this allowance from the total taxable income. The basic allowance is the single person's allowance which was £4,535 for the 2001–2002 tax year and it applies to everyone, including children.

Married couples used to qualify for the married couple's allowance but this was scrapped in the March 2000 budget, although the higher age-related allowance for those who were aged sixty-five before 6 April 2000 will still be given to pensioners. The rate of tax relief for the allowance is 10 per cent, which means that a pensioner couple aged between sixty-five and seventy-five qualifying for £5,365 of married couple's allowance can get a maximum tax break of 10 per cent of this or £536.50. The allowance is reduced for those whose income exceeds £17,600 a year. The married couple's allowance was replaced by the Children's Tax Credit, which was introduced in April 2001.

Income tax is levied at different rates for savings income other than dividends. The rates applying for the 2001–2002 tax year are 10 per cent for income in the starting rate band and 20 per cent for income falling between the starting rate and basic rate limits. The rates tax applicable to dividends are 10 per cent for income below the basic rate limit and 32.5 per cent above it. Income tax on savings and dividends is deducted at the basic rate at source so only those who do not pay tax and therefore want to claim this tax back and higher rate taxpayers who need to pay an additional amount of tax, need to declare these earnings to the Inland Revenue.

Most employees have income tax deducted automatically from their wages under the Pay-As-You-Earn or PAYE system. Employers calculate the tax due and pay it over to the Inland Revenue. Each employee has a tax code which tells the employer how much the employee can earn each year before paying tax. If the employee is entitled to the basic personal allowance of £4,535 then their tax code will include the letters 438 and no tax will be deducted from the first £4,535 of pay. The tax code is also used to collect tax due on taxable benefits in kind, employee perks such as company cars upon which the employee must pay tax.

Most higher rate taxpayers, the self-employed and those who have untaxed income (for example, from property rental), are sent a tax return each year. These returns, sent to one in three taxpayers, are sent out at the start of the tax year in April.

Under the new self-assessment system, they must be returned by specific dates or the taxpayer is fined and charged interest on tax owed. For those who want the Inland Revenue to calculate their tax liability the deadline for submitting forms is 30 September following the end of the tax year. For those who want to calculate their own tax liability, or are paying an accountant to do this for them, the deadline is 31 January following the end of the tax year. The 31 January deadline is also the final date for payment of outstanding tax for the preceding tax year. Failure to submit a tax return by 31 January incurs an automatic penalty of £100. There is also a 5 per cent surcharge on any tax still unpaid by the end of February and interest is charged on late payments of tax. Further fines and penalties are levied the longer the tax return and tax payments are outstanding.

Not all income is liable to income tax. In addition to certain state benefits being exempt, so are tax shelters including individual savings accounts (ISAs), personal equity plans (PEPs), tax-exempt special savings accounts (TESSAs) and some National Savings products and friendly society bonds.

In addition, taxpayers can reduce their tax liability by qualifying for tax relief. Although tax relief on mortgage interest was scrapped in April 2000, tax relief is still available on maintenance payments, certain investments (for example, into an enterprise investment scheme) and on pension contributions.

INDEPENDENT FINANCIAL ADVICE/ADVISERS

Known as IFAs, there are some 9,000 independent financial advisers across the UK. Not all financial advisers give impartial advice. Tied agents and the company representatives of financial institutions such as the insurance companies, banks and building societies sell only the products of that company, although a few banks and building societies do offer independent financial advice. IFAs can either be sole traders or national firms and some operate through a network that offers technical support and help with regulatory compliance.

IFAs earn their income in two ways. They can either take a commission from the company whose products they are recommending that you buy, or they can charge you a fee and rebate this commission to you. The interests of IFAs are promoted by an organization known as IFA Promotion which will provide you with the names and contact details of financial advisers in your area (see **Useful Addresses**).

IFAs are required to survey a range of products on offer before recommending one that best suits the individual's needs, which are assessed following a fact find. They should not be influenced by the commission paid on different products, but investors who are concerned that they might be can opt for fee-based advice instead. Four out of five IFAs offer the choice of paying commission or a fee, so in most cases there will be a choice.

The main drawback of using an IFA is that many of these firms are small and, as such, may not have expertise in all the areas which you need advice upon and may not be in business for many years to come. Also, just because a firm offers independent advice does not mean this is best advice. Several firms of IFAs were found guilty of personal pensions mis-selling – so poor advice is not just restricted to the salesforces of large life insurance companies. As most firms of IFAs still rely on commission to generate revenue, investors also need to be wary of churning, i.e. when an adviser regularly recommends that investments

are switched to other schemes to generate additional commission rather than boost investment performance.

(See also **Advice**, **Commission**, **Discount Brokers** and
Polarization.)

INDEPENDENT PENSIONS ACCOUNT

Pensions are one of the most confusing financial products
available and they have recently become even more bewildering. In addition to the basic State pension, SERPS (the
state earnings related pension scheme), company or occupational pensions, there are also personal pensions, stakeholder pensions and now the proposed independent
pensions account (IPA).

This pensions vehicle launched to coincide with the
introduction of stakeholder pensions in April 2001 is not
that new at all. The contribution limits remain the same as
for other pensions; the only difference is that the IPA
simply allows you to invest in unit trusts or open-ended
investment companies (OEICs) without the underlying
fund suffering stamp duty reserve tax – a tax unit holders
of unit trusts have to pay whenever units are bought and
sold. By scrapping this 0.5 per cent tax, unit trusts invested
within an IPA gain a small tax advantage.

The aim of the new account is to give pension savers a
sense of ownership, combined in many cases with a degree

of control over their pension savings. Aimed at those on modest incomes and with unsettled working patterns, IPAs will be flexible allowing varying contributions.

The IPA will not be a pension scheme as such. It will, however, provide the investment content of any sort of defined contribution scheme including personal, occupational money purchase, stakeholder and FSAVC pension schemes. The same rules that apply to those types of pension including contribution limits and tax relief will apply where IPAs are used. The aim is for investors to be able to move their IPA from one pension scheme to another easily and cheaply – vital as these days the average worker may move job seven or eight times before retirement.

When a transfer of this kind takes place, the terms of the new pension scheme will determine the choices available to the saver:

- the new pension scheme may be able to hold, and/or add to, the investment units held in the original IPA. In this case the saver can simply transfer the contents of the original IPA into a replacement IPA within the new pension scheme and carry on contributing as before;

- the new pension scheme may be prepared only to hold IPA containing units in pooled funds of its choice. If this is acceptable to the saver, units in the original IPA could be sold and a new IPA in the new scheme could buy for the saver units in the funds acceptable to the new pension scheme. Then further contributions into the new IPA would go into pooled investment funds acceptable to the new pension scheme;

- the saver could keep his or her existing IPA in the original scheme without adding to it further, and begin a separate new IPA through the new pension scheme.

The choices available for IPA transfers will be very like those available for ISA (and PEP) transfers. So long as the saved resources remain within the tax-privileged environment, a variety of transfers among providers is possible, subject only to the terms of the providers concerned. In the case of IPA transfers, there is of course an additional constraint that the saver cannot access their pension savings before retirement.

Whether unit trust pensions, which is basically what IPAs are, prove popular remains to be seen. Funds may have to cut costs to the overall stakeholder fee of 1 per cent if they want to compete – well below the 5 per cent initial fee and an annual management charge of around 1 to 1.5 per cent charged by many unit trusts. The IPA is also designed to be fully portable but this will depend on who offers the account. The theory is that you can start your own personal pension using an IPA as the investment vehicle and then, if you move jobs, join an occupational money purchase scheme, but instead of paying contributions into that scheme pay these contributions into your IPA. However, much depends on whether employers will allow you to transfer IPA investments across and how many pension providers offer these accounts. If they do not prove popular investors will find that, instead of being fully portable, they may have to leave their IPA behind while they join another scheme.

INDEX-LINKED

The rate of increase is linked to the rate of inflation. For example, pensions can be index-linked and rise each year in line with the rate of inflation in a specific month.

(See also **Inflation.**)

INDICES

The London Stock Exchange, in conjunction with the Faculty of Actuaries and the *Financial Times*, has developed a series of indices to cover the UK stock market as well as the main European markets. These indices are calculated to provide a guide to stock-market performance. Some indices such as the FTSE 100, or Footsie for short, have become household names, while others such as the FTSE SmallCap are less well known. The Footsie is an average of the share prices of the biggest 100 companies quoted on the stock market and is a real-time index in that it is continually updated. Since its launch it has spawned a number of index tracker unit trusts designed to mirror its performance. The constituent companies that make up each index change usually on a quarterly basis reflecting the growth or fall in value of companies. When a company is taken over or merges this also affects the composition of the index.

Another use for indices such as the Footsie is as a benchmark against which fund managers measure their own performance – all aim to outperform a chosen index to prove their worth. Other UK indices measure different sections of the stock market. The FTSE Mid 250 measures the performance of the 250 next biggest companies outside the top 100 and is also a real-time index. The FTSE 350 index combines the Footsie and the Mid 250 indices to provide a measure of large- and medium-sized companies. The companies included in this index account for about 90 per cent of the stock market.

Each industry sector within the FTSE Actuaries 350, such as mining or property, also has an index calculated called industry baskets. The FTSE SmallCap measures the performance of about 500 of the UK's smallest quoted companies. This index is not real time but is calculated at the end of each day.

Another well-known index, the FTSE Actuaries All Share, is the broadest measure of the UK stock market, although, despite its name, it does not include all shares. Some tracker funds track the performance of this index rather than the Footsie.

Although the main UK indices move in line with each other they do not necessarily move at the same rate. Depending on the stock market, the Footsie can either outperform the All Share or vice versa.

In fact, the FTSE produces thousands of different indices. Among the newer ones are the TechMark, which has a 100 and All Share index and covers companies committed to leading edge technology, the FTSE All Stars, the magic 28 stocks common to major European derivatives indices, and the FTSE Multinationals.

The European markets are covered by the FTSE Euro-track 100 and the Eurotrack 200. Other overseas stock markets have their own indices. The best known are the Nikkei 225 which covers the Japanese markets and the Dow Jones which measures United States shares.

INDIVIDUAL SAVINGS ACCOUNTS (ISAs)

The Individual Savings Account is a tax-free savings and investment scheme introduced in April 1999 to replace PEPs (personal equity plans) and TESSAs (the tax exempt special savings account).

There are three types of ISA and three different types of investment can be held in an ISA, which can make these schemes complex and difficult to understand. Some investors have even unwittingly flouted the rules and risk losing the tax-free status of their savings or investments as a result. Even so, the tax breaks of an ISA mean they have been incredibly popular.

ISAs are free of income tax and capital gains tax. Investors must be aged eighteen or over and resident in the UK to open an ISA and they can only hold an ISA on their own account – not jointly with, or on behalf of, anyone else.

The three types of ISA are:

- Maxi

- Mini

- TESSA-only

Maxi ISAs allow investors to invest the maximum ISA allowance with just one ISA provider. Mini ISAs allow investors to buy each of the investments from a different ISA provider. TESSA-only ISAs are for those with maturing TESSAs (these were five-year investments) who are allowed to transfer their capital (not any interest) into an ISA once their TESSA matures.

As a combination of two former investment schemes, ISAs can have three main investment elements:

- Share-based investments

- Cash deposits

- Life-insurance investments

Investors can opt to invest in just one or two of these or all three.

Stock-market based investments can include unit trusts, investment trusts, open-ended investment companies, government bonds or gilts, corporate bonds and shares. Cash deposits – or savings – are basic savings accounts, although some may be slightly more complex in that they may have tiered rates (a higher rate of interest the more is invested) or notice periods so investors cannot get access without losing interest. Life insurance investments should not be confused with life insurance. There is no life cover as part of these investments, instead they are investment funds run by life insurance companies.

The investment limits depend on the type of ISA – mini or maxi – and the type of investment. The total that can be invested in an ISA cannot exceed £7,000 in any one tax year (this runs from 6 April to 5 April). This limit applies until April 2006. The limit can either be reached through one Maxi ISA or through one, two or three different Mini ISAs. Cash savings are limited to £3,000. This limit is the same regardless of whether investors opt for a Maxi or a Mini ISA. Life insurance investments are restricted to £1,000 in this and future years, and once again this limit applies regardless of whether an investor has a Mini or Maxi ISA.

Stock-market based investments are slightly more complex. A maximum of £7,000 can be held in a Maxi ISA (this is the entire Maxi ISA investment limit). Investors who, for example, also want to invest in an additional type of investment such as cash, can invest up to £3,000 in cash and the remainder in stocks and shares provided they do not breach the overall investment limit.

Maxi ISAs mainly appeal to those who want to invest the full ISA limit in stocks and shares as the investment limit is higher than with Mini ISAs. Those who invest in a Mini ISA can only invest £3,000 in stocks and shares. As such they appeal mainly to those opting for a Mini cash ISA or who want to invest in cash and stocks and shares but buy these ISAs from different ISA providers.

The third type is the TESSA-only ISA which is only open to those who already have a TESSA which matures – or comes to the end of its five-year term – after 5 April 1999. A maximum of £9,000 of TESSA capital (not interest) can be transferred into a TESSA ISA and continue to grow free of tax provided the capital is switched within six months of the date the TESSA matures.

Each year investors can only take out either a Maxi ISA or up to the three Mini ISAs for different types of investment. Investors cannot take out a Maxi ISA and Mini ISA in the same tax year. However, the TESSA-only ISA limit is in addition to the other ISA investment limits.

In later tax years (which run from 6 April to 5 April) investors' options start fresh. Both Mini and Maxi ISAs investors can usually invest either a lump sum or make regular payments.

The next aspect of ISAs that investors need to get to grips with is that some meet the CAT standard and some do not. The CAT standard – which stands for fair Charges, easy Access and decent Terms and conditions – is voluntary. Once again the rules vary depending on the type of ISA. For the cash element of ISAs to be CAT-marked the ISA provider must make no charges, have a minimum transfer/investment of £10, allow withdrawals within seven working days or less and not pay interest that is more than 2 per cent less than the bank base rate. For stocks and shares ISAs to be CAT-marked the charges cannot total more than 1 per cent of the investment and the minimum saving must be no more than £500 as a lump sum per year or £50 per month.

For life insurance ISAs to be CAT-marked the charges must be no more than 3 per cent of the investment, there must be no penalty when the ISA is cashed in and investors must get back at least all the premiums that they paid three years or more before the date when the life insurance element is cashed in. Investors must be allowed to pay in as little as £25 a month or £250 a year. The fact that charges for life insurance ISAs are so much higher than for stocks and shares ISAs and the investment limit is much lower, has meant that comparatively few life insurance ISAs have been sold.

Some stocks and shares ISA providers claim that the low charges imposed by the CAT standard do not cover the costs of top fund management and as such investors will lose out. The pro-CAT-standard ISA providers disagree arguing that high charges eat into performance leaving investors worse off. This ongoing row within the financial services industry is likely to rumble on for several years while fund managers from either side of the debate wait for past performance figures to prove their point.

But where does that leave investors? If the financial services industry cannot agree, how can investors possibly know which type of ISA is best for them – one with a CAT mark or one without? For cash ISAs it is a matter of choice.

Some fail to meet the CAT standard because they have a high minimum investment or a minimum investment period or notice period. However, in return investors receive a higher rate. Provided investors know what the terms and conditions are of non-CAT-standard ISAs and are happy to abide by these, they should not lose out – and, in fact, will often be better off.

The CAT v non-CAT ISA debate is more complex when it comes to stocks and shares ISAs. With CAT-marked stocks and shares ISAs having no initial charge and a maximum annual charge of 1 per cent compared to a 4 or even 5 per cent initial charge and up to a 1¾ per cent annual charge on some non-CAT funds, there is a vast difference in costs between the two types of ISA. These higher costs will eat into investment returns. However, if the performance of a non-CAT-marked fund is much higher as a result then investors will not lose out and in many cases will gain. Where CAT-marked funds are a better bet is when there is little difference in performance, for example, with a tracker fund (a stock-market fund, usually a unit trust, that aims to track the performance of a stock-market index). In addition, those opting for an income-generating fund will find high charges will eat into their income. For other funds, performance should be as – if not more – important a consideration as charges when making an investment decision. Investors who make the investment performance a priority, and select a fund that is likely or expected to produce a greater return, can usually reduce the charges to those of a CAT-marked ISA by purchasing through a discount broker.

Those unhappy with their ISA provider can switch from one to another; however, only the same components can be switched. So they cannot move a cash deposit element of an ISA into a share ISA or vice versa even within a Maxi

ISA. Also once a withdrawal is made it counts against the normal ISA subscription limits for the year. So an investor who has withdrawn £3,000 from a cash ISA can then not reinvest £3,000 at a later date – once the investment limit has been used it cannot be used again.

As a result transfers must be made directly from one ISA provider to another – investors cannot cash in their investment and then reinvest this money with a different provider.

INFLATION

Inflation is no longer the threat it once was. Back in the mid 1970s inflation, which is basically the increase in prices, topped more than 25 per cent and in the late 1980s and early 1990s it reached double figures, leading to high interest rates, unemployment and recession.

In today's low inflation, low interest rate economy, inflation is still a key economic indicator with the government and the Bank of England, which sets interest rates, using it as a measure of how well the economy is performing. If there are signs that inflation is rising too sharply – the current aim is to keep it below a 2.5 per cent target – interest rates will rise.

Inflation is a very broad term. We refer to the retail price index (RPI) as the underlying rate of inflation. This index monitors the price or cost of a basket of items to determine how prices are rising. It includes essentials like rent, mortgage payments, fuel and food as well as clothing, electrical appliances, motoring expenditure and alcohol and tobacco. The items that make up the basket change to reflect consumer expenditure. For example, mangles, candles and rabbits for eating, which were all constituents of the index when it was devised in 1914, are no longer included, but childminder fees are.

However, the RPI is not the only measure of inflation. RPIX is underlying inflation minus mortgage payments. The Harmonized Index of Consumer Prices HICP was developed as a comparable measure of inflation for member states of the European Union. It is used by the European Central Bank as the target measure of inflation for the EMU area. HICP excludes some items covered by the RPI, including mortgage interest payments, council tax, road tax and buildings insurance. However, it includes air fares and personal computers, which were not introduced to the RPI until 1998.

The British Retailers Consortium uses its own index, the BRC shop index, made up of around two hundred items, and there are also producer output prices, producer input prices and house price inflation indices as well as wage inflation.

Inflation has a major impact on our lives, even though it is at an historically low level. State benefits rise in line with inflation and so do wages (although they tend to outstrip it), and rises in inflation can lead to higher interest rates and therefore dearer borrowing costs and mortgages.

Having so many different measures of inflation leaves raising prices, wages or benefit in line with inflation – or index linking – open to interpretation. For example, while most benefits are increased in April in line with the RPI rate in the preceding September, certain benefits such as Jobseeker's Allowance and income-related benefits generally rise in line with the Rossi Index, i.e. the RPI less certain housing costs.

INHERITANCE TAX (IHT)

The estimated number of taxpaying estates in 2000–2001 will be about 23,500 – around 4 per cent of all deaths. So very few actually pay this tax and it is fairly easy to avoid. IHT is payable on the balance of someone's money and property (their estate) including their property, jewellery, investments, cash, antiques, car and other chattels which exceed the nil rate tax band of £242,000 for the 2001–2002 tax year (this band usually rises each April following the budget) and is charged at 40 per cent. Even the estates of non-tax payers like the retired have to pay it.

There is currently no IHT payable between husband and wife, so when the first one dies the other does not have to pay anything. At the moment this applies only to married couples; if you are living together your partner will have to pay. However, if you are married, when the second spouse dies their estate is liable for tax if it is over the limit.

You cannot pay the tax by selling the home you inherit as tax has to be paid before the estate is released, so you may have to take out a loan to pay the tax if you do not have enough money of your own.

Gifts made before you die can be exempt from IHT but only if the donor survives at least seven years after giving them. These are known as potentially exempt transfers. If the donor dies before this time, the value of these gifts will be taxed on a sliding scale depending on how many years prior to death the gift was made.

There are ways to reduce the tax burden. The following are exempt from IHT:

- As many gifts of £250 or items to this value can be made as you wish (one to each person) each year.

- £3,000 a year can be given away without it being added back to the value of the estate on death.

- £5,000 can be given to your children tax free when they marry, £2,500 to a grandchild and £1,000 to anyone else.

- Combinations of these are allowed. For example, you could give your child money when they marry and another £3,000 in the same tax year. Any income you get from a job, pension or investments which is surplus to what you need can be given away. This does not include money made from the sale of capital such as land or shares which is liable to tax.

Many people wrongly believe that they can give their home to their children thinking this will avoid IHT. However, if you continue living in it, it is known as a gift with reservation and your inheritors will have to pay the full

IHT due unless you pay them a commercial rent. One way round this is for one parent to give their half to the children. As most couples own their homes jointly, you have to change the way you own your home to a tenancy in common. A solicitor can sort this out for you. A popular but complex way of avoiding IHT is to take out a life assurance policy held inside as a trust set up to benefit heirs. When a person dies, the proceeds of the policy fall outside the estate for IHT purposes and can be used by the heirs to pay any IHT bill on the rest of the estate. It is also possible to place assets inside an accumulation and main-tenance trust and maintain control over them even though technical ownership is lost. The trust protects the assets from IHT but can only be used to benefit heirs up to the age of twenty-five.

Although financial advisers can recommend ways to avoid inheritance tax, for more technical services such as drawing up a will or setting up a trust you should seek advice from an accountant or solicitor.

A lucky few may be able to use the official list of exemptions. This places many valuable articles such as paintings, prints, books, manuscripts and other objets d'art outside the Revenue's clutches. Anyone with a valuable object should apply in writing to the Capital Taxes Office in Nottingham. If the object is granted exemption it will be placed on the official list and should be made available for public display and for museums to borrow. If the object is subsequently sold, IHT becomes payable on the proceeds.

(See also **Wills**.)

INITIAL CHARGES

These can take the shine off even the best investments. Also known as front-end loads, they are the commission and expenses that investment or insurance companies deduct from investors' contributions before that money is used to buy shares or investment units. For instance, a 5 per cent initial charge is fairly standard for a unit trust. This means that for every £100 invested, £5 is taken in charges leaving only £95 to be put to work on the investor's behalf. So the investment has to grow by 5 per cent just to stand still.

In many cases the initial charge is used to fund commission payment to financial advisers – but they are not reduced if an investor avoids the middleman and goes direct to the investment company. However, it is possible to get back some of these charges by buying through a discount broker or using a fee-based financial adviser.

In addition to the initial charge there may also be an annual management charge. These should be explained in detail in the key features document all investors in life insurance, pensions, unit trusts and other collective investments should receive.

Unit-linked investments such as unit trusts or life insurance or pension policies invested in unit-linked funds, also have a bid/offer spread. This is the difference between the selling price (the price you pay) for the units and the offer price (the price you get when you sell). The initial charge will be included in this spread, which can often be higher

(6 per cent) – cutting the initial investment after charges even further.

INSIDER DEALING

Insider dealing occurs when someone trades in a company's shares after receiving specific information that has not been made public, which would affect the company's share price if it were widely known. Anyone from a director to a secretary – and even any person encouraged to deal after receiving tip-offs from such people – could know a company is about to announce unexpectedly big profits or a major trading deal. If they buy shares before that news is made public, in the hope of making a profit when shares rise, they are guilty of insider dealing. The same applies to those who sell in advance of bad news. These shady deals are illegal. However, private investors buying shares after finding that, for example, a company is putting staff on overtime or who sell after hearing that staff may be made redundant are unlikely to be caught out by the insider trading laws.

INSURANCE

See under **Accident Insurance, Car Insurance, Dental Insurance, Garden Insurance, Health Insurance, Holiday**

Insurance, House Insurance, Life Insurance, Pet Insurance, Pluvius Insurance (weather), **Sports Insurance, Wedding Insurance, Brokers** and **Premiums**.

INTEREST-FREE CREDIT

This, as the name implies, is the ability to borrow money on credit without paying any interest. Usually interest-free deals last for a year for electrical items and furniture and up to three years for cars. With most schemes a deposit must be paid and then the remainder of the debt paid in monthly instalments by direct debit. Watch out for 'nothing to pay for a year' deals that appear to offer free credit. Often, if the borrower does not clear the debt in full at the end of the year a penal rate of interest often approaching 30 per cent is charged.

INTEREST-ONLY MORTGAGE

As the term implies, the borrower only pays the interest on the outstanding loan during the term of the mortgage. At the end of the term, the outstanding debt – the original amount borrowed – is repaid usually from a savings plan such as an endowment policy, personal pension or an individual savings account (ISA) into which the borrower has paid a separate monthly premium. Interest-only mortgages may appear cheaper as the borrower is only paying interest not repaying capital each month; however, once the costs of an investment scheme to repay the mortgage at the end of the term are added to the total costs, they can be higher. Although borrowers do not have to take out a separate investment scheme and can instead repay the loan from the proceeds of the sale of the property, most lenders prefer borrowers to back their interest-only mortgage with an investment of some sort.

Interest-only mortgages were far more widespread in the late 1980s when the bulk of all mortgages were backed by endowments. Today repayments are more popular.

(See also **Repayment Mortgages**.)

INTEREST RATES

When we refer to interest rates, we usually mean the Bank of England base rate – the base rate of lending. Other interest rates such as mortgage interest rates, savings interest rates and money market and inter-bank interest rates reflect the base rate and move in line with its movements, although not necessarily by the same amount or at the same time. However, some interest rates, such as interest-tracker mortgage rates, are directly linked to movements in base rates. Interest rates are expressed as a percentage. A 6 per cent rate means that if you want to borrow £100 it will cost you £6 for the year – or if you were to earn 6 per cent interest on your savings and saved £100 you would earn £6 for the year.

For credit cards and overdrafts these interest rates may be expressed as a monthly rate, an annual percentage rate, APR (which includes other borrowing costs), or an effective annual rate, EAR. There are also gross rates (without tax deducted) and net rates (with tax deducted) as well as compound rates – if interest is added monthly, savers then earn interest on their interest which compounds up to a higher rate.

(See also **APR** and **Base Rate**.)

INVESTMENT TRUSTS

Investment trusts are stock-market quoted collective-investment companies that pool together the money of hundreds, if not thousands, of investors and invest this money on their behalf. Investors simply buy shares in the trust. This shareholder money – together with borrowed cash – is in turn invested in other shares as well as a wide range of other investments which depend on the invest-ment remit of the trust. The portfolio is run by professional fund managers and supervised by an independent board of directors.

Investors not only own shares that have the potential to increase in value, they can also earn a dividend from the fund. Investment trusts are what are known as 'closed-end' funds, which means that the number of shares is fixed unless there is a rights issue or the trust buys back shares.

Although the theory of investment trusts is very simple, they are in fact quite complex to understand – far more complex than, say, buying an ordinary share. For a start, although the value of the investment trust shares should rise and fall in line with the value of the assets the trust owns (the portfolio of shares and other investments), in practice this does not happen. Investment trusts often trade at a discount, which means that the total value of the investment trust shares is less than the total value of all the assets that trust owns. So if you sold off all the assets they would be worth more than the shares are worth. If the trust was wound up, therefore, shareholders would get back more than their shares are worth.

The reason why an investment trust's share price can be worth less than its net asset value (NAV) is simply a case of supply and demand. If there are more sellers and buyers the share price will be depressed. Most investment trusts trade at a discount mainly because there is less of an investment need for these trusts now that large institutions manage their own global portfolios of shares.

The discount adds an added risk to investing in investment trusts. Should the discount widen shareholders will lose out – however, should it narrow they would benefit from an added boost to their investment. Most trusts have a discount ranging from 2 to 20 per cent. An increasing number of share buy-backs to reduce the supply of shares is expected to help reduce these discounts. The abolition of advanced corporation tax, ACT, in April 1999 has helped investment trusts to do this without suffering tax losses. As they pay little or no corporation tax, the ACT on share buy-backs was often irrecoverable and acted as a disincentive to buy back shares.

The 275 investment trusts, which were developed in Scotland more than a hundred years ago to help finance the building of rail tracks in the US, now have a stock-market value of over £70 billion. The Foreign & Colonial investment trust has run continuously since it was formed in 1868 and has survived every war and financial crisis along the way. Its assets are now over £2 billion. The aim of investment trusts was to offer investors of moderate means the same advantages as larger investors by pooling their money together and that same principle remains today. However, in recent years the sector has been slowly shrinking.

The introduction of ever more complex and sophisticated investment trusts has attracted more interest in the sector. So-called split capital trusts – which issue more than one class of share to match the needs of different types of investors – have proved popular. Shareholders can now opt for predetermined growth, high income or high capital growth. With current low interest rates, the high yielding shares have particular appeal. As a result split capital trusts tend to trade at much smaller discounts – and sometimes even at a premium to their Net Asset Value (NAV).

Different types of share can also be used to help reduce tax – or even eliminate it. Zeros – the name given to zero dividend preference shares – give no income during their life but instead offer high capital growth.

As few investors maximize their capital gains tax allowances, they can pay no income tax (as they will be receiving no income from the shares) and either no, less or a lower rate of capital gains tax by deferring the gain to a time when it is more tax efficient. If the gain is less than the tax threshold they will have no tax to pay, if they defer the gain until they are a lower rate taxpayer (for example, after they retire) they can pay less tax. Investment trusts can also be held in an Individual Savings Account (ISA) so that all income and gains are tax free. A maximum of £7,000 of investment trust shares in any tax year can be sheltered in an ISA.

Other types of share include preference shares which offer a fixed rate of interest in the same way as bonds and offer a high level of income but little potential for capital growth. Convertibles are like preference shares in that they receive a fixed rate of interest, but differ in that they can be converted into ordinary shares at a set future date. As a result the income they pay is lower, but they do offer some potential for capital growth. Stepped preference shares are like zeros in that they offer a capital return in the form of a predetermined redemption value. But unlike zeros they pay annual dividends rising in steps at a fixed rate throughout the life of the trust. Capital shares generally pay no dividend and income shares pay some of the highest yields of any quoted shares, receiving all of the income during the life of the trust or all of it after stepped preference shareholders have been paid, if there are any.

Some trusts also issue warrants – which allow investors to buy the shares of a trust for a fixed price at a pre-agreed time in the future. This fixed price is called the exercise price. If the ordinary share price rises above the exercise price, the warrant holder can make immediate profits by exercising the warrant, acquiring the shares at the lower exercise price and then selling for the high price quoted on the stock market.

Investment trusts are split into categories based on their investment remit. These include UK general, High income, Japan, Venture and development capital, Endowment policies, European and Property.

The average performance of investment trusts is not that dissimilar to unit trusts although over the longer run both have failed to match the performance of the FTSE All-Share Index. Investment trusts, however, tend to be more volatile than unit trusts. While there are a few top performing investment trusts which have produced returns far outstripping the best unit trusts, there are also some very poor performing investment trusts.

Investment trusts are cheaper for investors than unit trusts which cost more (charges on unit trusts can be as high as 6 per cent on the initial investment and 1¾ per cent as an annual management charge). One recent study by the Association of Investment Trust Companies, which promotes these investments, found that unit trusts were 60 per cent more expensive than investment trusts. Most investment trust charges are 1 per cent or below and a few charge nothing at all. There will, however, be stamp duty on share purchases at the rate of 0.5 per cent.

You can buy investment trust shares from a stockbroker in which case you will pay a dealing commission. What makes investment trusts so accessible are the savings and investment schemes that many offer. These were intro- duced over ten years ago as a simple method of buying investment trust shares. Investors can use the schemes to invest a regular sum each month starting at around £25 or the occasional lump sum of £250 upwards and they pay very low charges. Known generically as savings schemes, they may also be called share plans or investment schemes to indicate that they are not solely for regular savings. They are flexible investments in that investors can increase or decrease regular payments and also stop investing and start at a later date all without penalty.

J

JOINT ACCOUNTS

Opening a bank current account in joint names is the most common way for couples to organize their finances and pay household bills. Usually only one partner's signature is required on cheques. The advantage of a joint account is convenience as all the family finances can go through one account. The disadvantage is that each partner is jointly liable for the debts of the other. So if one partner spends too much, refuses to pay his or her share of the bills or runs up a large overdraft, then the other partner is liable for these debts.

JOINT INVESTMENTS

There are two basic ways of sharing assets, holding them as joint owners or as tenants in common. Both systems apply to unmarried as well as married couples.

Savings accounts and other investments tend to be held under the joint ownership rules. Houses can also be held this way. The arrangement means that the assets are shared equally between both partners regardless of who actually pays for them. If one partner dies, their share of the assets passes directly to the surviving partner.

People can also choose to hold assets as tenants in common. This allows them to split ownership in other ratios rather than just splitting it equally. This proportion can more accurately reflect who pays, say, the mortgage. When a house or other asset is held by tenants in common, one person can leave his or her share to anyone in a will. Problems arise if someone in this situation dies without a will as the house will be passed on according to the rules of intestacy, so the other partner may not necessarily inherit it.

This means that if one partner of a couple that have been living together for years dies suddenly, his or her share of the house could automatically pass to his or her parents or siblings not to his or her life partner.

Many people base the decision on ownership on the inheritance tax implications of each arrangement. Bills can be cut by having a property held as tenants in common with each partner deciding to pass their share to their children on death – as long as the children are guaranteed not to force the survivor out of the house in their lifetime. When the second partner dies the total estate is reduced as half the house value has already been given away, reducing the total tax bill.

It is also useful to have some savings accounts held jointly. If a couple's assets are in the name of the partner who dies, the survivor may have to wait until probate has been granted before being able to withdraw any money. Holding accounts jointly means that the survivor has normal access to funds. Unless stated otherwise, most joint savings accounts are deemed to come under the rules of joint ownership rather than those of tenants in common.

There are other benefits to having joint accounts. A couple where one partner is a higher rate taxpayer and the other a lower-rate or non-taxpayer will generally have the interest on an account apportioned equally for income tax purposes. This means that half the interest will be taxed at a lower rate. It is possible, by agreeing in advance with the Inland Revenue, to have this interest split differently so a greater proportion is taxed at the lower rate or not taxed at all.

(See also **Cohabiting**.)

JOINT-LIFE ASSURANCE

Two people – normally married couples – can take out joint-life assurance contracts to pay out on the death of either the first or second named person on the policy or just on the first death. In this case, the surviving partner receives a tax-free lump sum payment and the policy then ceases with the survivor left with no life insurance cover.

These policies can be term assurance or whole-of-life assurance. Term assurance pays out on deaths that occur within a specific period, such as ten or twenty-five years, known as the term. If both policyholders survive until the end of the term then they get nothing back. This is the cheapest form of life insurance cover. Whole-of-life policies pay out whenever death occurs.

Joint-life assurance that pays out on the second death can be useful for tax planning purposes. On the death of a husband an estate normally passes to the wife through the husband's will and no inheritance tax is payable. But on the death of the wife, the estate is likely to pass to any children and inheritance tax may well be payable this time around. But the cash proceeds of a life assurance policy written to pay out on the second death (the wife's in this example) can be used by the children to pay off any inheritance tax bill. The policy must be held in trust, outside the estate, for this to work.

Joint-life assurance can be more expensive than a single life policy because insurers are faced with double the chance of a payout. Also, a husband and wife may be better off taking out two single life policies to produce two separate payments, and in many cases advisers recommend that couples take out separate life policies to vary the amount of cover between partners.

JUNIOR STOCK MARKET

The Alternative Investment Market (AIM) is often referred to as the junior stock market and is the stock market for small young, growing companies who want to raise capital by issuing shares.

(See also **Alternative Investment Market**.)

JUNK BONDS

These bonds are an infamous form of investment that came to prominence in the United States during the early 1980s. They featured in various Wall Street scandals towards the end of the decade. However, today investors should not be put off by the name 'junk'. Some of the fastest growing companies, including the Orange mobile phone group, have offered what are termed junk bonds to finance their growth.

Any corporate bond that is sub investment grade rated by one of the credit ratings agencies is referred to as a junk bond. As a result of this lack of credit rating, companies issuing these bonds must pay a higher rate of interest to attract investors. Provided the company performs well, and does not default, these bonds can benefit both the companies that issue them, as they can attract much-needed investment, and the investors, who can earn a higher return than from safer credit-rated corporate bonds or gilts. The fact that bonds can be repaid at a much later date than bank loans gives companies more time to be successful.

(See also **Corporate Bonds** and **Credit Ratings Agencies**.)

K

KEY MAN INSURANCE

This is insurance taken out by companies to protect the business from the death of a director or another important employee. The insurance company then reimburses any lost profits. This type of cover is often required by banks lending to smaller companies that rely on one or two key members of staff. It is also increasingly common for companies to take out critical illness insurance for vital employees.

KRUGERRANDS

These are gold coins minted in South Africa and used by investors as a convenient way of holding physical gold. But there are several other ways to invest in this precious metal.

Gold has traditionally been seen as a store of value with investors believing that by investing in gold they were protecting themselves against the ravages of inflation of a depreciating currency. Its universal appeal also made it an attractive investment in times of financial and political upheaval. However, this is no longer the case.

Sadly, gold has not bestowed the Midas touch recently on investors and the British government has been selling off its gold reserves. Even political and economic crises have done nothing to restore its fortunes. The 1987 global stock-market crash and the Gulf War had little impact on the price of gold.

These days it is easier and more profitable to inflation-proof assets with other financial instruments. The end of exchange controls and the rapid expansion of fast-moving foreign exchange markets means that people can switch out of depreciating currencies easily and quickly. Furthermore, unlike bank deposits and bonds, gold pays no interest, and is therefore expensive to hold when real interest rates (adjusted for inflation) are high. It is also expensive to insure.

Yet despite all this, some people cannot resist gold's lure. Private investors can buy either gold coins, such as Krugerrands or sovereigns, or gold bars from retail dealers. A single Krugerrand contains one ounce of gold and a sovereign contains half that much gold.

Investments in gold need not necessarily involve a physical holding in the metal – indeed it can be more expensive to hold it, as buyers who have gold delivered to them in the UK have to pay value added tax on the purchase price. This can be avoided by holding gold off-shore – though storage costs have to be put into the equation.

Some investors prefer to buy the shares of companies that mine gold or are involved in the gold-producing process in some other way. Investors can also put money into unit trusts or investment trusts that in turn invest in a portfolio of gold-related shares.

In 1996 gold was brushing US $420 an ounce. In August 1998 it hit a nineteen-year low of US $275 when deflation fears were at their peak. It then recovered slightly but only to around $280.

L

LEASEHOLD

One million flat owners and some 900,000 homeowners in England and Wales are leaseholders. Although they own their homes in many respects, in others they do not.

Most flats – and some houses – are owned on a lease-hold basis. This gives the leaseholder the right of possession, but not ownership, of a property for an agreed period of time – the length of the lease. Once the lease expires the leaseholder has no rights and must vacate the property.

The freeholder ultimately owns the property and issues the lease which sets out details of obligations (for example, no pets must be kept in the property) and ground rents payable. The freeholder also levies a service charge, which is the costs of maintaining and insuring the property divided among the leaseholders. The lessee is the person to whom the lease is granted – also known as the tenant – and the lessor is the person who grants the lease – or the landlord.

This system has its flaws: landlords are often faceless and sometimes even untraceable; work to maintain the property may not be done or done to a sufficient standard and service charges can be exorbitantly high. These factors and the fact that many flat owners who purchased lease-hold properties since the Second World War were seeing their leases come to an end led to the introduction of the Leasehold Reform Act in 1993. Under the enfranchisement rules flat owners could club together to purchase the free-hold which the landlord had to sell provided the criteria were met – and the tenants could afford the price. How-ever, the strict requirements of the law meant that many blocks of flats did not qualify, so a reform of the law is currently before parliament. As a result the right to buy the freehold will extend to a greater number of lease-holders.

Flat owners who do not want to collectively purchase the freehold, can individually extend their leases for an extra ninety years. They also have rights to challenge service charges and even demand an audit of the free-holder's books.

(See also **Freehold**.)

LEGAL AID

Legal Aid does not exist any more. The scheme is now called the Community Legal Service (CLS) and help with legal fees is paid from the CLS fund. However, as this type of help with legal bills is still referred to as Legal Aid, and as the changes to the system are comparatively recent, it is explained in detail under that term here.

The Legal Services Commission, which replaced the

Legal Aid Board on 1 April 2000, has responsibility for two
schemes – the civil scheme for funding civil cases as part
of the Community Legal Service, and a scheme for funding
criminal cases.

The CLS is developing local networks of people giving
legal help and advice – people like lawyers, the Citizens'
Advice Bureau, law centres and local councils. CLS Partnerships in different parts of the country set up these
networks. They look at the sort of help local people need,
then work to make sure the right services are in the right
places. The aim of the CLS is to have a CLS network up
and running in almost every area of England and Wales
by the end of March 2002. Some help and advice is free
and for those on very low incomes or with few assets there
may be help from the CLS fund. This fund can help pay
for divorce advice, advice on welfare benefits, credit, debt,
rent, eviction, mortgage arrears, job discrimination and
medical negligence.

Your lawyer will tell you whether you have a case that
meets the tests for help, what sort of help you will need
and whether you qualify for support to pay for it. Those
on a low income with little capital, may qualify for free
funding. The better off may be asked to pay part of the
costs. People on income support or income-based Jobseeker's allowance, or who receive the maximum tax credit
under the working families' or disabled person's tax credit
schemes may automatically qualify on financial grounds
for some help.

When assessing your income to see if you qualify for
aid, allowances are made for expenses such as income tax,

national insurance and providing for dependants. What you have after these allowances is called your disposable income. If your disposable income is £84 a week or less and your disposable capital is £1,000 or less, you will qualify for help under the scheme. Allowances are made against your capital for any dependants you have. The value of your home will only be taken into account above a specified limit.

Where further support is required, perhaps to bring court proceedings, then the LSC must also be satisfied that you have a good enough case before your case may be funded.

For higher levels of funding the income and capital limits are different from the initial help scheme and more allowances are made for expenses, for example rent and mortgage. Your disposable income for most of the higher levels of help must be below £8,067 a year and your disposable capital after allowances for your dependants must normally be below £6,750.

For very expensive cases you may still qualify if your capital is above the limit, and there are extra allowances for pensioners on low incomes. In some special cases involving children some applicants qualify regardless of their finances. If you are successful and you win or get to keep money or property with the help of CLS funding, you may be asked to put some or all of this money towards your solicitor or legal adviser's bill. This is called the 'Statutory Charge'. Where this applies, CLS funding acts as a loan.

If you don't qualify for help with your legal bills there

are other low cost or free ways to get access to legal help. The new no-win-no-fee or conditional fee system and the Small Claims Court can both give access to justice without breaking the bank. Ombudsmen schemes are also free.

(See also **Ombudsmen**.)

LEGAL EXPENSES INSURANCE

The cost of going to law can stop people getting justice. Help with legal bills from the Community Legal Service – formerly Legal Aid – is confined to an increasingly small number of people who satisfy a strict means test. If you're worried about not being able to get justice because you can't afford the prohibitive cost of going through the court, consider taking out legal expense insurance.

Many people already have some legal expense protection but don't realize it. These policies are often sold as add-ons to car insurance and household contents insurance policies.

The add-on to a car insurance policy will usually cover the cost of court cases following a road accident and pay for a hire car while you're off the road. The household version usually covers consumer disputes, personal injury cases and disputes with your employer. These policies often add between £7.50 and £15 a year to the cost of your insurance policy. A small price to pay considering the amount of legal cover they provide. In most cases there is a minimum claim of £250 and the maximum cover can be as high as £50,000. Members of trade associations and unions may also be provided with free legal insurance.

Most services provide twenty-four-hour legal help lines but note that the insurer may only back your case if they think you have a good chance of success.

LEVERAGE

Leverage is the word preferred in the US for what we call gearing and is the ratio of a company's debts to its equity. In other words, the ratio of borrowings to its share capital. People who like to take risks when it comes to investment will borrow money to invest. Such people are said to be gearing up. However, borrowing to invest is very risky because if the market falls you stand to lose some of your investment and also some of the money you have borrowed.

(See also **Gearing, Investment Trusts**.)

LIBOR

LIBOR stands for London Inter Bank Offered Rate. It's the rate of interest at which banks offer to lend money to one another in the so-called wholesale money markets in the City of London. Money can be borrowed overnight or for a period of in excess of five years.

The most often quoted rate is for 3 month money or 3 month LIBOR, which tends to be used as a yardstick for lenders involved in high-value transactions. They tend to quote rates as points above LIBOR. So if 3 month LIBOR were (say) six per cent, a bank may choose to lend to another bank at (say) 6.25 – a quarter per cent or 25 basis points above 3 month LIBOR.

Lending to individuals tends to be based on base rates which are set by the Bank of England. Base rates tend to be less volatile. However, some home lenders offer mortgage rates linked to LIBOR. Once again the 3 month rate is the basis for these loans. Minimum advances tend to be high – as much as £250,000 in some cases – and the rate that the loans are fixed above LIBOR is usually 1.5 per cent or more. Bear in mind that LIBOR-linked borrowing by individuals is higher risk and not cheaper than standard mortgages which offer much larger discounts and are more flexible. Another drawback of LIBOR-linked mortgages is that the rate may only be reviewed every quarter so borrowers will not benefit immediately from changes in base rates.

The LIBOR rates are set each day at 11 a.m. by leading banks but rates fluctuate throughout the trading session according to sentiment about the outlook for base interest rates. LIBOR rates are listed each morning in the *Financial Times* and other newspapers.

Banks also offer to borrow money in the wholesale money markets. The rate is called the London Inter Bank Bid Rate (LIBID).

LIFE ASSURANCE

No one likes to think about their own mortality which is why they say life assurance is sold, not bought. It should be taken out by anyone with dependants or debts, such as a mortgage, or both, who does not want to leave a legacy of financial problems behind them when they die.

Yet, even though buying peace of mind for yourself and your family can cost as little as a few pounds a month, ten million adults in the UK don't have any life assurance at all.

There are several different types of cover but the cheapest, most basic and most popular is term assurance. It pays out a tax-free lump sum if you die before the term of the policy is up. However, if you don't die, you don't get anything back. It is often taken out to protect a mortgage, running for the same period as the home loan so that if the borrower dies within this period the debt is cleared in full.

Monthly premiums are determined by age, health and lifestyle. They tend to be cheaper for women (because they tend to live longer) although they increase for both sexes as they get older.

If there is any hereditary illness in the family or if you smoke, premiums will be higher. Most companies will test applicants to see if they have nicotine traces. It takes twelve months after giving up to be considered a non-smoker.

The easiest way to find the most suitable policy is by going to a broker who can compare products for you.

There are different sorts of term assurance:

- Flat rate cover – gives you a set amount of cover for the term of the policy.

- Decreasing life cover – usually goes with a repayment mortgage. The size of the mortgage decreases as you pay it off therefore so does the amount of cover.

- Family income benefit – another form of decreasing cover. Instead of a lump sum, your dependants receive a yearly income if you die within the term of the policy. The amount of income they would receive decreases each year you remain alive.

- Increasing term assurance – the premiums and benefits are increased each year in line with inflation. This is usually needed by people who want extra cover because of salary increases or starting a family.

- Renewable term assurance – also known as extendable term insurance. It can be renewed at intervals, usually of five years, without the policyholder paying the rate for their age at the time. This can make it more expensive initially but at least the policy is guaranteed to be renewed regardless of the state of your health.

- Convertible term assurance – gives you the option to convert to a whole of life or endowment policy with the same company. The main advantage is that you can convert to the new policy without 'medical evidence' so the state of your health is irrelevant. This option is mainly for those who want to guarantee insurability throughout the term and, if necessary, for life.

Do not mistake 'renewable' for 'reviewable'. Reviewable term assurance is cheaper than the others, but the life company will review their premiums – so they could go up significantly. With most other forms of term assurance, the premiums stay the same throughout the term of the policy.

The term assurance market is very competitive and it is possible to shop around to cut premiums significantly. You can switch policies at any time. However, if you are much older you may find that your premiums cost more than when you first took out a policy.

Whole of life assurance, as the name suggests, covers you for the rest of your life, not just for a fixed term and, unlike with term assurance, your family is guaranteed to receive a lump sum when you die. Therefore, it is more expensive.

You can either choose the amount that will be paid out (the sum assured) or invest your premiums in the hope that they will provide a larger lump sum when you die. The cost of the first option will depend on the amount of cover you are buying. The advantage of the second option is that you can choose a level premium that you can afford – but if you die early, you could leave your family with a very small legacy as there will have only been a short period for your investments to grow. If you do pick this option, it is wise to get financial advice to choose the right investment fund.

Endowment policies are more of a savings scheme than a life insurance policy. However, they do include some life insurance cover – usually enough to pay off your mortgage if you have an endowment loan. Like term insurance, the endowment policy only lasts for a set period, usually the twenty-five-year life of a mortgage – but unlike term assurance you do get a pay-out at the end whatever happens to you. If you die, the mortgage will be paid off in full. If you live until the endowment policy matures, it should produce enough to repay the mortgage although recent poor performance by some policies means this is not always guaranteed. As a result, instead of paying a level premium (the same amount every month) for the term of the policy, some homebuyers have been asked to pay in extra each month to guarantee their debt will be repaid. Endowments should generally be avoided; there are better types of investment and cheaper forms of life cover.

Savings schemes offered by life insurance companies are often confused with life insurance policies. With-profit bonds, maximum investment plans and other investment schemes offer no life assurance at all.

Another form of life assurance that many people have – although they may not be aware of this fact – is death-in-service benefits. This is the life assurance provided by your employer if you have an occupational pension scheme. If you die while working for your firm, your family can expect to receive around three or four times your annual salary as a tax-free lump sum.

LIMIT ORDER

A limit order is the instruction an investor gives to his stockbroker setting out how much he or she is prepared to pay for particular shares. It means that investors can specify in advance which shares to buy once they hit a particular price. So an order can be placed, for example, for XYZ shares at £3 and when the price drops to that level the broker will execute the share deal. Limit orders can also be placed specifying the maximum price the investor is willing to pay or a minimum price below which a share should not be allowed to fall before it is sold.

LIMITED COMPANY

A limited company limits the liabilities of shareholders to paying for their shares in full. They are not responsible for the debts of the company unlike a sole trader or partner who has not incorporated his or her business and is therefore personally responsible for the business's debts. However, in practice, directors of limited companies are often liable for business debts as they are often required to sign a personal guarantee. A bank will often require that directors of a company put up personal property, such as a family home, as security for any business loans.

It is possible to buy a pre-formed limited company off-the-shelf for less than £100. Companies selling off-the-shelf pre-formed limited companies advertise their services in the classified and business sections of newspapers. Although the pre-formed company will have a name it will probably not be the one you want. But once you have purchased it you can apply to have the trading name changed.

Although they are simple and easy to set up, the responsibilities of owning a company should not be taken lightly. There are requirements to have at least one director and a company secretary, the company must be registered at Companies House, the powers, obligations and internal regulations of the company must be set out in two documents, the Memorandum of Association and the Articles of Association, annual returns must be filed to Companies House and the statutory books open to public inspection. There are fines for those who fail to meet these requirements. (Companies house will fine those who are late in delivering their accounts – fines for private companies range from £100 to £1,000 depending on how late the return is, and for public companies from £1,000 to £5,000.)

To be listed on the London Stock Exchange or the Alternative Investments Market a company must become a public limited company or plc, which means it is publicly rather than privately owned.

LIQUIDITY

Liquidity describes the ease with which assets – shares, bonds, etc. – can be bought and sold. Some assets such as shares in the FTSE 100 are highly liquid because they are actively traded. Whereas shares in the Alternative Investment Market, which are not heavily traded, are illiquid. The more liquidity there is in a market, the more competition, which generally means that market makers offer narrower margins.

LISTED COMPANY

This is a company whose shares have been listed by a stock exchange. For shares to be accepted by the Quotations Committee of the London Stock Exchange, the company's financial position and reputation will have been examined. If these are satisfactory, the shares are admitted to the Official List of securities dealt in by members of the Stock Exchange.

LLOYD'S OF LONDON

Lloyd's used to epitomize quality and fair play in the City of London, but now has an image tainted by corruption scandals and big losses following the near collapse of the insurance market in the 1990s. For many, the well-heeled, middle-class individuals whose capital provided the backing for Lloyd's complex insurance operation had only themselves to blame for being too greedy and too complacent to check exactly what they were getting into. But people who have been ruined by Lloyd's losses say that in many instances they were the victims of one of the biggest corruption scandals this country has ever seen.

Lloyd's is a market. Just as the stock market is the market for companies' shares, Lloyd's is the market for insurance policies. Lloyd's sets itself apart from other insurance markets in the way it is organized and the range of risks people can find insurance for under one roof – from policies that pay out when a ship sinks to insuring a footballer against breaking his legs, as well as more mundane events such as car thefts and burglaries.

The market began in the 1680s in a coffee house near London's Tower Wharf where ship owners and sea captains regularly met to discuss maritime issues. Merchants agreed to insure ships and their cargoes in return for a down payment or premium.

The trappings of its seventeenth-century origins are still retained by Lloyd's despite its high-tech City building. Anyone visiting will still see the Lutine Bell on the main underwriting floor. The bell from a captured French frigate was rung to signal news of overdue ships – once for bad news, twice for good.

In the late 1980s the Lloyd's market was rocked by scandal as various high-profile Lloyd's underwriters (who agree to take on a risk and assess the premium) and brokers (who approach underwriters to take on risks) ended up in court, charged with defrauding the market. Then a series of natural disasters such as hurricanes, asbestos-linked claims from the United States and man-made disasters such as oil spills left the market nursing heavy losses.

Lloyd's investors known as Lloyd's Names, the rich individuals whose personal wealth supported the market and who had unlimited liability, were then faced with mounting losses. Some have been ruined, some have sued and many have left the insurance market. The number of Names has fallen from 34,000 in 1992 to just 3,300 in 2000. The number of syndicates (Names join together to form syndicates when accepting business and are represented by an underwriter who accepts risk on its behalf) has also fallen sharply from 156 in 1998 to 122 in 2000.

Although private individuals are now returning to the market, and providing limited rather than unlimited liability, the Lloyd's market is still for the wealthy who already have large investments and are looking to add to their portfolios, rather than for the more average investor.

While Lloyd's is expected to make a £725 million loss for 1998 (it takes several years for accounts to be finalized as claims need to be submitted), these losses no longer fall mainly on private individuals.

The market has restructured in recent years and now 35 per cent of capital is provided by professional insurance and reinsurance companies. Individuals have less of a role to play and of those that remain many have converted from having unlimited liability to limited liability and these names now provide over £1 billion of cover.

LOAN TO VALUE (LTV)

The loan to value ratio is the ratio between the size of the mortgage you are seeking and the mortgage lender's valuation of the property. Most lenders have a maximum LTV of 95 per cent although some do offer 100 per cent mortgages which means you can borrow the entire cost of a property without paying a deposit. For some of the best deals, however, lenders may require a 25 or even 30 per cent deposit. Borrowers who have high LTVs have little equity in their property and therefore risk falling into negative equity if property prices fall or their debt starts to mount because they fall behind on monthly repayments. Those borrowing more than 90 per cent of the property's value may also have to pay mortgage indemnity guarantee, also known as a high lending fee, which can add up to £1,000 to the cost of buying a home.

(See also **Mortgage Indemnity Guarantee**.)

LOANS

See under **Personal Loans**.

LONG-TERM CARE

Long-term care is one of the political and economic hot potatoes of the early twenty-first century. Thanks to medical advances, the ageing population (who are living longer but often require help with day-to-day living) is putting a huge burden on the state.

Life expectancy for sixties baby boomers is sixty-eight for men and seventy-four for women – up an average of ten years on the pre-war generation. By 2041 the pension population will reach its peak at one in four people as the 10 million babies born in the sixties boom swell the figures. And, with genetic research into the ageing process making leaps and bounds, living to a hundred could become routine.

The retirement age was originally set at sixty-five because most people didn't live much longer than that. However, today's elderly can expect a long – if not healthy – retirement. Around one in three women and one in five men spend their last years in a nursing home, currently around half a million pensioners. This is the problem. Who should pay for this care? The government or the individual? Some 40,000 pensioners a year have been forced to sell their homes to pay for this care, something the New Labour government promised to address. However, despite a commission being set up to look into the issue of long-term care and hopes that this would lead to free personal care for all, fewer numbers of elderly residents of care homes will get help after all (apart from in Scotland where the elderly now receive more help than pensioners south of the border).

The government has decided to make nursing care in a nursing home free, benefiting 35,000 elderly people. However, there are nearly half a million older people in residential nursing homes who need personal care – help with dressing, bathing, etc. If they do not qualify for state help with their care home fees they will have to pay for this because they have savings or an income that puts them above the means-tested threshold, although these thresholds have been raised in recent budgets.

In 1993, the Community Care Act radically changed the way in which state long-term care is paid for in the United Kingdom when responsibility as to who should receive state care was transferred from the Health Service to Local Authorities and means testing was introduced. Individuals must pay towards the maintenance of their care until their total assets – including their home, cash, shares, etc. – is reduced to £16,000. With nursing home fees topping £20,000 or even £30,000 a year, these assets are quickly eroded. When the value of assets falls below £8,000, some contribution to care will still have to be made. It is only when the assets are reduced to £3,000 or less that full support is provided. There are exceptions. The house of the person who has moved to a nursing home is not taken into account if it continues to be occupied by the person's partner. This is also applicable if the home is occupied either by an incapacitated relative or a relative who acts as a carer.

The fact that so many elderly people face the prospect of paying for their own long-term care, which often means selling the family home, eating into savings and investments and leaving very little as an inheritance to the next generation, has led to the development of long-term care policies. The aim of the insurance is to provide cover so that should you develop a long-term disability or illness as you grow older the costs of care will be met. The policy will pay out to provide care, either at home or in a residential or nursing home. Generally, to be able to claim benefit, the insured has to show that he or she is unable to perform at least three day-to-day activities such as eating, washing or dressing.

Like private medical insurance, the cost of cover will be determined by the area in which you live and the cost of care locally. Cover can be arranged for a fixed number of years or indefinitely. Most plans are paid for by monthly premiums but they are not cheap.

There are three main types of policies: an insurance-based plan or pre-funded plan, an investment or bond-based plan and a plan designed for someone needing care immediately. With the insurance scheme a monthly or lump-sum premium is paid and the policy pays out enough to pay for care fees. The drawback is that if the policyholder dies or only spends a short time in a care home, then the premiums are not recoverable. With an investment scheme the individual can get their capital back but they tend to be expensive. Immediate care contracts involve purchasing an annuity.

Before taking out a long-term care policy you are advised to seek advice from a financial adviser. They sell these policies on behalf of life insurance companies. It is best to seek independent advice so that you get a choice of a range of products. Age Concern (see **Useful Addresses**) also has useful literature.

How far ahead should people start planning? Most financial products cost less the longer you plan ahead as you then have more time for your investments to grow. However, with long-term care products there is a down-side to planning ahead. If you take out a long-term care product and then die without needing to go into care, your investment is wasted. Hence the fact that long-term care products are taken out post-retirement when the individual can assess his or her likely needs.

M

MARGIN TRADING

This enables you to take a position on a stock without having to put up the full value of those shares. Instead you put up a margin deposit as collateral. This is normally around 10 per cent of the contract value. You can either go long (which means buying) or go short (which means selling) the stock. As such you can gamble on share prices falling – something you cannot or would not want to do if you own shares directly. Margin trading is also known as contracts for difference trading.

MARKET MAKERS

Market makers do exactly that – make markets in shares. By shopping around from market maker to market maker it is possible for a stockbroker to find a better price for a trade. Although prices vary only fractionally, if large amounts of shares are traded this can make a significant difference. Some online share dealing services offer this best-price service. Market makers may actively try to encourage/discourage trading by changing the prices they quote to tempt buyers and sellers into the market. However, they are a dying breed. In October 1997, the London Stock Exchange introduced order driven share dealing for the shares in the FTSE 100 index starting a process which will eventually do away with market makers (they'll be replaced by Retail Service Providers).

For shares outside the FTSE-100, the London Stock Exchange continues to operate a system of competing market makers all of whom are obliged to make a continuous two-way price, that is, to offer to buy and sell securities.

MEANS TESTING

To ensure that state benefits are targeted at those in greatest need, some are only payable to those on low incomes either because they are not working or are in poorly paid employment. Means testing is the process by which the claimants' means are tested to see if they qualify. Expensive to administer, it is a means of rationing public funds. However, a reluctance by some claimants to be means tested and the amount of information required can sometimes deter people from getting the benefits they are due.

MID PRICE

Shares and units in unit-linked funds and unit trusts have a buying and selling price. This is known as the bid-offer spread. However, the price of each unit or share printed in newspapers is the mid price – the average between the two. It is sometimes also referred to as the middle market price.

MIRAS

This stood for Mortgage Interest Relief at Source and was the tax relief given to homebuyers to encourage them to buy their own homes. Steadily eroded over the years it was finally abolished in April 2000 although some pensioners with home income plans still qualify for tax relief.

MONETARY POLICY COMMITTEE

Set up in 1997 by the Chancellor of the Exchequer, Gordon Brown, the Monetary Policy Committee is the Bank of England committee that decides the level of interest rates. Before its formation, interest rate decisions were largely political. However, the government no longer has a say in the base rate, but still sets inflation targets and the Bank of

England must then set interest rates at a level consistent with achieving the target.

The committee consists of nine members including the Bank of England Governor, the Deputy Governor and second Deputy Governor and six other members – two from the bank with responsibility for monetary policy and market operations – and four recognized experts members from outside the bank. The committee meets monthly to discuss and vote on whether to raise interest rates.

MONEY PURCHASE SCHEMES

These are pension schemes where the pension paid out upon retirement is dependent on how much you invest, how well these investments perform, the charges taken from the fund and annuity rates when you retire. They are increasingly being offered by employers as an alternative to final salary schemes, which pay out a pension dependent not on what is paid in but on salary at or near retirement and the number of years of service for that employer.

Personal pensions and stakeholder pensions are also money purchase schemes.

(See also **Additional Voluntary Contributions, Occupational Pension Schemes, Personal Pensions** and **Stakeholder Pensions**.)

MONEY TRANSFER

Money transfer services enable you to transfer money round the world quickly. It is an ideal service if you want to send money to relatives abroad or someone runs out of cash while travelling. These companies, such as Western Union and MoneyGram, can transfer money in minutes. Major banks and some building societies also offer a similar service but this may take a few days. Charges for money transfer start at seven pounds.

MORTGAGES

With more than 4,000 different mortgages on offer, this is not only a competitive market but also an increasingly complex one. Where once there were just a few alternatives and limited choices – an endowment or a repayment mortgage? – there is now a bewildering choice of home loans on offer from a growing number of lenders. This makes it difficult to compare different products to find the one most suited to your needs.

Borrowing money to buy a home still remains the biggest financial commitment most people will undertake and yet while they may spend three months or more looking for their dream home, most buyers still spend less than three hours looking for the right mortgage. The consequences of this apathy can mean an extra £10,000 or more in mortgage payments and being saddled with a mortgage for far longer than is necessary.

Mortgages tend to be taken out for twenty-five-year terms, although there is nothing to stop borrowers taking out shorter or longer-term mortgages. The amount advanced is based on the income of the borrowers with most lenders restricting the amount of loan to an income multiple of 2.5 to 3 times salary for a single purchaser and 3 times the first salary plus the second, or 2.75 times joint income for joint purchasers. However, some lenders will offer to lend far more if the purchaser has other income or is likely to see their income rise rapidly. There is an added restriction to how much buyers can borrow, the loan to value (LTV) ratio. Most lenders will not advance more than 90 or 95 per cent of the property's value.

The two basic types of mortgage are repayment and interest only. Interest-only mortgages backed by endowment policies were the most popular at the start of the 1990s but that situation has reversed and repayment mortgages are now more widely sold.

With a repayment mortgage the borrower pays interest on the loan plus an element of the capital (the amount borrowed) each month so that by the end of the term of the mortgage all the capital is repaid. The advantage of these loans is that the borrower is guaranteed to be debt free at the end of the mortgage term and also will see the amount owed decrease over the years.

With an interest-only mortgage, only the interest is paid on the amount borrowed with the buyer usually taking out an investment scheme that should grow sufficiently to produce a lump sum capable of paying off the mortgage debt at the end of the policy term. Traditionally the investments sold to back mortgages were endowment policies, but since the returns of these have fallen more flexible, cheaper and better performing individual savings accounts (ISAs) are the preferred investment. It is also possible to use a personal pension to repay a mortgage. The advantage is that there is tax relief on the premiums. However, borrowers have to wait until they retire to pay off the mortgage or reach fifty (the age at which personal pensions can be taken) and will have less retirement income to live off when they retire.

There are several other varieties of mortgage which are all types of repayment mortgage. Current account mortgages or all-in-one accounts that combine a mortgage with a current account, savings and loan account to minimize interest payments. Flexible mortgages which allow borrowers to vary, stop, restart, over and underpay their monthly repayments. Offset mortgages which keep different financial products such as savings, loans and the mortgage in different pots but at the end of each day the credit balances are offset against the debit balances to reduce the amount of interest the borrower is charged.

In addition there are daily interest mortgages that calculate the amount of interest the borrower is charged on a daily basis. Using this so-called daily rest system saves borrowers significant amounts of interest particularly if they pay in additional sums over and above the minimum monthly payment required.

Traditional repayment mortgages charge borrowers

interest on money they have already repaid as the interest calculation is based on the amount outstanding at the start of the year and no account is taken of any repayments made. Daily interest calculations are a requirement of the new CAT standards for mortgages.

In addition to selecting the type of mortgage, borrowers need to choose the way the interest is charged. Borrowers can have either fixed-rate, capped-rate or discounted-rate mortgages.

With a fixed rate the mortgage rate is fixed or set at a pre-agreed rate for a certain period, usually up to five years. After that the rate reverts back to the standard variable rate which is the rate most existing borrowers pay and is usually higher than the fixed rate. The advantage of these mortgages is the borrower knows exactly what rate he or she will pay in the first years of the loan. The disadvantage is that if general mortgage rates fall during this period, the borrower could be tied into a higher rate than other borrowers.

With a capped-rate mortgage the interest rate will not rise above the pre-agreed capped rate during a pre-agreed period – again usually up to five years. The rate then reverts to the standard variable rate. Although these borrowers will pay more if interest rates rise they will never pay more than the capped rate so should be paying far less than other borrowers. The advantage is that if general mortgage rates fall these borrowers will benefit, unlike those who have fixed-rate mortgages.

With a discount-rate mortgage the rate charged is at a

fixed discount – for example, 2 per cent – below the standard variable rate charged by that lender for a certain period of time.

The rates on tracker mortgages are guaranteed to track rises and falls in the Bank of England base rate. The rates are usually well below the standard variable rate which often rises and falls by a different amount to the movement in base rates. In addition, lenders are often quick to pass on interest rate increases to borrowers but slow to pass on cuts.

Some mortgages are annually adjusted which means that the monthly repayments only change once a year. However, this does not mean the rate of interest charged stays the same. The interest rate changes in line with movements in base rates and if the borrower is paying a higher amount than needed or less this is taken into account at the end of the year when the monthly repayments are set for the next year. Annually adjusted mortgages usually have their monthly repayments adjusted in the spring and help to make budgeting ahead easier.

Rates are not the only issue. Additional costs such as arrangement fees can push up the total cost of the mortgage. Some lenders may also insist that borrowers take out certain insurance products such as house insurance as a condition of the loan. However, these policies are often far more expensive than can be purchased independently. This conditional selling is not permitted if the mortgage is to meet the CAT standard.

Redemption penalties can also push up the cost of a

mortgage. These are charged when the borrower wishes to cash the mortgage in – and even if they only want to repay part of it – during the redemption period which is usually the same length as any fixed, discount or capped rate. Extended redemption penalties extend longer than the cheap rate. Penalties can add up to over £1,000 or several months interest.

Special rates are often offered to first-time buyers and those who remortgage (i.e. switch their mortgage to a better rate without moving home, which accounts for around 30 per cent of all mortgages). Often any legal, survey and arrangement fees will be reimbursed. As added incentives some lenders offer cashbacks, a cash lump sum once the mortgage has been completed which can sometimes amount to hundreds if not thousands of pounds. It is also possible to take out a further advance on a mortgage, increasing its size to pay for major items of expenditure such as home improvements.

(See also **Buy-to-let**, **Mortgages**, **Endowments**, **Flexible Mortgages**, **Loan to Value**, **Redemption Penalties**.)

MORTGAGE INDEMNITY GUARANTEE

Also known as a high lending fee, the MIG is a premium paid by borrowers who take out mortgages with a high loan to value ratio (i.e. borrowing more than 90 per cent of the property's value), although a few lenders no longer charge this fee. It pays for an insurance policy to protect the lender, not the borrower, against the loan falling into arrears or defaulting. So although borrowers pay for the cover, they get no protection at all. Often amounting to £1,000, the MIG premium is usually added to the loan at the outset so the borrower then pays interest on this premium pushing up the costs further. The new CAT standards for mortgages require that no separate charge for mortgage indemnity guarantee insurance is made to borrowers.

Although MIG is charged on loans above a certain LTV it may actually be calculated as a percentage of borrowing above 75 or 80 per cent. This is because historically it was charged on loans with an LTV above this level. It is charged as a percentage of the amount over this level. So a 95 per cent mortgage on a £100,000 property could have the MIG calculated on the difference between £75,000 and £95,000 or £20,000. The percentage charge ranges from 5 per cent to 10 per cent, with the higher the rate charged the higher the LTV. So if MIG was charged at 10 per cent, the borrower in this example would pay £2,000 in MIG.

You cannot shop around for the best MIG deal, but have to buy the one your lender chooses. However, as costs vary – and some lenders do not charge this fee – it is worth comparing costs. Another alternative is to save up a larger deposit, more than 5 or 10 per cent, in order to escape paying MIG.

MORTGAGE PAYMENT PROTECTION INSURANCE (MPPI)

This is insurance taken out to ensure the mortgage is paid if you are unable to work because of accident, illness or redundancy. Policies usually cover the monthly mortgage payments for twelve months although some also offer twenty-four-month cover, although this will be more expensive.

Around 700,000 people are made redundant every year and around 2 million are unable to work for a year or more due to sickness according to research by CGU Direct. The odds of suffering a serious illness which requires at least six months off work are one in sixteen.

However, many homebuyers wrongly believe that they can rely on the State to cover mortgage payments. The State pays only the interest on mortgages and then only after thirty-nine weeks off work. A change in State benefit now means that more than three-quarters of homeowners would receive no help at all if they lost their jobs.

However, MPPI is not suitable for everyone. Industry estimates suggest that just over half of borrowers would benefit from it. So while it is worth considering, no one should feel pressurized into buying it. Those who have secure employment with good redundancy and sickness terms may feel they do not need cover along with those who have large amounts of savings, small mortgages or dual incomes.

You can often pick and choose the type of cover you need. Most policies cover accident, sickness and unemployment, but you may be able to buy just one or two of these types of cover. So if, for example, your insurance covers you for accident and sickness leave you may want to cut the costs of cover by buying only unemployment insurance.

As with all insurance policies there are exclusions. Redundancy at the start of the policy is excluded, along with pre-existing medical conditions and you cannot take out MPPI after becoming unemployed. No policy pays out immediately.

Lenders charge a set amount per £100 of the monthly repayments. Prices for cover do vary and some companies offer free introductory periods – but check what price you will be paying after that.

If a mortgage is paid jointly and both people are working, it is possible to take out MPPI for half the mortgage in the name of the borrower who has the least secure employment, assuming it is very unlikely that both of you would be unemployed or unable to work at the same time.

MORTGAGE REGULATION

With so many different mortgage products available, choosing the best one to meet a borrower's particular needs is time consuming and difficult. That is why many borrowers seek advice. But how reliable is that advice?

The Mortgage Code was introduced to improve standards of advice and to persuade the government that statutory regulation of mortgages was unnecessary. It was introduced by the industry in 1997 and is a voluntary code of practice. However, concerns about the information given to borrowers and criticism of high redemption charges imposed by some lenders, meant that the lenders could not stave off being regulated. Now mortgages have been brought into line with other financial services products and are regulated by the new Financial Services Authority.

The aim is to end loans that cannot be easily compared; those that are expensive to escape; the hard-selling of endowments and expensive insurance; and misleading interest rate offers and hidden charges.

However, the FSA will not cover mortgage advice – only information and advertising – something consumer groups feel will leave borrowers still vulnerable to mis-selling. The FSA regulation is designed to complement the voluntary Mortgage Code which does include the advice given to potential borrowers. But once again there are flaws in this system.

There are three levels of advice, so borrowers need to check which they are receiving.

- The top level is advice and a recommendation as to the most suitable deal. In order to select the best mortgage to meet the borrower's needs, the lender needs to ask questions about the borrower's needs and circumstances. The advice given and the reasons behind it must then be summarized in writing. However, lenders do not often offer this level of service.

- The second level is information but no specific advice on the different types of mortgages available. The borrower can then review the information to make an informed decision for themselves.

- The third and most basic option is information on only one mortgage deal. So if the borrower has seen an advertisement for a particular loan and requests details of just that one product, then this is all they will receive.

Lenders and advisers should declare at the outset which levels of service are available so that borrowers can choose the one they want. Most big lenders offer all three levels of advice.

The Mortgage Code also covers intermediaries – estate agents and financial advisers – which account for about half of new mortgages. From May 1998, lenders subscribing to the Code will accept business only from intermediaries who also sign up to it.

Intermediaries must tell potential borrowers whether they search the whole market to find the best deal or whether they operate with a restricted panel of lenders or use one particular lender. They should also disclose commission that lenders pay them and any fees they may charge.

There are drawbacks with the code. Consumer groups have found that advisers do not always mention the code or the level of services available. Also if the lender does not offer the most suitable type of mortgage the borrower may never know. So if a homebuyer would be better off with a flexible mortgage or one that charges interest on a daily basis, they may not be told this if the lender does not offer that product.

A third level of consumer protection was introduced in 2000 – CAT standards. However, these are voluntary so not all lenders need meet the requirements and, even if they do adopt them, it may be for only a few mortgage products.

The CAT standard, which stands for low Charges, easy Access and fair Terms, requires that lenders:

- Make no separate charge for mortgage indemnity guarantee insurance

- Calculate interest daily – known as daily rests

- Charge no fees for arranging the mortgage although there can be a booking fee of £150 for fixed or capped mortgages

- Have an interest rate that is no more than 2 per cent above base rates for variable rate mortgages (this is well above that charged by most lenders)

- Have no redemption charges for variable rate loans and no extended redemption charge for fixed or capped rate loans

- Allow early repayments at any time

- Not make buying any other product – such as insurance – a condition of the loan

However, the CAT standards do not cover advice and in fact preclude borrowers paying fees to brokers, who give mortgage advice.

Although this combination of measures should ensure borrowers get clearer information about mortgage products, and should get rid of unfair clauses, they only go some way to addressing the problem of poor and misleading mortgage advice.

MUTUALS

Mutually owned organizations are owned by their members rather than shareholders. In the case of building societies these are certain types of saver and borrower, and in the case of life insurance companies they are investors in the with-profits policies of that company. In addition, friendly societies are mutually owned organizations.

Building societies are the mutually owned organizations that have been grabbing the headlines in recent years with many coming under attack from carpetbaggers trying to force conversion into banks (known as demutualization) in pursuit of windfalls – free shares or cash. In addition many of the smaller societies have merged. As a result the number of societies have dropped from 2,286 in 1900 to just sixty-eight at the start of the new millennium. Life companies are also losing their mutual status mainly from take-overs by larger quoted companies with Scottish Widows and Equitable Life both being sold and losing their mutual status.

However, there has been a backlash against demutualization – not just from mutual organizations like the Building Societies Association but also from members of the public. In the late 1990s the shares of former building societies turned banks failed to sparkle, potential windfalls fell in value and the arguments in favour of maintaining mutual status began to sink in. Mutuals, as they do not have to pay dividends to shareholders, can make their customers a priority and therefore offer better value. Over the life-time of a pension plan or mortgage these benefits can far outweigh the short-term gains of a £500 or £1,000 windfall. As a result some societies have successfully staved off being forced to demutualize including the larger Nationwide and the smaller Leek United. As a result, mutuality – which looked under threat a few years ago – is likely to remain a powerful force in the financial services sector.

(See also **Building Societies, Windfalls**.)

N

NATIONAL DEBT

This is the total amount borrowed by successive governments that is still outstanding. Once a major threat to our
economy, in recent years government surpluses have been
used to reduce the amount owed dramatically.

In the March 2000 Budget alone, Chancellor Gordon
Brown was able to clear £12 billion off the national debt.
This is a situation likely to continue for some years to
come. This is known as public sector debt repayment
(PSDR) and is the opposite of the more familiar public
sector borrowing requirement (PSBR).

To finance the national debt the government can:

- Issue Gilts which are government bonds

- Raise money from National Savings

- Issue Treasury bills for short-term borrowings

- And also use Net foreign currency

Ever since 1694 (the year the Bank of England was formed)
governments have borrowed money. In the first place
this was to finance wars. From the end of World War II

government borrowing has been used to finance spending on more constructive things such as the welfare state.

The current target is to reduce public debt to 35 per cent of the country's gross domestic product (GDP) – a measure of our economic activity which is basically the value of all goods and services produced by the nation. By 2003 the target is to bring this percentage down further to 33 per cent.

NATIONAL INSURANCE CONTRIBUTIONS

Everyone gets a National Insurance number as a sixteenth birthday present from the Department of Social Security. From then on they have to pay NI contributions or NICS unless they earn less than the lower NIC threshold which, for the 2001 to 2002 tax year, is £87 a week. Those in receipt of certain state benefits and those who are registered as unemployed receive national insurance credits. No contributions are paid on earnings above an upper earnings limit which, for the 2001 to 2002 tax year, was £575 a week.

Men over sixty-four and women over fifty-nine no longer pay NICs – with this age limit for women due to be equalized with the male retirement age over the next few years.

The theory behind national insurance was that it would

pay for a variety of state benefits and the state pension. However, rather than an individual's contributions being used to pay their pension when they retire, the burdens on the state from the ageing population means that today's workers are paying for the generation that has already retired with nothing being set aside for their own futures.

NICs come in various classes:

- Class 1 is by far the most common type and is paid by employees and their employers. Those earning more than the employee's earnings threshold of £87 a week pay contributions of 10 per cent on all earnings up to the upper earnings limit. There is a reduced rate for some married women and widows, however, this is now being phased out. Employers also pay a contribution, but they do not start to pay until earnings exceed the employer's earnings threshold which, for the 2001 to 2002 tax year, is £87 a week. Employers pay NICs at a higher rate of 11.9 per cent and, unlike employees, employers have no upper earnings threshold so must pay contributions on all earnings. There are reduced rates for employees who are members of contracted-out occupational pension schemes, which means that members of these schemes are not members of the state earnings-related pension scheme (SERPS). Class 1A contributions are paid on company cars and fuel made available for private use at the rate of 10 per cent with these contributions paid by the employer only – not the employees.

- Class 2 national insurance contributions are the flat-rate payments made by the self-employed. The self-employed may also have to pay Class 4 contributions. For the 2001 to 2002 tax year these contributions are just £2 a week. Those earning less than £3,955 do not have to make any contributions.

- Class 3 NICs are voluntary flat-rate contributions made by the non-employed or the self-employed who earn less than the Class 2 earnings limit. They are paid to secure social security benefits for which they would not otherwise qualify.

- Class 4 contributions are paid by the self-employed based on their taxable profits between £4,535 and £29,900 a year. These are calculated at the same time as income tax.

The payment of national insurance contributions is vital to secure state benefits including the basic state pension. Contrary to popular belief not everyone qualifies for the full pension – only those who have paid NICs for at least 90 per cent of their working lives or have had NIC credits for periods of unemployment. It is possible to buy extra years of contributions to ensure that a larger pension will be paid. However, not all NICs give the payee the same rights to benefits. The self-employed, for example, are not entitled to Jobseeker's Allowance should their business fail as this is only payable to those who have made Class 1 contributions.

NATIONAL SAVINGS

Ever since 1861 the public has been asked to lend the government small amounts of money through their savings to boost the nation's coffers. National Savings gives the government a convenient way of doing this from private investors.

The products offered by National Savings come in the form of savings accounts and fixed-term investment bonds sold through post offices. They are a risk-free way of investing for income or growth.

The idea of a government-backed savings scheme was the brainchild of Lord Palmerston's government which launched the Post Office Savings Bank. The then Chancellor of the Exchequer, William Gladstone, soon realized that the deposits could be used to finance government business as well as encourage thrift among ordinary wage earners.

Although National Savings does not offer the best rates on the market, its products are, nevertheless, competitive and better than average, and in addition some offer tax-free interest – a valuable bonus particularly for higher rate taxpayers.

The products offered by National Savings include:

- The Ordinary Account: Generally paying a very low rate of interest, this instant access account is, surprisingly, one of the most popular savings accounts, partly because of customer apathy. Savers do not realize they can shop around to get a far better rate of interest. Although the first £70 of interest a year is tax free, this tax break hardly makes up for the low rate of interest.

- Investment Account: This one-month notice account pays interest gross – without tax deducted – which must be declared to the Inland Revenue. The minimum investment is £20.

- Savings Certificates: These certificates, which run for either a two- or five-year term, have a minimum investment of £100 and are tax free. The rate of interest is fixed at the outset. However, to get the maximum rate of interest they have to be held for the full term.

- Index-linked Certificates: These have the same terms and minimum investments but instead of paying a fixed rate of interest they pay a set amount above inflation. They appeal when there are fears of inflation rising. These are also tax free.

- Fixed-rate saving bonds: These are issued over different periods. The current bonds in issue are for six months, one year, eighteen months and three years. The minimum investment is £500 and the rate of interest is fixed at the outset. Interest is paid net of tax at the lower rate (currently 20 per cent).

- Capital Bonds: These are five-year investments with a minimum £100 investment and a fixed rate of interest that is paid gross but liable to tax. Although these bonds can be cashed in before their five-year term is up, there will be loss of interest.

- Pensioners Guaranteed Income Bonds: These are either two- or five-year investments that pay a fixed rate of interest gross – but liable to income tax – aimed at people aged sixty and over with a minimum £500 to invest.

- ISA – individual savings account: National Savings also offers its own version of the tax-free savings scheme with this ISA qualifying for the CAT Standard.

- Children's Bond: This is a five-year bond that pays a fixed rate of interest on a minimum £25 investment.

- Income Bonds: The interest rate on these is not fixed, the notice period is three months although earlier access is allowed with an interest penalty and the interest is paid gross but must be declared. A minimum £500 investment is required.

In addition, matured issues of savings certificates earn the general extension rate – a less than competitive rate for those who have forgotten or not got round to switching their matured investments to a new savings product.

NEGATIVE EQUITY

This term came to prominence in the property slump of the early 1990s; negative equity means that a homebuyer owes more in mortgage debt than the property they are buying is worth. A combination of soaring mortgage rates and falling property prices led to millions of homebuyers suffering from negative equity. Most were trapped in their homes unable to sell until property prices recovered enough to repay the mortgage debt. The recovery in house prices led to the introduction of negative equity schemes whereby borrowers could move to a new home and often borrow up to 125 per cent of the loan to value (LTV) provided they had sufficient income and a good credit history.

NET

This is an amount after tax has been deducted. For example, your net salary is the amount you actually get as take-home pay. The net rate on your savings is the amount they will earn after tax is deducted. The net rate is always lower than the interest rate advertised which is the gross amount.

(See also **Gross**.)

NET ASSET VALUE (NAV)

The value of a company's underlying assets. In the case of an investment trust, this is based on the market price of the shares and other investments owned by that trust.

(See also **Investment Trusts**.)

NEW ISSUES

This term is most commonly applied to the shares issued by companies joining the stock market for the first time. It may also refer to subsequent share issues by companies that are already quoted on the stock market.

New shares are issued in order to raise extra capital, either to repay existing company debts, or to fund further expansion of the business. Sometimes these shares are placed with existing clients of the stockbrokers involved in the flotation. But some stock-market debutants will also make an offer for sale of at least a proportion of the shares to the general public.

Details of new share issues are published in a prospectus – a brochure whose function is partly to market the shares to potential investors and partly to fulfil statutory obligations. These include the provision of specific information about the company, the background of the issue and the appropriate risk warnings.

NO CLAIMS BONUS

Also known as a no claims discount, this is the bonus policyholders who are claim free receive as a 'reward' for being careful. Traditionally only given to motorists, who can receive a maximum discount of up to 75 per cent on their premiums which is usually earned after six years of no claims, these discounts are now also being offered as an incentive to homeowners to keep their property safe. Motorists gradually build up their no-claims bonus over several years. It is so valuable that many drivers also insure their no-claims bonus so that, if they have to make a claim, it will not be lost.

NOMINEE ACCOUNTS

These are accounts set up by stockbrokers to hold shares on behalf of private investors. A nominee account is increasingly common as a way of holding shares as paper-less trading takes over from paper share certificates. Faster settlement of shares – the time in which shares must be paid for is now just three days – means that private investors who want to trade on a regular basis cannot afford to wait for delays while cheques and certificates are sent by post. As a result stockbrokers generally recommend that investors open a nominee account. One will be required if the investor wants to trade through Crest, the electronic share settlement system.

Although the account is in the name of the stockbroker, the investor is still the beneficial owner of the shares. Investors need to check that they will still receive free copies of annual reports and company accounts, will still be entitled to attend company meetings and be entitled to any shareholder perks once they are no longer listed on the company share register. Shareholders should automatically receive any dividends to which they are entitled.

Despite the move to paperless trading, nominee accounts will not entirely replace share certificates. Those who hold shares for any period of time may still want to have a paper certificate which they can then take to a stockbroker when they need to sell.

(See also **Crest, Online Share Dealing**.)

NON-STATUS MORTGAGE

These are mortgages where no income details are required. Suitable for the self-employed who do not have the required three years' accounts demanded by many lenders, they generally require a substantial deposit of between 25 and 50 per cent of the property value and borrowers are usually charged a much higher than average interest rate.

These types of loans are now less common and self-certification mortgages, which require details of income but no proof, offer better value. The maximum loan to value (LTV) of these loans is usually 75 to 90 per cent and some lenders restrict these mortgages to the self-employed.

O

OCCUPATIONAL PENSION SCHEMES

Some 11 million people, or virtually half the workforce, are members of company pension schemes. In addition, around six million retired people receive payments from a company scheme.

There are two main types: final salary (or earnings-related) schemes and money purchase (or defined contributions) schemes. Final salary schemes are still dominant, but there is a continuing but slow trend to introduce money purchase schemes which tend to be cheaper for employers to run.

With final salary schemes the pension paid on retirement is based on the employee's salary at or near retirement and the number of years service (membership of the scheme). Generally the calculation is done as a fraction – 1/60th of final pay for every year of service. So after forty years the employee is entitled to a pension of 40/60ths of final pay or 2/3rds. Both the employer and employee usually pay into the scheme, although some well-funded schemes may grant to the employer a payment holiday. In other cases, the scheme may be non-contributory which means that the employee does not have to make contributions. Upon retirement the employee can usually choose whether or not to convert part of the benefits into a tax-free lump sum or take a higher pension, although some schemes will automatically pay a lump sum.

With money purchase schemes, the employee normally contributes more than to a final salary scheme. The pension paid on retirement depends on how much has been paid in (by both the employer and employee), how well this money has been invested, the charges deducted, how much is taken as a tax-free lump sum on retirement and annuity rates at the time of retirement.

Some schemes are contracted out of the state earnings related pension scheme (SERPS), which means that both employers and employees make lower National Insurance contributions. However, the employee is no longer entitled to the state top-up pension, SERPS. If the scheme is contracted in, employees receive SERPSs as well as the company pension.

Members of occupational schemes can also make additional voluntary contributions (AVCs) to boost their pension. These top-up schemes are offered by the occupational schemes. Those who want to buy their AVC elsewhere can buy a free-standing AVC (FSAVC) from an outside provider, usually an insurance company.

As with all pensions, occupational schemes are tax-efficient. All contributions made by the employee attract tax relief at that employee's highest rate. So it only costs a higher rate taxpayer £60 to contribute £100 – the remaining £40 is tax relief. However, the tax does not have to be reclaimed because pension contributions to an occupational scheme are made out of gross earnings, before tax is deducted. Other tax benefits of a pension are that the fund grows free of tax and upon retirement a tax-free lump sum can be taken from the fund (up to certain limits).

However, these tax breaks aren't unlimited. Employees can only pay in a maximum of 15 per cent of their earnings up to an earnings cap, which for the 2001 to 2002 tax year is set at £95,400. In addition, the maximum pension that can be taken upon retirement is two-thirds of final salary.

In addition to these two main types of occupation scheme, employers may also offer group personal pensions, personal pensions owned by the individual employee but with the arrangements set up by the employer who usually also makes a contribution. Employers who do not offer any form of employer scheme may soon have to offer stakeholder pensions to employees instead. Only the smallest employers are likely to be exempt from this requirement. A few employers will make contributions to a personal pension plan if the employee does not wish to join a company scheme.

Most experts say that occupational schemes offer better value than personal pensions. This is because the employer pays for the management and setting up of the scheme, usually makes a contribution and offers additional benefits such as death-in-service benefits (life insurance of up to four times salary) and a widow's and dependants pension. The only drawback with occupational schemes is that they are not that flexible. It is common now for most employees to have between five to nine jobs during the course of their working lives and as such they may build up a number of small pension entitlements with several employers. To get the best deal from an occupational scheme employees need long periods of continuous service.

When members change jobs they have three choices: they may leave the money to continue growing in their old scheme (where it must grow by at least 5 per cent or inflation, whichever is the lower); transfer it to the new company scheme; or transfer it into a personal pension plan. The transfer value is calculated by the actuary of the old scheme. However, many employees fail to take their pension with them and often forget where they have built up a pension entitlement. The Pensions Tracing Service can help track down any missing pension entitlements of which there are an estimated £6 billion.

If you are given the option of joining a company pension scheme, you are generally advised to accept unless you plan to remain with the company for only a short period of time (less than two years) and already have your own pension arrangements. Even in this case, it may be worth asking if your new employer will contribute to your personal or stakeholder pension.

If you need advice as to whether or not to join a company scheme you can talk to the scheme's trustees who will often put you in touch with a scheme adviser such as an actuary. If you talk to a financial adviser remember that the adviser will only earn money (commission) by recommending a personal pension and will not earn a penny from recommending you join a company scheme unless you are paying the adviser on a fee basis.

Although joining an occupational scheme is generally best advice you still need to check:

- Are there any restrictions on who can join? You may find that you need a minimum period of service.

- What is the type of scheme? Many employers now offer only a money purchase scheme for new employees and not a final salary option.

- How much does the employer pay in?

- Does the employee make any contributions?

- What other benefits are offered? Death-in-service (life insurance), spouse's and dependant's pension, etc.

- What are your options if you leave employment?

- What benefits are offered if you decide to take early retirement?

Following the Mirror Group pension scandal, where hundreds of millions of pounds of present and future pensioners' money was found to be missing from the company's pension fund, the Pensions Act was introduced. It came into force in 1997 and was designed to remove the uncertainty surrounding the use of pension funds and improve consumer protection. The Occupational Pensions Regulatory Authority supervises the new system of rules.

OFFSHORE ACCOUNTS/ INVESTMENTS

The term 'offshore' conjures up images of tax-exiles, tycoons and shady individuals on exotic Caribbean Islands hiding their millions from the tax man. True, many off-shore centres cater for this trade mainly for tax purposes – particularly those island nations that service the million-aires and billionaires of the United States. But the UK has its very own offshore satellites that provide perfectly legal and safe havens for more ordinary taxpayers and investors.

The main offshore centres for UK residents are Jersey, Guernsey, the Isle of Man and Bermuda. All these are recognized by the British government and hold designated territory status, which means that their systems of financial regulation and investor protection are considered to be at least as good as that offered by our own regulatory system. These offshore centres offer investment funds such as unit trusts and investment trusts, bank and building society savings accounts and life insurance.

Why, though, should a UK resident want to put money offshore? There are two reasons: tax and investment free-dom. UK investors can open a savings account offshore and delay paying tax on any interest earned and therefore earn interest on their gross interest boosting their returns. Depending on when interest is credited to an offshore account, it is sometimes possible for UK residents to defer paying income tax for between eighteen months and two years. The only snag is that rates paid by some offshore accounts – and most of the major banks and building societies have offshore subsidiaries – are often poor compared to the best buys in the high street. As a result investors may be better off with an onshore taxable account. Although some savers may be tempted to fail to inform the Inland Revenue of their savings it is an offence and is known as tax evasion.

The other tax break is that income and capital gains tax can be deferred until the taxpayer is a lower rate or non-taxpayer, for example, after retiring. This is known as tax avoidance and is perfectly legal. With offshore unit trusts, accumulation funds pay no income. As such the tax liability only arises when investors repatriate the assets to the UK. However, at this stage the gains are taxed as income not capital. This means investors can enjoy growth that compounds gross before paying tax and can defer that tax bill for several years. People who intend to retire abroad can also use offshore accumulator funds to place long-term savings outside the UK tax net.

The other type of offshore unit trusts are distributor funds. These must pay out 85 per cent of their income as dividends, which are taxable. Any other profits are taxed as capital gains.

OMBUDSMEN

The eight financial ombudsmen schemes have been replaced by the new Financial Ombudsman Service which is bringing all complaints under one one-stop scheme.

The financial ombudsman's role is to act as an independent arbitrator when disputes between personal finance companies and their disgruntled customers reach an impasse. Most, but not all, areas of the financial services industry are covered by the ombudsman scheme (although the lines between the previous schemes were sometimes blurred which will be less of an issue once the single scheme is fully up and running). The public are not charged for the services, which are only available for cases that have not been through the courts. The ombudsman can award compensation and their rulings are normally binding on the company involved, although the individual may still be able to take his or her case to court.

Some ombudsman schemes will still fall outside the Financial Services scheme. The Pensions Ombudsman looks after occupational pensions and some queries concerning personal pensions, mainly to do with administration errors, but does not consider state schemes. Complainants must first contact the Occupational Pensions Advisory Service (OPAS).

The Inland Revenue Adjudicator considers most complaints concerning personal taxation, including overpayments and the behaviour of Revenue staff. However, this scheme does not look at any problems to do with tax law. The first port of call is your local tax office.

ONLINE BANKING

There are two types of online or Internet banking services: those that simply enable existing current account and savings account customers to access their accounts via the Internet and those that can only be operated via the Internet. The former are far more popular as existing banks and building societies can simply offer customers the same product, just a different means of accessing it in addition to the telephone, post and visiting a branch. Internet-only banking is still in its infancy with only a few services up and running. They do, however, offer higher savings rates and cheaper borrowing rates than conventional bank and savings accounts.

The main advantage of online banking is convenience; you can access your account whenever it suits you rather than just during banking hours. Nearly all of the main high-street banks now give their customers access to their branch-based current and savings accounts online. Customers can pay bills, check on standing orders and direct debits as well as look over current account statements and transfer money to other accounts – their own or other people's. With most banks it is also possible to apply for loans, insurance and credit cards, request cheque books and paying-in books.

To sign up, go to the bank's web site and follow a series of instructions on the screen, filling in information about yourself and your bank account. This includes passwords which no one but you and the bank's computer will know – so your money should always be safe, although some banks have suffered from major security scares. The web site or your bank should give you details of the technical specifications you will require.

Although online banking can save time, the sign-up procedure is not yet instant. The bank still has to send a form to be signed for confirmation and the whole process can take up to ten days.

The other sort of Internet banking is done completely online. Online savings accounts usually pay better rates than most high-street banks because online services do not have the expense of running branches. Money can be withdrawn through Link cash machines and with some accounts it can be withdrawn or paid in at the Post Office. When you set up this sort of bank account it takes a little longer. As you would be opening a whole new account rather than just accessing an existing one, you need to send forms of ID and proof of address – which in some cases will not be returned unless specifically requested. The self-employed should be warned that there is often a long list of requirements including providing annual accounts. Then, as with traditional banks, a form is sent to you to be signed. Again, this can take up to ten working days.

With some accounts you will be required to pay in your salary or a minimum amount each month so you may find it difficult to try out more than one account at the same time.

The other drawbacks are that virtual banking is impersonal. There are times when you need to speak to someone either about your money or about technical problems and you do still have to go to the branch or cash machine to withdraw cash.

Despite online accounts selling themselves for their convenience, not all of them are completely twenty-four hour – they may be closed for a few hours after midnight, for example. This would not affect most people but it could be inconvenient for some. With some banks, customer help lines are open much less than twenty-four hours. Many banks are offering free Internet access to attract customers, but check out the cost of the technical help line which can be as much as 50p a minute. And bear in mind that free Internet access means there are no monthly charges, not free time online. You will still be paying the cost of a local call for your surfing time. Anyone who uses the Internet frequently may be better advised to look for an account which does have a small monthly charge but gives free time online during the evenings and weekends.

ONLINE SHARE DEALING

One of the fastest growing areas of Internet financial services, online share dealing enables investors to buy and sell shares far more quickly and cheaply than before. The type of service offered by online stockbrokers is execution only which means that no advice is given (although some online brokers offer additional services such as company information and broker tips).

In peak periods of trading, some online brokers have run into difficulties keeping up with demand so investors need to check the reliability of the service. In most cases, investors need to open an account and send off a cheque before they start trading, so although the Internet can be fast it is not instant. If your bank offers online stockbroking facilities this can make it quicker. In order to set up the account you will need your National Insurance number and banking details so have them to hand. You will also need to have money in your trading account before you can start to cover the amount of your order. Money can be transferred by cheque or direct debit. An account with an e-broker is a good idea if you want to trade more than once. That way money can be deposited or taken out directly, secure passwords set up and trading is easier.

A few services offer real-time prices, which means that the share price displayed is the price you pay or will be paid. Other, cheaper services, may have a short time delay on this information. With online share dealing services you are usually required to have shares held in a nominee account and settlement is usually through Crest.

Minimum commission charges start around £10 per deal – always check both minimum and maximum commission. In some cases you will pay a set commission – normally around 1 per cent of the trade and in other cases there is a flat fee. A very few sites allow you to trade without paying commission at all but there may be a subscription fee instead.

Remember that if it costs £25 to buy and £25 to sell a £500 trade and there is a 5 per cent spread on the shares, even if the market moves 15 per cent you will still not make a profit. There is also stamp duty of 0.5 per cent to pay on all share purchases.

Also ask if there is a minimum deposit to open and trade on account and if there is a limit order service that enables you to deal at a specific – but not the current – price. Some online brokers offer 'price improver' services. They shop around market makers to get the best price on share deals and although the price may be only a fraction different, these savings soon add up. Online dealing can generally get a better price than if you deal through your bank or even a telephone service, particularly if the share price you get is the closing price (the price at the end of the trading day) rather than the real-time price.

Online share dealing has led to the advent of day trading, where private investors buy and sell shares on the same day – but it's not as lucrative as you might think. Surveys show that as many as 70 per cent of day traders lose money once costs are deducted.

When choosing an online broker, there are certain guidelines to follow. Firstly, try the site out to check if it is reliable (even at busy times when it can be hard to log on) and find out what the back-up is if the system fails – a phone help line, for example. This should be listed on the web site.

Watch out for hidden or extra fees – administration

charges, Crest account fees and annual management fees like the frequent trading membership fee. Not every site offers the same amount of information. Find out what research, charting and other services are offered and how much they cost.

OPEN-ENDED INVESTMENT COMPANIES (OEICs)

As financial acronyms go, OEICs – pronounced oiks – do not exactly sound enticing. Most OEICs are formerly unit trusts that have converted from being trusts into companies. As such investors buy shares in the OEIC instead of holding units as with a unit trust.

So why convert from a unit trust to an OEIC? There are benefits for fund management companies in that OEICs are cheaper to run. This is because most OEICs are umbrella funds – with one OEIC and a number of sub-funds, so the management costs are lower. In some cases, fund managers have even seen this as an opportunity to rationalize the number of funds they offer. However, this does not necessarily lead to cheaper charges, although one leading fund manager has predicted savings will be between £11 and £49 over five years assuming £3,000 – so the savings when they do occur are not large.

From the investor's point of view charges should be lower, pricing simpler to understand and switching between funds far easier. The key difference between OEICs and unit trusts is single pricing. Whereas units have a buying or offer price and a selling or bid price with a bid-offer spread of around 5 per cent between the two, OEICs have just one price. As a result, when a unit trust is converted into an OEIC some investors can expect a small increase in the value of their assets. However, the charges can still be the same – it is just that instead of being incorporated into the bid-offer spread they are identified and paid for separately. This makes the charging more transparent and easier to understand. Single pricing should also make it easier for investors to calculate the value of holdings.

OEICs accounted for nearly a quarter of all investment fund sales in 1999 and the number of providers offering OEICs has grown rapidly.

The fact that OEICs are companies makes them similar to investment trusts. But whereas investment trusts are closed-ended in that they have a set number of shares, OEICs are not. So while the value of investment trust shares can fall and even trade at a discount to the value of the trust's assets when there is little demand for the shares, with an OEIC shares are issued on demand and there is no limit. The price of each share is not dependent on supply and demand and is simply calculated by dividing the assets of the company by the number of shares in issue. The value of the shares will therefore always reflect the value of the assets, so there is no question of them trading at a discount.

(See also **Unit Trusts**.)

P

PAYMENT PROTECTION INSURANCE

Also known as creditor insurance, this protects – or pays for – your loan, mortgage or credit card payments in the event that you lose your job through redundancy, sickness or accident. When taken out in conjunction with a credit card, the minimum monthly payment (usually three or five per cent of the outstanding balance) will be paid until the cardholder can resume earning. When taken out with a mortgage, this type of insurance is known as mortgage payment protection insurance (MPPI). When taken out in conjunction with a personal loan the insurance covers the monthly payments until the policyholder resumes earning or, with some policies, in the event of sickness until the loan is repaid in full. Some payment protection policies also offer some life insurance cover and clear the debt in full in the event of death.

As with all insurance policies, payment protection has exclusions. Pre-existing medical conditions, those on short-term employment contracts and claims within the first month or so of the policy may all be excluded. The self-employed will usually find that they are not covered for unemployment unless they have been forced out of business involuntarily. All policies have an excess period (typically thirty days) during which you must be sick or unemployed before any benefit is paid. Most policies also have an initial exclusion period just after the policy has started, when unemployment claims won't be accepted.

Payment protection is usually sold alongside the credit or loan agreement and the person selling it to you will probably have no financial expertise. So it is vital that you know what you are buying and whether you need it.

The insurance may cover you against redundancy but not a pay cut or pregnancy. Also, as borrowers usually take out these policies when they borrow money, they do not tend to shop around and may not realize that even if the loan/mortgage/credit card rate is competitive the payment protection insurance may not be. Lenders should not make a loan conditional upon the borrower taking out insurance.

P/E RATIO

This is the profit per share compared to share price. It represents the number of years of current year earnings it will take for the current share price to be repaid. It is a way of comparing companies against each other.

Companies with higher PE ratios tend to be those with greater prospects. Companies that are more mature and those that carry a greater risk of contraction tend to have lower PEs.

While the PE is based on last year's profits the PE forecast looks ahead to future profits and is based on brokers' average forecasts. It is therefore a valuable tool for investors.

PERKS

Several companies offer perks to some, if not all, of their shareholders. One of the best known is P&O, the shipping company, whose generous channel ferry travel concessions are thought to account for the unusually large number of private shareholders on its register. Others offer books of money-off vouchers, or a one-off discount every year to shareholders. The more generous companies provide a set discount on all purchases or those made in a specific area of the business. A wide range of goods and services is available, from cars, clothing and credit cards to wines and washing machines.

No one should invest in a company solely for the perks. Investment performance is more important than 15 per cent off a hotel room. The one exception is if you qualify for an on-going discount and use the service or buy the goods on a regular basis.

Stockbrokers' nominee accounts can sometimes cause difficulties for people whose investment portfolios include shareholder perks as some companies will not supply the extra benefits to shareholders in nominee accounts.

PERMANENT HEALTH INSURANCE (PHI)

Despite the name, this type of cover insures your income rather than your health and pays out if you are unable to work because of accident or illness. PHI usually provides an income of up to three-quarters of your earnings minus any benefits or other income you receive each month. Benefit is payable until you recover or reach retirement age – hence the term 'permanent'.

Different policies demand different levels of disability before they will pay out; some will pay if you cannot do your own job, others only if you cannot do any job at all, which would seriously restrict who can claim. Insurers categorize policyholders by job, ranging from high to low risk, so you should inform your insurer if you change job. Lower risk includes accountants, office workers and hairdressers while high risk includes builders and HGV drivers. Policies for men are around half the price of those for women.

PHI is expensive but taking out a budget version could leave you without enough to live on. One option is to defer payment. By opting to wait thirteen weeks after you become unable to work, or even longer, the cost of the premiums is cut – by nearly half in some cases. This would work only for those with savings or if your employer would provide sick pay for a few months.

PHI is generally recommended for the self-employed

who if, for example, they suffered a fractured leg which meant they could not work would otherwise suffer financially as they do not have the luxury of an employer to give them full sick pay.

(See also **Critical Illness Cover**, **Mortgage Payment Protection Insurance**.)

PERMANENT INTEREST BEARING SHARES (PIBS)

Building societies issue PIBS as a way of raising money. Although they are called shares and are listed on the stock market, PIBS work just like bonds. They pay interest half-yearly, normally at a fixed rate, although one or two issues pay a variable rate of interest. The interest is paid out net, which means that non-taxpayers must claim tax back from the Inland Revenue while higher rate taxpayers must declare a further tax liability.

When buying PIBS you are in effect lending money to the building society, which pays you interest in return. PIBS are more risky (but only slightly) than a building society's savings account and thus pay higher interest rates to compensate. In the unlikely event of a building society going bust, holders of PIBS would have to wait in line behind all other creditors before getting a pay-out.

PIBS must be bought through a stockbroker and there are plenty of issues with minimum investments of £1,000 although others require at least £10,000 or even £50,000. Unlike most bonds, PIBS do not have a maturity date at which the investments are redeemed by building societies and the original capital paid back. This lack of a repayment date means investors who want to retrieve their capital have to sell the shares on the stock market through a stockbroker. There is no guarantee that the price you receive on selling will be higher than the price paid and investors could therefore end up losing money. However, as investors are attracted by the high level of fixed income, they may feel that this is a risk worth taking.

PERSONAL BANKING

Not to be confused with private banking, personal banking services offer a more personal service in an era when banking has become impersonal – but for a price. Customers are either selected for this service or qualify when they take out a gold card or a packaged account (one where the customer pays a fee even when in credit). The customer then deals with a personal account manager or management team directly.

Other benefits vary from bank to bank but include cheaper overdrafts and loans, a small free overdraft buffer zone, free travel insurance and account sweeping and a personal account manager to provide specialist advice and help manage your money.

However, with the average cost of these accounts currently around £100 a year, the benefits need to be weighed up. Your own bank will offer you only their products, not the best on the market. Also you could well get cheaper overdraft rates by moving to a different bank anyway.

PERSONAL EQUITY PLANS (PEPs)

Withdrawn from sale in April 1999, personal equity plans were highly popular tax-free investment schemes. They were replaced by the new individual savings account (ISA). However, just because investors can no longer invest new money in these schemes, does not mean that they are obsolete. Some £70 billion is still invested in PEPs and most of those who invested in them are advised to keep their money in this tax shelter for as long as they can afford. Once a PEP is cashed in the tax breaks are lost for ever.

Personal Equity Plans invest in stocks and shares or collective investments that invest in the stock market such as unit trusts, open-ended investment companies (OEICs) and investment trusts. There were two types of PEP allowance. In addition to a general PEP allowance of £6,000 investors could invest a further £3,000 a year in a single company PEP, a PEP that invested in the shares of just one company.

Those who took advantage of all the PEP allowances given since they were first launched in 1987 could have £100,000 sheltered in these tax-free schemes. The fact that

PEPs were available for so many years and proved so popular, means that far more is invested in these schemes than ISAs. Yet many PEP investors have failed to monitor the performance of their PEP portfolios even though their money could be languishing in a poorly performing fund.

Even though no new PEP investments are allowed, it is possible for investors to switch from fund to fund from the same PEP provider or even switch to a different PEP provider and not lose their tax breaks. The investments cannot be cashed in and reinvested – the money must be transferred directly from one PEP provider to another. Before switching, investors need to bear in mind the costs – there will be the bid-offer spread on sale of the existing PEP and a new set of charges to pay on the new PEP.

PERSONAL LOANS

There are two sorts of loan – secured and unsecured. Personal loans, whether they are called car loans or con-solidation loans, are usually unsecured which means the lender takes no security for lending you the money.

With a secured loan, if you do not keep up repay-ments, you could lose your home, the asset most lenders require as security for your debt. These loans give security to the lender, not to you, and as such have traditionally offered lower rates to borrowers. However, tough compe-tition in the loan market means that the best-buy personal loans now offer lower rates, so, unless you find it difficult to get credit, there is no need to offer your home as security.

As there is a greater risk to the borrower with secured loans, the rates tend to be lower than some unsecured loans – but often not lower than the very best rates on offer of an unsecured loan.

Loan rates are almost always cheaper than overdraft or long-term credit card rates so are a cheaper way of borrowing. It is generally expected that you will set up a direct debit to repay the loan. However, note that the loan rate quoted in advertising may be the best rate and could vary according to your circumstances and credit history. Also loan rates may vary depending on how much you want to borrow (with larger loans having a lower rate) and for how long. Check whether the rate quoted includes payment protection insurance or not. This will continue to pay the loan for you if you are unable to pay it because of illness or unemployment. But this insurance makes the loan much more expensive – around £250 a year – and you may not need it if you have good employee benefits and are not borrowing a significant amount.

Loans are generally taken out for a fixed period of time with monthly repayments paying the interest on the loan plus an element of the amount borrowed, so that at the end of the term of the loan the debt is repaid in full. Many companies charge a penalty if you want to pay the loan off early, typically one or two months' interest.

PERSONAL PENSIONS

Generally, those who are given the chance to join an occupational or company pension scheme (one run by their employer), should do so. Of the population, 10.5 million have a company pension, 10 million are in a personal pension but 14.5 million people over the age of sixteen have made no retirement provision at all. The number who have failed to provide for their financial futures would have been far higher but for the introduction of personal pensions in 1988. The downside of this is that millions of those who took out personal pensions were mis-sold these schemes by salesmen who were after the lucrative commission they could earn.

Now the government is planning to try once again to encourage more of the population to provide for their own retirement by introducing a new type of personal pension, the stakeholder pension. Although the costs of these schemes will be lower and they will represent better value for investors, there will still be a place for personal pensions particularly among those who wish to contribute more than the maximum allowed by a stakeholder scheme, £3,600 a year.

It is estimated that total contributions to private pension plans administered by insurance companies in 1999 was £46 billion and that this figure is set to double by 2010. In the same period, stakeholder pensions are likely to grow to take 45 per cent of the market.

While both types of pension scheme have the same tax

breaks with all contributions (up to the limits allowed) qualifying for tax relief at the policyholder's highest rate and the pension fund growing tax free, there is one fundamental difference. Personal pension contributions can only be made out of earned income. Stakeholder pension contributions can be made out of any income or capital – so they will appeal to the non-working and non-earning as well as employees and the self-employed.

Personal pensions can be bought by any working person under seventy-five who is not a member of an occupational scheme. Contributions cannot be made to a personal pension and an occupational pension at the same time unless the worker has additional earnings (other than from his main employment) from which to make personal pension contributions.

The investment limits for personal pensions are higher than for occupational schemes and rise according to age starting at 17.5 per cent of net relevant earnings for the under thirty-fives and rising to 40 per cent for the over sixties. Contributions can either be made on a regular basis with the policyholder committing to make monthly (although sometimes quarterly or annual) contributions for a set number of years until retirement. The other option is to make a single contribution – a one-off lump sum. The latter is a more flexible method as it does not tie you to a particular pension provider or commit you to regular payments.

Personal pensions have traditionally been very inflexible as investments and in the past policyholders were penalized for stopping contributions (for example, after they were made redundant) or wanting to vary their retirement date. But the advent of stakeholder pensions has forced pension providers (mainly the life insurance companies) to make their policies more flexible.

Personal pensions are money purchase schemes which means that the pension paid out at the end depends on how much has been paid in, how well this money has been invested, the charges taken out and, on maturity, the annuity rates available. On retirement, which can be from age fifty, a tax-free lump sum of 25 per cent of the accumulated fund can be taken by the investor. The rest must be used to buy an annuity (an income for life) before the retiree reaches seventy-five.

What made personal pensions so popular when they were first launched was the fact that employees could use an appropriate personal pension to opt-out or contract-out of the state earnings related pension scheme (SERPS). Rebates of SERPS contributions were then paid by the Department of Social Security into the personal pension boosting contributions – or in some cases, making up the only contributions to that personal pension. Initially, the incentives to contract-out were tempting for younger employees (older workers were advised to stick with SERPS), but the rebates have been gradually eroded and some of those who have only SERPS rebates paid into their personal pensions have found them poor value because of high charges. The proportion of the fund containing the DSS contributions is known as your protected rights.

(See also **Stakeholder Pensions** and **State Earnings Related Pensions**.)

PET INSURANCE

Insuring your pet against accident or illness is part of responsible pet ownership. Your car or dog is more likely to need medical treatment in a year than you and treatment is not cheap: vet bills account for about 30 per cent of the cost of owning a dog, and the most common animal injury, a broken leg, can cost up to £300 in veterinary bills for a cat and £1,000 for a dog. Yet even though half of all households own a pet (5.3 million households own a dog and 5 million a cat) only a fraction are covered by insurance. One in three pets in this country is ill each year but only one in seven is actually insured.

Policies for cats and dogs cover vet fees, death by accident or illness, advertising and reward if the pet is lost and third party liability if your pet injures someone. There is also cover if your pet runs away or is stolen. As with all insurance policies there are limitations and exclusions. There may be a limit, for example, of £1,500 in respect of each illness or accident, and exclusions from policies usually include vaccinations, pregnancy, spaying or castration. Owners also have to pay the excess on each claim and some companies will not pay out for more than twelve months if the animal has a chronic or recurring problem.

Not all insurance companies will take on older pets and those which do tend to increase the premium and excess. As your pet is more likely to need treatment as it ages, it's a good idea to get cover while it is still young which can be continued as it gets older. Premiums are relatively inexpensive at around £5 per month for a cat and £8 or £9 for a dog.

The government's new Pet Travel Scheme means dogs and cats can now be taken abroad. Some insurance companies include cover in the standard price, some charge extra.

Some other animals can be insured, such as horses and a few exotic animals but it is not possible to insure koi carp or other aquatic animals.

PHONE AND POSTAL ACCOUNTS

Savings accounts conducted by post or phone rather than the customer dealing directly with a branch of the bank or building society often pay double the rate of interest of branch-based accounts. They are also a convenient way of saving for anyone who does not live near a branch. However, in return customers do not have access to the branch.

Accounts are opened by sending an application form, cheque and proof of address and ID (this will be needed if you do not have an existing account with that financial institution) by post and in return the saver receives a certificate of investment stating the amount paid in. Paying in and withdrawal slips are then sent to the customer. Every time money is put in or taken out, an acknowledgement is sent.

For those banking by phone, passwords and pass numbers are set up for security. In addition, some phone and postal accounts offer savers a cash card so that they can get easy access to cash via ATMs. Alternatively, those with phone accounts can call up and ask for money to be transferred into any current account. The interest rates may be even better if you limit the number of withdrawals you make a year.

There are also some current accounts which can be run over the phone. Many banks now offer customers the option of contacting them by phone rather than go into branches to check on balances, order cheque or paying in books or transfer money. Again, passwords/numbers are set up for security. Alternatively, some current accounts are telephone only and operate twenty-four-hour services so you can bank when it suits you. However, if you do need to pay in a cheque, you can do it at a branch.

PLUVIUS INSURANCE

This is insurance against weather spoiling an event. The main reasons for taking it out are to protect against bad weather ruining a wedding reception in a marquee, a summer fête or a sporting event. Wedding insurance policies will cover every aspect except the weather which is where pluvius policies can provide cover. In the event of a claim, the insurance covers the cost of hiring the marquee, catering, flowers, chair and table hire as well as portaloos and other essentials if the weather is a wash-out. The cover

starts from when the marquee is erected until the beginning of the reception – unless the ground is too water-
logged or high winds make it impossible to put up at all.

Prices vary according to the time of year and the location, as some parts of the country are wetter than others.
The policy must be bought at least fourteen days before a
wedding in May to September and up to six weeks in
advance for the rest of the year.

It is also possible to insure other outdoor events from
village fêtes and cricket matches to hot air balloon and
charity events. These are mostly costed by the hour
and the policy pays out for rain (depending on how much
falls), wind or even bad light. This part of pluvius insurance is not cheap though and would only be worthwhile if
a charity event was likely to raise a considerable amount
of money, for example. Only one company specializes in
this form of insurance – Zurich.

POLARIZATION

This technical term is rarely referred to outside of the
financial regulators and the financial trade press. Polarization was and still is one of the main areas of consumer
protection. It was introduced to make a clear distinction
between advisers and financial firms who work independently and those who are owned by or tied to just one
financial institution.

As a result investors know whether they are dealing

with an impartial adviser or one that sells only the products/investments of one company. By law, anyone conducting or advising on investment business must inform clients of their status.

However, the polarization rules could be diluted following a review by the chief city watchdog the Financial Services Authority (FSA). The Director General of Fair Trading has ruled that the polarization rules significantly restrict or distort competition and has recommended that the polarization rules should remain in place but only for investment products linked to life assurance. In respect to advice on collective investment schemes such as unit trusts he asked that the rule be removed.

At the time of writing the situation is still under review. However, it is likely that stakeholder pensions and CAT-marked ISAs will fall outside the polarization rules. In the meantime, investors are advised to check the status of anyone from whom they receive financial advice.

(See also **Independent Financial Advice**.)

POLICYHOLDERS PROTECTION ACT

This 1975 Act of Parliament protects investors and policy-holders of life insurance companies. In the unlikely event that an insurance company might fail, an individual's investment is protected and compensation for 90 per cent of any outstanding claims will be paid without limit.

POUND COST AVERAGING

This is a useful side effect of regular saving that makes a virtue out of falling markets. Regular saving involves drip feeding often small amounts of money into the stock market on a monthly basis.

Most regular savers invest through the monthly saving scheme offered by unit trusts, open-ended investment companies and investments trusts. They, therefore, do not have to worry about timing their investments for when shares are good value or, at least, not about to fall.

Investors with large lump sums to invest can put all their money into the stock market on one day but if the market falls the next day, week or month they will have to wait for prices to recover just to break even (and that does not take into account charges). So the investor could lose, say, 10 per cent of their original investment in the first year. However, investors who drip feed actually benefit from stock market falls. Instead of buying shares on just one day, they will be buying on twelve different days during the year. As prices fall during the course of the year, investors can buy more shares or units for their money – so when prices rise they have more shares or units to their name and stand to benefit more. When prices rise, they will be buying fewer shares or units but benefiting from stock-market recovery.

Of course, if the market rises throughout the year, those who invested a lump sum at the start would be better off. So pound-cost-averaging only works when markets are volatile as regular savings then smooth out the stock-markets' peaks and troughs.

PREFERENCE SHARES

These are similar to gilts except that they are supported and guaranteed by large companies and not by the government. Preference shares will offer higher yields than gilts due to the additional risk of being backed by a private company rather than the government and are bought by investors for their income.

(See also **Zeros** or **Zero Dividend Preference Shares**.)

PREMIUM BONDS

These bonds are issued by National Savings and, despite the Lottery, they continue to grow in popularity. There are now more than 23 million bond holders. One advantage they have over Lottery tickets is that they can be cashed in if you don't win – so you get your stake back.

The minimum bond holding is now £100 and the maximum £20,000. By the law of averages, you can expect to win 10 prizes of the minimum £50 and three of £100 every year if you hold £20,000 worth of bonds, but there are no guarantees. If you did win this amount it would represent a return of 4 per cent on your money – and it is tax free which makes it worth nearly five per cent for lower-band tax payers.

If you do win a prize National Savings will write to you for up to eighteen months, but if you have still not replied by that date they give up; so it is important to notify them of any change of address. The bonds themselves cannot be inherited but their value can be – they have to be cashed in. The bond will continue to be entered in the draws up to a year after the death of the bond holder and the winnings go to their estate. Consequently, if you do inherit any, it could be worth leaving them in the draw for a year before cashing them in.

(See also **National Savings**.)

PREMIUMS

These are the monthly payments you make on your insurance policies. However, premium has other meanings in the world of finance. Some investments, such as investment trust shares, can be traded at a premium which means that they are worth more than the underlying worth, or net asset value, of the trust.

(See also **Investment Trusts**.)

PRIVATE BANKING

This frock coat and top hat service has its roots in the days of Jane Austen and Napoleon Bonaparte. During the first two hundred years of its existence it relied on the landed gentry and other members of the privileged classes to provide business. But, in recent years, the industry has begun to widen its net and include pop stars, Internet millionaires, lottery winners and wealthy retirees.

The principal function of a private bank is to assume total responsibility for the general financial affairs of their customers, so they offer more than just basic banking facilities. Investment management is also a key part of the service with a full one-stop fund management advisory service which includes stockbroking, tax, legal and trust planning services.

Although the most well-known private banks – Coutts & Co., Child & Co. and C. Hoare and Co. – are still in existence and still have clients whose families have been customers for generations, they have been joined by newer names. The major banks such as Barclays have their own private-banking divisions.

In general, customers need to have a minimum level of income of £100,000 or assets in excess of £250,000, although some banks consider each individual case on its merits and the high-street banks set lower levels of income and capital for their customers. Private banking is different from personal banking, which merely offers a more personal service.

Private banks can offer an advisory management service or a discretionary one depending on the client's needs. A fee of a percentage of the value of the portfolio, usually around 1 per cent, is charged.

PRIVATE MEDICAL/HEALTH INSURANCE

Private medical insurance offers people an alternative to the National Health Service. PMI policies are available from a growing number of insurers including the provident associations BUPA and Western Provident as well as insurance companies. Some 6.5 million of the population – around 10 per cent – are covered by private medical insurance although two thirds of them are provided with it as a benefit-in-kind by their employers.

The average cost of private medical insurance premiums is £750 a year, rising to over £1,000 as policyholders get older. Those who make a number of claims usually find that their next year's premium rises sharply.

One of the cheaper options is the budget plan, which an increasing number of people are choosing as average premiums are about a third of fully comprehensive PMI. This complements rather than replaces the NHS; the patient uses the NHS unless the wait is longer than six or twelve weeks, depending on the treatment and the policy. Otherwise, treatment is private. If you do opt for the NHS treatment, the policy pays a cash sum anyway. Some of these plans also cover the cost of outpatient treatment up to a certain limit but generally only if it follows directly on from treatment as an inpatient.

Standard private medical insurance offers a range of cover at a range of prices; you can insure individuals or whole families. The benefits include the cost of hospital treatment as well as physiotherapists, dentists and opticians as well as other specialists, sometimes including complementary therapies like acupuncture or osteopathy. Many policies also cover day-case admission where an overnight stay is not necessary, or the cost of a parent staying in the hospital with a child.

Be aware of the limitations of policies though.

- Pregnancy or fertility treatments are excluded.

- There may also be limits on the amount you can claim for each element per person per year. For example, you may only be allowed to claim for £200 specialist consultation fees in one year.

- There may be an excess which means you will only be able to claim back a proportion of the claim or may have to pay the first £50 or so of the claim.

- Cover for treatment provided in the first three months of the policy may well be excluded.

- Pre-existing medical conditions treated up to three years before the policy starts will also often be excluded.

- Any claims related to any long-term incurable conditions like cancer or Alzheimer's are excluded. HIV or AIDS will not be covered.

- Treatment for mental illness is excluded from most policies.

- Treatment outside of the UK will be excluded.

- Some policies limit the number of nights a year you can spend in hospital before you have to start paying yourself.

The biggest factor in determining the level of premiums is your age: the older you are, the more likely you are to need treatment and so the premiums will be higher. Your sex, medical history and the medical history of your family as well as whether or not you smoke will also affect the cost. A medical examination will often be required before you take out insurance.

PRIVATIZATION

Selling off the family silver, as the late Harold Macmillan once described privatization, turned Britain into a nation of fortune-hunting stock-market speculators in the 1980s and 1990s. Many of Britain's twelve million shareholders still own shares that were issued following the privatization of utility companies such as British Telecom.

However, the push to privatize as many state-owned

companies as possible under the Conservative government of Margaret Thatcher has now been replaced with a vigour for another way to raise private finance for public services and at the same time boost efficiency, known as the private finance initiative. PFI involves a public/private partnership with private companies paying for facilities such as new hospitals and then being paid a regular income to lease them back to the public sector.

Q

QUOTED COMPANY

This is the colloquial term most people use to describe companies that have sold shares in their businesses to the public by obtaining a listing on a stock market. In Britain most companies that go public join the Official List run by the London Stock Exchange. It is possible to become a quoted company and obtain a listing on other exchanges such as the Alternative Investment Market (AIM). So why do companies go public and how do they do it?

There are more than 2,000 quoted or listed companies on the London Stock Exchange. There are four main reasons why a company in private ownership might want to go public or float. These are as follows:

1. access to capital

2. growth

3. prestige

4. increased visibility or publicity

With these advantages come three main obligations for a public company, which are:

1. accountability

2. responsibility

3. regulation

Public companies and their directors have to comply with an enormous amount of regulation. The rules exist primarily to ensure that a fair, equitable and efficient market is maintained at all times in the market for shares for all participants, be they investors or the companies themselves.

The Stock Exchange enforces the rules that relate to a company obtaining a quote on the Official List. The listing rules are commonly known as the Yellow Book. Then there is the Companies Act, which lays down the laws on disclosure of interests in shares. This enables public companies and their shareholders to identify significant shareholdings. The Act also sets out the rules for company investigations. Under Section 212 a public company is allowed to find out who its shareholders are at any point in time. Public companies are obliged to keep a register of shareholders' names. Shareholdings may also be held through a nominee company. A Section 212 investigation forces a nominee to reveal who the real shareholder is.

The initial listing or flotation can be used to issue more shares in a company. The investors who buy the shares provide extra capital for a company, which it can use to fund future growth. Later on, the Stock Exchange provides various means for companies to raise extra cash. Going public allows a company to use the capital raised from issuing new shares to pay off bank loans, a process known as swapping debt for equity, while borrowing money from the bank in future might be easier for a public company than a private one.

Access to capital is perhaps the main reason why a company uses a Stock Exchange to go public. The Stock Exchange fulfils a dual function. Raising capital for companies and then providing a means for investors to sell their shareholdings for cash if they wish to get out.

To win a place on the official list company directors must prepare a prospectus. This provides investors with a complete picture of the company, including its trading history, financial record, management and business prospects. There are three methods for companies to go public and become a quoted company. The most appropriate method depends on cost and whether or not new money is to be raised.

The three methods are:

1. Offer for sale. This allows a company to invite subscriptions from both institutional and private investors. The shares available may be new ones being sold for cash or existing ones held by current shareholders. The offer for sale is organized by a company's sponsor, normally a firm of stockbrokers. It will also be underwritten. This means that for a fee a sponsor will buy any shares left over after the offer for sale closes in order to make sure that a company's aims are achieved. Application forms and prospectuses should be advertised in the national

press. The offer normally takes place at a fixed price per share.

2. Placing. This is a low-cost, low-key affair, with no widespread advertising and less publicity, and is the most common method for going public for small companies. A placing allows a company's sponsor or stockbroker to offer new or existing shares selectively to its own client base, be they institutions or private clients.

3. Introduction. Shares can be introduced to the Official List by companies that already have a widely held share capital with 25 per cent already in the public's hands. In an introduction no money is raised and no new shares are issued. As a result there are no underwriting costs and only small advertising requirements. An introduction is the least expensive way of flotation.

Already quoted companies can issue new shares to existing shareholders to raise extra cash through a **Rights Issue** (see entry). Shareholders will expect quoted companies to pay a dividend, normally paid in two amounts: an interim dividend, and a final dividend six months later. Dividends are paid on ordinary shares, the main form of capital issued by quoted companies. To raise capital companies can also issue bonds, which pay investors a fixed amount of interest each year. Some arrange for options and warrants to be issued, linked to their ordinary shares. Other types of capital issues include convertibles, preference shares and convertible preference shares.

R

REDEMPTION PENALTIES

When you take out a loan or mortgage you usually borrow the money for a fixed term – the period over which you agree to pay it back. If you want to pay it back early, some companies will penalize you and charge you extra to cover the interest they will lose. These are known as redemption penalties.

With personal loans the most common penalty is two months' interest. For example, you borrow £5,000 for three years at a rate of 14.5 per cent with monthly repayments of £174.40. Over three years this would cost you £1,278 in interest. If you decided to pay off the loan after two years to save yourself interest, you could be charged a penalty of two months or £348.80. You would still have saved yourself ten months' interest but the lender is recouping some of their losses.

With mortgages, you may be tied in for a certain amount of time and if you want to switch mortgages before that, you will have to pay a penalty. In most cases redemption penalties are only charged during a low-rate period. So if you take out a fixed-, discount- or capped-rate mortgage with this special rate charged in the first five years, the penalty will apply if you cash in all or part of the mortgage during those first five years. In some cases there may be extended redemption penalties – this means that you will still be charged a penalty even after the low rate ends. So you could be locked in for a further six months or a year after the cheap rate has ended. In some cases paying the redemption penalty may be worthwhile if you can save more than the penalty by switching to a far cheaper rate. Mortgages that meet the CAT standards are not allowed to charge extended redemption penalties and there are limits on the size of the penalty that can be charged.

REMORTGAGE

This is when a homebuyer switches mortgages without moving home. The costs of remortgaging can be as high as £750 although many lenders do reimburse or pay for some or all of these costs. The fees involved can include administration fees, legal and survey fees as well as arrangement fees.

REPAYMENT MORTGAGES

With a repayment mortgage the borrower pays the interest on the outstanding debt and a proportion of the capital (the original amount borrowed) each month so that at the end of the mortgage term the debt is cleared in full. So unlike interest-only mortgages, they guarantee to repay the loan.

Although most mortgages are arranged over twenty-five years, they don't have to be and borrowers do not have to revert back to a twenty-five-year mortgage every time they remortgage or move house.

By opting for a shorter-term mortgage borrowers increase the amount of capital they repay in the early years. Although it may appear that little capital is repaid in the first few years of the loan, assuming an interest rate of 7 per cent and an £80,000 loan on a twenty-year term, the borrower would repay around £11,000 of capital after five years and £17,000 after seven.

The capital repaid creates equity in the property for the next house move, which is one advantage of a repayment mortgage. Also the current low-inflation, low-interest rate environment means it makes sense to repay a mortgage debt as quickly as possible as inflation does not erode the value of the debt as fast as it used to do. In the days of rampant inflation a mortgage debt would halve in real terms – after the effects of inflation – every decade. So it paid to have a mortgage for a long period as half the battle of repaying it was done for the borrower in terms of inflation.

The only drawback of a repayment loan is that it will appear to be more expensive initially because borrowers are paying the interest and an element of the debt. However, borrowers taking out interest-only loans should bear in mind that they will usually have to pay into a savings scheme to pay off the mortgage debt at the end of the term and this will push up the monthly costs.

REPOSSESSION

Repossession proceedings are started by mortgage lenders when borrowers fall into arrears. Generally borrowers need to be at least six months behind on payments before proceedings by the lender to take possession of the property are instigated as most lenders try to help homebuyers who are having difficulties making payments. Borrowers can often have their payments suspended, negotiate reduced payments for a short period or sell their home to repay their mortgage before their arrears mount up and they find themselves in negative equity. Once a borrower has fallen into arrears and their home has been repossessed by the lender, they will find it very difficult to get credit or another mortgage in future.

Once the lender takes possession of the property, it is then sold to repay the mortgage, any outstanding debts and accrued interest, as well as the costs of repossession and sale. As a result, borrowers are usually advised to sell themselves before repossession proceedings start as they will generally get a better price and the costs will be lower.

If the lender is left with a loss after the property has been sold, it can then pursue the borrower for this short-fall. In the past mortgage lenders have been able to begin procedures to recover debts from former mortgage borrowers up to twelve years after a property has been repossessed. However, in 2000 mortgage lenders agreed that in future they will not institute recovery actions more than six years after the sale of a property in possession.

RETAIL PRICE INDEX (RPI)

The Retail Price Index is a measure used to track the buying power of money and is often referred to (not altogether accurately) as inflation, or the cost of living index.

The original cost of living index which began in 1914 was much more limited than the modern version. It covered basic necessities like bread, potatoes, clothing, lamp oil and candles but not, for instance, fresh fruit, biscuits and cakes or electricity.

Now there are many different types of inflation calculation and governments tend to use the one which suits them best when calculating benefits and interest rates.

The RPI All Items Index includes essentials like rent, mortgage, fuel and food as well as clothing, electrical appliances and motoring expenditure. DIY, Council Tax, leisure goods, foreign holidays and toys are added in as well. Then there is the RPIX which is the RPI excluding mortgage payments.

The index is intended to reflect the cost of practically everything including travel and entertainment. It no longer includes mangles and rabbits for eating, but does include condoms and childminder fees. Some products are excluded though because, according to the Central Statistical Office, they are too difficult to assess. These include life assurance, betting, cash gifts, income tax and National Insurance contributions.

The RPI is compiled from about 130,000 separate quotations collected each month, mainly by people going to shops all over the country. The figures are then divided into five broad groups: food and catering, alcohol and tobacco, housing and household expenditure, travel and leisure. The index is weighted to give more importance to some elements than others. A percentage rise in the price of bread has four times the effect on the index as a similar increase in the price of butter, for instance.

The whole operation is overseen by an independent advisory committee whose members include consumers, retailers, employers and employees. There are also other terms used to describe inflation: headline inflation includes changes in mortgage payments and underlying inflation does not.

Inflation at the end of the nineties hit the lowest it has been since 1963. In the mid seventies, it soared to nearly 27 per cent. The advantage of high inflation is that it boosts the value of homes and stimulates the housing market, but prices in the shops keep going up. Low inflation means shop prices stay the same while wages, benefits and pensions hardly go up at all.

In times of high inflation, you could rely on it to erode the value of your mortgage as anyone who bought a home in the 1970s will remember. But low inflation and low wage rises could keep the cost of repaying a loan a bigger burden for a longer time. Annuity rates also fall in times of low inflation which means that pensioners get less returns on a lifetime of pension saving for retirement.

(See also **Inflation**.)

RIGHTS ISSUE

An invitation to existing shareholders to acquire additional shares in a fixed proportion to their holding is known as a rights issue. It is how a quoted company raises new capital by issuing new shares after its initial flotation on a stock market such as the London Stock Exchange. Rights issues must be made to present shareholders in proportion to their existing shareholdings – this rule is known as pre-emptive rights.

The capital raised from a rights issue is used for a variety of purposes, such as funding an acquisition, paying for investment or paying off debts. To persuade shareholders to subscribe to a rights issue the new shares will be offered at a discount to the market price. A company might have five million 20p shares in issue at a market price of 100p. It decides to make a rights issue of one new share for every four held at 75p a share. An investor who owns four shares has an investment worth £4 (4 x 100p). If that investor takes up his or her rights, he or she will end up with four shares worth £4 and one share worth 75p, making a total of five shares costing £4.75 or 95p a share, known as the ex-rights price. As you can see from this example, by diluting the share capital (issuing more shares) the price of each share will generally fall initially.

Alternatively, investors can split their rights. This allows investors without enough cash to subscribe for their full rights to buy some of their rights.

ROLLING SETTLEMENT

This is the system for paying for shares you have bought and receiving the proceeds from shares you have sold. The stock market used to have settlement dates when shares had to be paid for, which could be anything from a few days to three weeks after purchase or sale. However, this was replaced by rolling settlement, which means that payments are made at a set time after purchase of shares *not* on a set date. Settlement is currently three working days after purchase or, if you are selling, the shares have to be supplied within three working days. The fact that settlement now takes place so quickly (until recently it was five working days), has led to increasing numbers of individual shareholders holding their shares electronically through Crest or having them held in nominee accounts so that they do not have to supply or wait for paper share certificates – something that can easily take more than three working days.

S

SAVE AS YOU EARN

Save-as-you-earn or SAYE schemes are employee share schemes that enable staff to save a regular amount each month towards buying shares in their employer's company at a future date. These schemes give employees the option to buy the shares rather than committing them to purchasing them. However, employees are usually better off buying the shares as when the option is granted it is usually at a discount of up to 20 per cent of the current market price. Once they have saved their fixed amount (between £5 and £250 a month) for three, five or seven years, the shares have usually appreciated in value.

(See also **Employee Share Ownership**.)

SCHOOL FEES PLANNING

Recent figures from the Independent Schools Information Service show that the cost of a private school education is currently around £6,000 a year for day students and £12,000 a year for boarding students. The total cost of educating a child privately including primary and secondary schooling as well as university could amount to as much as £200,000.

There are several ways to finance these fees. One option is to pay out of existing savings or income, but this is probably a possibility only for the lucky few. Some families may have grandparents willing to pay a lump sum or make regular payments to meet school fees. Or plan ahead with some sort of school fees planning.

Start as early as possible – you will have longer to set money aside and it will have longer to grow. Also choose the most flexible and tax efficient investments available. You do not have to opt for a cleverly packaged schools fees plan from an insurer. These can be expensive and difficult to get your money out of if you have a change of heart about private schooling, or realize that due to a change in circumstances you can no longer afford it.

For those with five or less years to plan ahead, a savings scheme will often be the best option as there is less risk than with a stock-market investment. For those with longer to plan, an investment scheme linked to the stock market such as a unit trust, investment trust or open-ended investment company will often be recommended. Both savings and investments can grow tax free if they are bought via a tax-exempt individual savings account, i.e. an **ISA** (see entry).

A common plan sold by insurers is a package of endowment policies with maturity payouts designed to coincide with annual school bills. Regular premiums to pay for the policies are funded out of parents' income. Returns are only average but involve little risk. Maturity payments when they arrive can be spent on other things if private schooling is no longer a priority, but early encashment will result in poor surrender values.

If parents have already selected the school of their choice, finding out if that school offers any school fees planning schemes is worthwhile. With a composition scheme, parents pay a lump sum before their children start school. This is invested by the school and is then used to pay bills as they arise. If the lump sum is paid over early and invested well, parents can make big savings over the years. Parents should check what rate of return a school needs to earn to pay fees and where the money is invested. Parents may also be penalized if a child does not attend the school chosen or leaves early.

SHARES

These are issued by companies who want to raise capital from investors to expand or improve their business. In return, investors expect to share in a company's profits. They do this by receiving regular dividends from the company, usually twice a year in the form of an interim and a final dividend. Any company can issue shares, be it a private company or a public company with shares listed on a stock market. Mostly people read or hear about shares issued by public companies, as they are the most widely available and the most widely held.

The most common type of share owned by private

investors is the ordinary share. Holders of these are entitled to a dividend and also to a vote at company meetings. Although the directors of the company (who sit on the board) run that company, the shareholders own it. Ordinary shares can carry the most risk, but also the biggest potential return. Some companies have more complicated share structures than simply issuing ordinary shares. They issue different types of shares and bestow different voting rights on different classes of shareholders.

However, in most cases ordinary shares make up most of the company's equity capital. This is capital that is entitled to a variable and hopefully growing dividend. Participating preference shares are also classed as equity capital. Most preference shares have a fixed dividend that must be paid before other shareholders, while participating preference shares can receive a dividend above the fixed pay-out.

Share prices are closely monitored by investors and stock-market commentators. A share price is determined by the supply and demand for it in the market. If demand is strong, a price will rise. Demand, though, is based on investors' perception of a company's fortunes, and if the future looks bad investors will sell and the supply of the shares on the stock market will increase, thus forcing the price down.

Some share prices languish simply because the companies that issued them are not well understood and they are not noticed by investors even though their businesses may be doing well and their prospects good. These shares are said to be undervalued. A perceptive investor can buy these undervalued shares and make a killing once the rest of the market catches up.

The share capital of investment trusts – particularly split-capital investment trusts – may be different with investors buying income, capital and preference shares as well as warrants.

Shares in companies quoted on the alternative investment market, AIM, are often known as penny shares.

SHARE CLUBS

Also known as investment clubs, these clubs are groups of friends or work colleagues who pool their resources to invest in the stock market. By forming a club they increase their buying power and spread the risks of investing as by pooling cash they can buy a larger number of shares than they could afford as individuals. In addition, they benefit from the knowledge of all the members of the club.

The number of share clubs in the UK has grown rapidly in recent years with over 8,000 now in existence. Most club members have never invested before. Anyone over eighteen can set up a club with most having between two and twenty members.

Before you start, it is essential to draw up a constitution, which includes details of what happens should anyone want to leave and the amount that everyone has to invest each month. The average is about £25 to £30. Also set a minimum deal size of at least £750 otherwise dealing charges and stamp duty could mean your profits will be too small. Add in a 'no blame' clause as well for the inevitable mistakes.

As long as one member of the club knows the basics, you can learn as you go. There are plenty of magazines and web sites with information to help. Choosing a chairman or chairwoman, a treasurer and secretary is important too. Then decide whether you are going to use a broker or invest directly yourselves online.

Joining ProShare, the organization that promotes share ownership, means that you can get useful information on how to run the club as well as about the stock market. This is the only organization in the UK so far which provides an independent and exclusive service dedicated to helping individuals set up and run investment clubs. They provide a manual, magazine and general advice on every aspect of running a share club.

SHARE EXCHANGE SCHEMES

Fund management companies running investment trusts and unit trusts will often offer to buy small parcels of shares cheaply and reinvest the proceeds in one of their own funds. This saves investors from having to sell the shares themselves. Sometimes the fund managers will waive the charges altogether. However, investors should not be seduced by low or no charges and should remember that they are swapping one investment for another and should satisfy themselves that it is an investment worth buying.

SHARE OPTIONS

Share options are associated with fat-cat bosses. However, there are schemes that are targeted specifically at workers rather than high-earning executives. These include the savings-related share-option schemes known as Save-as-you-earn schemes, or SAYE, which give employees the option or right to buy shares in their company at a future date, and the new all-employee share plan introduced in 1999. However, these are generally referred to as employee share schemes rather than share options.

Company share-option plans are usually restricted to a small number of employees and are often known as executive or discretionary share-option schemes. They give the option to buy shares at a fixed price on a set date. The option price (the price you will pay for the shares) must not be less than the market value of the shares at the time you are given them. As the name implies, you only have an option to buy the shares – if you don't want to buy them you don't have to. The total value of shares which can be held as options cannot exceed £30,000.

(See also **Employee Share Ownership**, **Save As You Earn**.)

SPLIT CAPITAL TRUSTS

These are a type of investment trust, and one that issues different types of shares to meet the differing needs of investors.

(See also **Investment Trusts**.)

SPORTS INSURANCE

Four million people a year visit their GP with a sports injury and another 14 million injuries are treated at home. Anyone who plays football in the park at the weekend should be aware that more people are injured in amateur football than in professional. And an injury can lead to financial loss – particularly for those who are self-employed and may be unable to earn a living after suffering an injury.

Most standard accident, sickness and unemployment policies do not cover sports injuries, and, of the ones that do, they have greatly varying levels of cover, so consider the type of injuries you are likely to suffer from your particular sport. Unless you are taking part in a very hazardous sport, the cost of the premium is calculated according to your occupation.

If you belong to a club it could work out cheaper for the club to take out a policy for all of the team members – including subs and occasional players. On average, the cost of insuring a cricket team is about ten times cheaper than insuring a football team. Policies will pay out a weekly amount to anyone who is injured and unable to work. This will not be as much as their salary but should cover extra expenses.

If you should injure someone else who then sues you, standard third-party insurance should cover this and is included in your household insurance package. However, do not rely on your household insurance to cover the full value of your equipment when it is taken outside the house, especially if it is very expensive. Only household policies that cover all risks insure possessions taken out of the home and then there are limits on the value of each item. There are also limitations with car insurance policies. Some policies pay out only up to £100 for anything stolen from the car even if it is locked in the boot.

Lost bicycles are covered under household policies, but you will have to tell your insurer that you want yours covered and may be charged an extra premium.

SPREAD BETTING

This is a very risky way to speculate on share price movements. Unlike traditional betting which has fixed-odds that give you a multiple of your stake if you win, and therefore all that is at stake is your bet if you lose, spread betting gives you bigger winnings the more right you are – and greater losses the more wrong your judgement. The risks are even greater as when you bet on a share you only need to put down a deposit which is a percentage of the maximum you could lose. The spread betting company then makes a quote for the price of a share on a given date in the future. You decide whether it will be higher or lower. The higher it goes the more you win and vice versa.

STAKEHOLDER PENSIONS

The pensions mis-selling scandal of the late 1980s and early 1990s (when millions of investors were misled into taking out a personal pension plan when they may have been better off remaining in a company pension scheme) led to deep mistrust of the pensions industry. This, combined with apathy and a belief that pensions were unaffordable, has left a large proportion of the population – some 10 million workers –with no private pension provision at all.

To address this the New Labour government decided to introduce a new type of personal pension, the stakeholder pension. This officially goes on sale in April 2001, although pre-stakeholder or stakeholder friendly pensions were available for a year prior to the official launch.

Much thought has been given to how stakeholder pensions will be sold to avoid another scandal. However, as the charges for stakeholders are so low – a maximum of 1 per cent – investors may have to pay an additional fee if they want advice.

The chief city regulator of the Financial Services Authority has outlined proposed rules for the selling of stakeholders. At the time of writing it was proposed that decision trees would be adopted to help consumers make the right choice on whether to join a stakeholder scheme. It is hoped that this, combined with consumer information and training and competence standards for the staff who will be giving out information on stakeholder pensions, will reduce mis-selling.

Stakeholders are primarily aimed at those on low incomes, although they will also appeal to non-working mothers, employees who do not have the option of joining an employer's scheme and the self-employed.

What are the main features of the stakeholder scheme?

- They have a simple and transparent charging structure, unlike many existing personal pensions.

- Charges are limited to 1 per cent per annum.

- The minimum contribution can be as low as £10.

- Contributions can be stopped, re-started and varied without penalty.

- Tax relief is given at the top rate of tax (as with all pensions).

- Unlike other pension schemes, contributions can be made out of unearned income, so non-working mothers, for example, can still have a pension plan. With other pension schemes contributions can only be made from earnings from employment or self-employment.

- The maximum contribution in any one year is limited to £3,400.

- On retirement up to 25 per cent of the pension fund built up can be taken as a tax-free lump sum.

STAMP DUTY

This is a tax levied on the transfer of shares and property and is paid by the purchaser. On share sales the rate of tax is 0.5 per cent, but it is always calculated in multiples of 50p per £100 or part thereof. So if someone buys £2,300 of shares the duty would be 0.5 times £2,300 which equals £11.50. Anything between £2,301 and £2,400 would be charged at 0.5 times £2,400 which equals £12.

The stamp duty on shares is nothing compared to that paid on property. In successive budgets, the rate of stamp duty has been increased hitting those who own more expensive homes in the south-east hardest. As the UK rate of stamp duty on property is still below that of the European average there are fears that the level will increase further.

Anyone purchasing a property worth less than £60,000 escapes paying stamp duty. Above this level the rate of tax starts at 1 per cent. It then increases in bands depending on the value of the property. In the March 2000 budget there were further increases in the rate of duty with it charged at 3 per cent on properties worth over £250,000 but not more than £500,000, and then at 4 per cent on properties worth over £500,000.

STANDARD VARIABLE RATE

This is the mortgage rate that most borrowers pay – hence the term standard. It is variable in that the rate rises and falls in line with the Bank of England base rate. However, the margin above the base rate can vary, unlike with a tracker mortgage which rises and falls a set percentage above the base rate. Also the standard variable rate does not always move as soon as base rates are changed. Lenders can delay passing on cuts in interest rates and pass on any rises quickly boosting their profits.

STANDING ORDERS

These work in the same way as direct debits in that an agreed amount of money is taken out of your account at agreed intervals. However, with a standing order, the amount is chosen by you rather than by a third party like the gas or cable company. So while your mortgage will be paid by direct debit so that the lender can vary the amount deducted depending on the mortgage rate, a subscription to a club or union at a fixed amount may be paid by standing order.

Although standing orders are reliable, they don't come with the same in-built guarantees as direct debits which are regulated by the Direct Debit Scheme.

(See also **Direct Debits**.)

STATE EARNINGS RELATED PENSION (SERPS)

Started in 1978 by Labour minister Shirley Williams as an add-on to the basic state pension, SERPS is paid out of a worker's National Insurance contributions, with benefits based on the amount earned in a lifetime. However, the self-employed and those in contracted-out pension schemes do not pay towards this state top-up scheme.

Also fewer and fewer employees are members of SERPS as, since 1988, they have been allowed to contract out and have their relevant NI contributions paid into a company pension scheme or a personal pension. This incentive to opt out of SERPS was designed to help the government reduce the state's pension bill and offer people the opportunity to turn their National Insurance contributions into a bigger pot by investing in a personal pension run by an insurer or fund management company. The SERPS element of the pension is known as protected rights.

Over the years the level of SERPS rebates has been adjusted. Generally, older employees receive a larger rebate as an added incentive to contract out. However, it is these workers who would often be better of remaining within SERPS. Much depends on how well their rebates are invested. It is possible to contract back into SERPS at a later age.

Generally, men aged 44 or over and women aged 37 or over are advised not to contract out of SERPS or to contract back in if they have contracted out at an earlier age. This will not be possible, however, if they are members of a contracted-out company pension scheme as they will not have an option. They do have a choice, however, if they have their SERPS rebates paid into a personal pension.

A string of government decisions over the past couple of years have served to undermine the value of SERPS and make it far less attractive. Benefits for those retiring after 2000 are being reduced significantly. By 2010 benefits will fall by £600 million a year. This reduction in benefits will continue to hit people retiring over the ensuing thirty years. By 2020, the reduction will amount to £1.3 billion a year, by 2030 it will be £2.5 billion and by 2040 it will be £2.9 billion. These figures are calculated at today's values.

The changes to the SERPS benefit calculations are retrospective, which means people have made contributions based on benefit calculations that have now been replaced by less generous ones.

STORE CARDS

These work in the same way as a credit card but can be used only at a particular shop or group of shops. There are often perks such as discounts on goods when you first take out the card (10 per cent off your first purchase is a common incentive to take out a store card) but interest rates are very high compared to credit cards.

However, if you pay off the full balance each month by the required payment date, all your borrowing is free. If you are late paying or do not pay the full amount, you will usually be charged interest from the day you spent the money. Some store cards have a budget option where you pay in a set amount every month and can then borrow up to twenty-four times this amount.

One way to make the cards work for you is to take one out if you have a lot of spending to do, for example if you need to buy a lot of furniture – and take advantage of the initial discounts offered as an incentive. Then pay off the whole amount at the end of the interest-free period, using a cheap rate credit card, money you have saved up, or a much lower rate loan.

Don't confuse store cards with Reward cards which offer points for every pound you spend which can then be redeemed for goods or cash.

STUDENT ACCOUNTS

Banks offer some of the best banking deals available to students. It is in their best interests. For once a customer has opened a current account they are usually a customer for life – it is still more common to change your spouse than your bank account. In addition, undergraduates will become the high net-worth individuals of tomorrow, the profitable customers that all banks want to attract.

The main attraction of the student current accounts is an interest-free overdraft. Some banks offer this only in the first year, others for the entire course with an increasing limit. The account can also be used for a period after graduation which varies from six to twelve months.

In some cases, the account is automatically transferred to a graduate account which may offer an interest-free overdraft for up to three more years, but the limit will decrease every year as the student is expected to be working and repaying debts. Some banks also offer cheap loans to graduates for five years at a much lower rate than other personal loans.

Bank accounts for students offer various incentives in the hope that these new customers will stay with them after graduation. These should never be a factor in choosing the account though. They range from interest on current accounts in credit to book and CD vouchers or Railcards.

When choosing a student account what should I check for?

- The limit on interest-free overdrafts and how it changes during the course.

- The charges for going over the limit – some banks charge around 30 per cent.

- Whether you can bank by phone or Internet for convenience.

- What happens after you graduate?

STUDENT LOANS

Student debt is a fact of life, particularly now that many students must pay their own tuition fees. In addition to parental contributions, student loans continue to be a main source of income.

The Student Loan Scheme has been in existence since 1990 and a new student support loan was introduced for new entrants starting after September 1998. Both schemes offer students a source of finance to help meet their living costs whilst at college or university. From the academic year 1999/2000 the government brought in means testing where 25 per cent of the student support loan is means tested. This means testing replaced the existing system of maintenance grants and, depending on parental income, students were required to meet up to £1,000 towards the cost of tuition fees by using these loans or other means.

Unlike other sources of funding, student loans are subsidized by the government with an interest rate linked to the Retail Price Index allowing students to borrow finance at a rate of interest equal to the rate of inflation. This means the amount of money they pay back is equal in real terms to the amount they borrowed.

The figure that a student can borrow varies annually and is different for each scheme. It also depends on where the student is studying (there is a higher amount for London) and if they are living at home. Final-year students are eligible for a lower rate as funding is not required for the full summer period.

On leaving his or her degree course, the student must repay the money borrowed. Under the original mortgage-style scheme, the borrower is eligible to start repaying the loan the April after they graduate or otherwise leave their course. However, they can apply to defer these repayments if their gross income is less than 85 per cent of national average earnings (currently this figure is set at around £19,000 gross per annum but is reviewed annually). Repayments are collected by direct debit from the borrower's bank account. Depending on the number of loans taken out, repayments are either spread over sixty or eighty-four months.

Under the newer schemes (student support loans) the borrower is eligible to start repaying when their earnings have reached £10,000 or more per annum. The majority will have their gross earnings collected by the Inland

Revenue via their employer, i.e. directly from their salary. The repayments are calculated as a percentage of gross income – currently 9 per cent – above the £10,000 threshold. A graduate earning £20,000 a year would take thirteen years to pay off a £10,000 loan assuming interest rates remained at 2.5 per cent.

With both schemes, if the borrower's income falls beneath these threshold figures, collection of repayments will stop.

SUBSIDENCE

This occurs when the earth (usually clay) under your house shrinks and the building starts to move. The tell-tale signs are cracks in brickwork particularly around windows and doorframes. It is particularly common on the clay soils of the south-east. To rescue the house it is often necessary to underpin it by building deeper foundations and then to repair any damaged brickwork and straighten any uneven lintels and doorframes. However, even if the problem is corrected successfully, your property may still be difficult to sell because another insurer may be reluctant to take on the risk of a further claim.

Subsidence is the opposite of heave where the house moves upwards as the ground swells under it. This can happen when a tree growing near to a property is chopped down and there is suddenly an increased amount of water in the soil causing it to swell.

As soon as there are signs of subsidence, contact your insurance company. The average claim is currently about £8,000 and the average excess payable on this sort of claim is between £1,000 and £2,000.

SUPERMARKET BANKS

The main advantage of banking at the supermarket is convenience – financial services are available at the same extended hours as the store is open, not just during banking hours. It is now possible to have current and savings accounts at the supermarket as well as loans, many kinds of insurance, credit cards, pensions and mortgages.

In general, the rates will not be the very best, but they will beat most of the high-street competition. In some areas where bank branches are closing supermarkets could become the easiest option for those wanting financial services, and supermarket tills can be used to withdraw cash where free ATMs are not available, saving the customer money.

Each supermarket will have one or two products well worth considering and some which are not so good, so treat them like a pick and mix rather than buying everything from one. In addition to savings, loans and credit cards, you can buy insurance products.

At some supermarkets, if you use their credit card to buy food, you could get extra club card points. You should also check out if they have phone and Internet access to financial products – whether you can buy online or just get information.

SURRENDER VALUE

The amount you will receive back if you cash in an investment such as an endowment policy before the policy term is up.

(See also **Endowments**.)

SWAPS

One of a number of financial tools invented during the 1980s, swaps were engineered to meet the increasingly complex needs of big business. But the sight of whizz-kids making big profits for themselves and clients by using such schemes tempted some less than suitable users into the hothouse atmosphere of the City of London. Famous cases involved such organizations as Hammersmith and Fulham Council, which were eventually banned from using swaps by the courts.

Companies who want to borrow money use interest-rate swaps either to reduce the cost of borrowing or to match interest payments to their expected income.

Swaps are based on the idea of comparative advantage. One company will be able to borrow money by issuing bonds on different rates and terms compared to another. For instance, company A may want to borrow money at a fixed rate, which means it will be sure of how much its repayments on the bonds will be and can match these repayments with its income. But it may be able to issue bonds more cheaply it if pays a variable rate of interest. On the other hand company B may want variable rate finance but can only borrow on a fixed rate. Both would be better off by issuing the bonds they are able to, and then swapping their interest payments. Swaps are organized by merchant banks, which match one company with another.

SWEEPING

In order to make sure all of your surplus money is earning interest, some banks will arrange a sweep. This means that if there is over a certain amount of money in the current account, it will be swept into your savings account where it will earn interest or a higher rate of interest. Should the balance of the current account fall below an agreed limit, or if you have a big spend, then money is swept back to cover it.

For a sweep to work, you do have to have a savings and current account with the same bank but high-street banks' savings accounts rarely offer the best rates on savings so bear this in mind.

At the moment, few banks offer this service free; the rest

make it available only to customers who have opted for personal banking with a monthly charge. It is also possible to arrange your own sweeping if you have an online bank account.

T

TAKEOVERS AND MERGERS

When one company wants to swallow up another it mounts a takeover or merger. Takeovers can either be agreed or hostile. Agreed takeovers are often invited and involve the board of the target company recommending the takeover offer to shareholders. A hostile bid is uninvited. The aggressor makes an offer to the target company's shareholders which it hopes they will accept. Shareholders vote as to whether or not they want the takeover to go ahead.

TAXES

See **Capital Gains Tax, Income Tax, National Insurance Contributions** and **Stamp Duty**.

TELEVISION/TV BANKING

Television banking is an alternative to phone or Internet banking with the same twenty-four hour-convenience. It does not replace the high-street branch account but offers an additional way to manage your money. Customers can keep track of their current and savings accounts, pay bills, transfer money between accounts and review standing orders or direct debits. It is also possible to order foreign currency, arrange health or life cover or request a mortgage. (It's still advisable to shop around though as better rates elsewhere could outweigh the convenience.)

Customers will be assigned a special ID number and a separate security number. This number is entered on every visit and takes you straight into your own account. In order to use the service you currently need to be a cable television subscriber or to have a digital satellite dish and a box linked to an existing phone line. The TV remote control is effectively used as a mouse to select the options and the TV screen serves as a computer screen.

The main disadvantage is that it is not possible to print out any record of transactions as you can on a computer.

TERM ASSURANCE

See **Life Assurance**.

TESSAs

The Tax Exempt Special Savings Account, more commonly known by its acronym TESSA, was withdrawn from sale in April 1999. However, it still plays a major role in the finances of millions of savers who still have some £30 billion invested in these tax-free savings schemes which first went on sale in January 1991.

TESSAs were replaced by the new Individual Savings Account, ISA, which is a combination of TESSAs and PEPs. Although withdrawn from sale, existing TESSAs can continue to grow tax free and investors can continue to invest their yearly allowance until the five-year term of the TESSA is up. The total that can be invested in a TESSA over the five-year term is £9,000 with £3,000 in the first year followed by £1,800 in years two to four and £600 in year five subject to the overall £9,000 limit.

Once the TESSA has matured after five years, it is possible to retain the tax breaks by investing in a TESSA ISA. However, only the capital invested in the TESSA, up to the maximum of £9,000, can be switched into the TESSA ISA, but not any of the interest earned. Those whose TESSAs matured before they were withdrawn from sale could have invested in a follow-on TESSA. Once again, only the capital but not any interest could be rolled over into these schemes.

TESSA rates are generally poorer than ISA rates now that TESSAs have been withdrawn from sale. (Although some banks and building societies have started to pay compensation to TESSA savers who can prove they are worse off than ISA savers.) The lack of tough competition among providers means that many have taken the opportunity to cut rates knowing that some TESSA savers will take no action as they believe they are trapped in their scheme. However, it is possible to switch TESSAs to get a better rate and still retain the tax breaks. Not all TESSA providers accept transfers from other TESSAs, but many do and the rates can be significantly higher. However, investors cannot cash in one TESSA and then try to open another. The transfer must be made directly from one provider to another.

TRACKER FUNDS

These are unit trust funds that aim to track the movements in a particular stock-market index – usually the FTSE All Share or the FTSE 100 or Footsie. They are passively rather than actively managed funds in that there is no fund manager buying and selling shares on a regular basis to try to improve the performance of the fund. Instead, the shares that make up the fund are selected to reflect the index as a whole. These share holdings are only changed when the shares that make up the index change.

Many fund managers fail to even match the performance of the stock market which is why tracker funds were first introduced and became so popular. At least investors were guaranteed that their investments would perform as well as the stock market as a whole (there is, however, a slight underperformance to take into account the charges). The fact that tracker funds have low charges (there are no expensive fund managers to pay) also boosted their appeal. However, there has been a backlash against tracker funds in the past year or so. Investors can do better if they pick a good performing actively managed fund. The gamble is knowing which funds will perform well.

(See also **Active Management**, **Indices** and **Unit Trusts**.)

TRAVELLERS' CHEQUES

The main advantage of these is security – you cannot cash them without proof of identity, usually a passport. If they are stolen, you are automatically covered for their value and many suppliers will undertake to replace them for you within twenty-four hours (although this will depend on where you are in the world). For added security, make a list of the numbers printed on them and keep it separately, as well as details of the twenty-four-hour international help line of the supplier.

Travellers' cheques have certain advantages over other

forms of holiday spending. Outside of cities and big towns it may be hard to find a bank to change sterling or an ATM to use your credit or debit card. Some outlets may not accept credit cards and few travellers want to travel with large amounts of cash. However, many hotels and retailers will accept travellers' cheques as a form of payment. Travellers' cheques are not available in every currency, but in certain parts of the world international currencies such as US dollars are widely acceptable.

The drawback to travellers' cheques is that you do have to pay commission twice – once when you buy them and then again when you cash them. They will therefore cost a little more in terms of commission than if you were just changing currency, but they are generally sold at a better rate of exchange. Shopping around for the best rate can make a difference as some high-street banks charge twice as much as others and travel agents generally give the worst rates.

TRUSTS

One of the most efficient ways of avoiding, or reducing, inheritance tax, is to shelter the relevant assets in a trust. It is also a useful way of avoiding income tax and capital gains tax.

Trustees are appointed to look after the assets held in a trust on behalf of the people who are supposed to benefit from the trust's proceeds, known as the beneficiaries. Trustees are the legal owners of the trust's assets and are obliged to act in the best interests of the beneficiaries.

Trusts need to be set up with the help of professional advice. The trust is usually created by a document, the trust deed, which names the people involved and sets out the terms of the trust. Trustees should be given the widest possible powers of investment and delegation and the terms should be as flexible as possible in case of unforeseen eventualities. Once created, a trust is almost always irrevocable, even if the person who set up the trust (the donor or settler) is also a trustee, although it may be possible to secure a variation on the original terms through the courts.

There are several types of trust. The main ones are:

- Accumulation and maintenance trust. These minimize inheritance tax, normally for the benefit of children and grandchildren. The income may be used for education and maintenance among other things, and advances may be granted on request.

- Absolute trust. A useful tool in the avoidance of income tax and capital gains tax (CGT). It gives beneficiaries sole entitlement to both income and capital, with the proceeds payable at age eighteen. For inheritance tax purposes, the assets are a potentially exempt transfer, which means they are tax-free provided the donor survives for seven years.

- Interest in possession trust. This trust pays income to named beneficiaries. The capital may be paid to a second named beneficiary on death of the first – a child on the death of the mother, for instance. Useful for inheritance tax planning or CGT avoidance.

- Discretionary trust. This allows trustees to pay income or capital to people in a specified category such as children or grandchildren. It may be used to save income tax, CGT and inheritance tax.

(See also **Inheritance Tax**.)

U

UNIT TRUSTS

Unit trusts are the most popular way of investing in shares because the initial investment needed is relatively modest, the risks of investing are spread among a wide number of shares and the costs are low.

Investors also have the option of investing on a regular monthly basis or investing a lump sum. This means that those with as little as £50 a month to set aside or £500 as a lump sum can have access to the performance of the stock market, but without the high costs of directly investing in shares. With minimum dealing charges to buy shares starting at £10 to £15, investing £100 or even £250 is not economic.

Also investors get access to greater purchasing power. A single investor may only be able to afford one or two shares, whereas the unit trust will invest in dozens of different companies (usually fifty plus). As an individual, if one share performs badly the investor can lose significantly. The trust can absorb a few poor investments as the risks of investing are spread so widely.

To spread the risks further, many investors invest in several individual trusts to build up a unit trust portfolio. This can then meet different investment needs, for example, a long-term low-risk growth fund for long-term security, a higher risk speculative fund to gamble on a quick profit and some overseas funds so the investor is not dependent on the UK market alone.

The other benefit is that the investment decisions are made by a fund management company so the investor does not have to make his or her own investment decisions.

Unit trusts are also very flexible. There is no minimum investment period so investors can get to their money at any time without penalty. Investors can increase their investment or withdraw part of it and if their investment priorities change they can switch to another fund, for example, one that has a more cautious approach to investing.

Unit trusts are therefore ideal for those who want to invest in the stock market, but without having to make their own complex investment decisions, without having to pay high costs and with relatively small sums of money.

Historically the stock market has outperformed savings accounts, which adds to the appeal.

On regular savings of £50 a month, an equity investment in a UK All Companies fund outstripped the returns on a savings account deposit after five years by £1,421. The difference increased to £6,188 over ten years and £14,484 after fifteen years.

First introduced some seventy years ago, unit trusts have now become the bedrock of many investors' portfolios. More than £250 billion is managed by unit trust fund managers for more than 14 million unit-holder accounts. However, unit trusts do not just appeal to private investors. Pension funds, unitized insurance investments (insurance products investing in unit trusts) and in-house insurance investments (life companies' own funds) also account for a significant amount of unit trust investments.

Unit trusts are a type of collective investment, which simply means that the money of hundreds – if not thousands – of investors is pooled or collected together and then invested.

Run by fund management companies and fund managers (these can be independently owned or part of larger financial institutions such as life companies, banks and building societies), each trust fund is divided into equal portions – or units.

Anyone investing in the fund is allocated units in proportion to the size of the investment they have made.

The price of these units is governed principally by the value of the underlying investments held by the fund.

So if the underlying investments – which in turn are affected by rises and falls in the stock market – rise in value, the value of each unit will increase.

Investing in a unit trust is fairly straightforward. Investors can either deal directly by buying from the unit trust group itself, or they can buy units through an intermediary such as an independent financial adviser. Banks, building societies, life insurance companies, fund managers, financial advisers and Internet investment brokers all sell unit trusts.

Although the costs of investing in unit trusts can be as little as 1 per cent of the amount invested, some trusts have much higher charges.

These charges are included in the spread – this is the difference between the price you pay for your units (i.e. the offer price) and the price you get when you sell (the bid price).

The offer price – the higher of the two – can be as much as 5 or 6 per cent more than the bid price. So even if the value of the units was the same on the day the units were bought and the day they were sold, investors will still be 5 or 6 per cent worse off.

So investors need to wait until the unit price has risen by more than that amount in order to make a profit.

The spread covers commission paid to the financial adviser who sells the product as well as dealing costs. Most trusts are valued daily and the buying and selling prices for unit trusts are published in the financial press. However, some papers may only print the mid-price – halfway between the two.

A newer type of unit trust known as an Open-ended Investment Company or OEIC only has one price for its shares – there is no offer-to-bid spread.

The spread on unit trusts is why they – along with all stock-market based investments – should ideally be seen as a minimum three- to five-year investment. That way investors have a greater chance of recouping the costs of investing (and hopefully make a profit) and should be able to ride out any rises and falls in the stock market.

It is, however, possible to reduce these costs. Included in the charges is usually a commission payment of around 3 to 5 per cent for the adviser (or salesman) who sold the investment. However, an increasing number of financial intermediaries now rebate their commission usually by investing the commission in additional units which can reduce the initial costs of investing to zero.

In addition to the initial charge, there is also an annual management charge which is usually between 0.5 and 1.5 per cent.

Although unit trusts spread the risks of investing by investing in a wide range of shares, risks do vary from trust to trust.

Any stock-market based investment carries a risk and unit trusts come with the warning that the value of your units can fall as well as rise.

To help investors select the unit trust most suitable to meet their needs, trusts are split into investment sectors. These reflect the geographical as well as specialist nature of the investment remit of the fund manager.

The most popular unit trust funds invest in the UK stock markets; however, overseas trusts investing in markets such as Europe, the USA and Far East also feature in the top sales (depending on whether these markets are in favour or not). As such the use of unit trusts as a means to diversify into global stock markets for relatively little cost should not be overlooked.

The largest investment sectors are UK All Companies, UK General Bonds and UK Equity Income. These have a very wide investment remit. UK Smaller Companies, European and Far East funds are slightly more specific in their investment remit and, finally, property, UK gilt and global emerging markets funds have an even tighter investment remit.

Unit trusts can have two types of units in issue: income units and accumulation units. With income units, any income distributions made can be paid out to the client or reinvested to buy further units.

With accumulation units, any income distributions are automatically rolled up in the price of the units. In most cases, where accumulation units are available and income is not required by the investor, accumulation units will be purchased.

Any gains made on investments within a unit trust are not liable to tax. This makes unit trust more tax efficient than dealing in share purchases. However, income taken by investors from a unit trust or gains made on the sale of units are liable to tax.

Any income payments received are paid with some tax deducted. Investors must declare this income on their tax return. However, basic rate taxpayers need not pay any more tax. Only higher rate taxpayers are liable for additional income tax.

Capital gains tax may also be payable on the sale of units if the investor's gain (profit) from the sale of the units exceeds (along with any other gains) the capital gains tax threshold. CGT is then paid at the investor's top rate of tax on any gains above the threshold.

It is, however, very easy for investors to avoid paying

any income or capital gains tax by investing in a unit trust via an Individual Savings Account, or ISA.

(See also **CAT Standards, Individual Savings Accounts, Investment Trusts, Open-ended Investment Companies.**)

V

VALUE ADDED TAX

This tax is collected by suppliers of goods and services on behalf of Customs and Excise. The current rate on all but a few exempt or zero-rated goods is 17.5 per cent. Insurance, finance and education are all exempt; food, children's clothing, books and newspapers are zero-rated.

Businesses must register for VAT if their annual taxable turnover is above the VAT threshold, currently £54,000. Each VAT registered business has a VAT number and if you are charged VAT you are entitled to ask for this number to check that VAT is being deducted by a registered business.

VENTURE CAPITAL TRUSTS

Designed to encourage individuals to invest in certain types of small higher-risk trading companies not listed on the stock exchange, Venture Capital Trusts offer significant tax breaks to those prepared to invest in these unquoted companies.

Invented by Chancellor Kenneth Clarke in his 1994

budget and introduced on 6 April 1995, venture capital trusts spread the risk of investing in unquoted companies by spreading investments among a large number of different investments.

In this respect VCTs are similar to investment trusts. They are run by fund managers with investors purchasing shares in the VCT which in turn invests the money raised in trading companies, providing them with funds to help them develop and grow.

Because the shares of a VCT are listed on the London Stock Exchange they can be sold in the same way as any other Stock Exchange quoted investment.

The main attraction of VCTs is not the investment potential but the tax breaks. VCTs investors are entitled to various income tax and capital gains tax relief and VCTs are entitled to exemption from corporation tax on any gains arising on the disposal of their investments. Investors are not only exempt from income tax on dividends from ordinary shares in VCTs – known as dividend relief – they also receive income tax relief at the rate of 20 per cent for the tax year in which an investment is made in VCT shares – provided that they are held for at least five years.

Investors are also exempt from capital gains tax on gains arising on disposals of ordinary shares in VCTs and can defer capital gains on the sale of assets provided that gain is reinvested in a VCT.

The maximum that can be invested in a VCT is £100,000 per tax year and tax reliefs are given on both new and secondhand shares.

Tax relief is given once shares have been issued and the

investor tells his or her Tax Office and sends in a certificate provided by the VCT. The income tax relief reduces the investor's income tax liability for the tax year in which the VCT shares are issued. Any relief which cannot be used in that year is lost.

Tax relief will be lost if the investor disposes of shares less than five years after they are issued.

Although VCTs cannot invest in companies quoted on the official list of any stock exchange, their shares may be listed on the Alternative Investment Market of the London Stock Exchange (AIM) or dealt in on OFEX.

Most companies qualify to be included in a VCT, however, there are some exemptions including companies dealing in land, commodities, futures, shares and other financial instruments, those providing legal or accounting services, property developers, farmers and hotel management companies.

W

WAIVER OF PREMIUM

For an extra premium, you can insure premiums – or monthly contributions – into a personal pension or life insurance contract against you being unable to afford them due to accident, sickness or unemployment for a limited period of time, usually a year. This cover is important as some (particularly older) policies are very inflexible and if you fail to keep up with regular monthly premiums you can be penalized. Even if there are no penalties, the fact that you do not pay into your policy for several months can impact severely on the final pay-out.

WAP – WIRELESS APPLICATION PROTOCOL

One step on from Internet banking, WAP banking enables customers to get access to account information and transfer money from a WAP-enabled mobile phone. It means that banking can be done any time, any place and anywhere.

WAP technology is a platform which allows Internet

content to be viewed through a mobile phone device such as a WAP telephone, a pager or a personal organizer. The Internet content is stripped down to a basic text format.

Some banks have sites that are more advanced than others allowing customers to look up mortgage quotations and calculate the cost of a personal loan. It will not be long before most banking transactions and even share dealing can be done using a WAP phone. Currently WAP services are free, although customers do have to pay for the cost of the call. Some financial service providers have been issuing free WAP phones as an incentive to customers to take up these new services.

To access a financial site such as one run by a bank, those with WAP phones can go via a 'portal' – often run by the mobile phone company – which links users to a range of useful sites. Or they can go directly to the WAP address of the bank or other financial institution.

WAP addresses are similar to web addresses except that they start with the letters wap instead of www. So the wap address may be wap.mybank.co.uk instead of www.mybank.co.uk.

WARRANTIES

Usually known as extended warranties or extended guarantees, these insurance policies are taken out to pay for repairs to household electrical items, computers and even cars for a certain period of time. For most domestic appliances the warranty lasts for five years. The reason why these policies are known as 'extended' is that appliances are usually covered by a free guarantee in the first year of ownership.

The extended warranty market is worth over £400 million a year, but fewer than one in five householders buy a warranty when purchasing a domestic appliance partly because of the cost. In most cases a warranty covers the cost of parts and labour. If the machine is beyond repair, you should get a replacement or cash repair. They are available from three main sources: the retailer selling the goods, the manufacturer or a specialist insurance company.

Warranties have been exposed as poor value for money. While a warranty on a washing machine may cost up to £200, the average cost of repairs during the warranty period is nearer to £50. It is possible to buy a cheaper policy from an insurance company that will cover all domestic items, not just one. In addition, some credit and gold cards will cover appliances for free if they are bought using the card and registered within a certain period (up to sixty days) after purchase.

WARRANTS

Warrants allow investors to buy a certain number of a company's shares at a fixed price at a fixed time in the future. They are issued both by investment trusts and trading companies. Warrants are either handed out free to investors as part of a new share issue or can be bought on the stock market, as they are quoted securities in their own right.

Warrants can make the investor money in several ways. If the warrant price rises the warrants can be sold at a profit. Or the investor can keep the warrant with the intention of exercising it. Or, as warrants are high risk, they can be combined with a low-risk portfolio of gilts or other bonds to provide extra growth potential.

An investor exercises a warrant when he or she wants to take up his or her right to buy the underlying shares. The price is fixed by the terms and conditions of the warrant and is called the exercise price or strike price. Exercising a warrant normally only becomes worthwhile if the cost of the warrant plus its exercise price is *less* than the price of the ordinary shares in the market. So if a company's warrants have an exercise price of 200p and the ordinary shares in the market are trading at 225p, then it is worthwhile exercising the warrants and subscribing for more shares, as an immediate profit of 25p per share is available. In this case the warrants are said to have an intrinsic value of 25p.

In a small number of circumstances it is worth exercising a warrant when the exercise price is *above* the ordinary share price. This happens when the exercise price and the ordinary share price are close together and the cost of buying the shares through a stockbroker, including dealing commission, is higher than exercising the warrants.

The most common issuers of warrants are investment trusts. While warrants give holders the *right* to buy a trust's shares they do not impose an *obligation* on the investor to do so. Warrants do not always have to be exercised on a specific date in the future. Sometimes they can be exercised during a specific period, such as three weeks.

The big attraction of warrants is that they give investors exposure to the performance of a trust's shares, but at a fraction of the cost of the shares. Warrant holders do not receive dividends. Many recent investment trust issues have handed out free warrants – normally one free warrant for every five ordinary shares – as a sweetener to investors.

Exercising a warrant means new shares have to be issued to satisfy the warrant-related demand. This can dilute the trust's net asset value (NAV). Investors may well see investment trusts publish two sets of performance figures, showing both its net asset value assuming all outstanding warrants were exercised – the diluted NAV – and the undiluted NAV, which makes no allowance for the effect of warrants.

Two other important terms to remember are warrant gearing and warrant premium. Gearing is expressed as a ratio – the share price divided by the warrant price. If the share price is 150p and the warrant 45p, the gearing is 3.3. This figure tells investors that the warrant gives them full exposure to the fortunes of the shares but at only one-third of their cost. The higher the gearing the more exposure at a fraction of the cost.

A warrant's premium is the percentage by which the warrant price plus the exercise price exceeds the share price. If the exercise price is 100p and the warrant price is 44p with a share price of 120p the premium is 20 per cent

(24 as a percentage of 120). In this case the shares would have to rise by 20 per cent before it becomes worthwhile to exercise the warrants.

WEDDING INSURANCE

The average wedding now costs over £11,000 so for many people insurance could be a wise choice. Policies cover damage to wedding outfits, photos or videos, loss or damage of wedding presents, flowers and wedding rings. If anyone is injured on the day or the wedding car does not turn up, then the policy will also pay out. The reception can also be covered in case the caterers do not turn up or something happens to the (indoor) venue to make it unusable. It is even possible to include the wedding cake in the policy. The cost and range of cover does vary greatly so check out several companies. As a rough guide, basic policies cost between £40 and £50.

Some household contents insurance policies will automatically cover a period before and after the wedding to protect anything wedding related while it is in the house as long as the company is notified the wedding is taking place – damage to gifts, wedding clothes, flowers or food, for example, will be covered.

For insurance against weather ruining an outdoor reception, see **Pluvius Insurance**.

WILLS

The main purpose of a will is to ensure that decisions about how your property – your estate – is divided upon death are made by you and are carried out as you would want. If you die intestate (without a will) your belongings are divided up by the state. Each year some 53,000 people with estates worth more than £5,000 die intestate. If no relatives can be traced to inherit, the taxman gets the lot.

It is a myth that if you are married your spouse will get everything so you do not need to make a will. He or she will only get everything up to £125,000 plus your personal possessions. Anything remaining is divided in two:

- half goes to any children over eighteen

- half goes in trust during your spouse's lifetime with your spouse having access only to the income, not the capital. On the death of your spouse, this half also goes to your children.

This means that if your home is worth more than £125,000, your spouse could lose their home.

If you are married with no children, the spouse will get everything up to £200,000, plus your possessions, with the remainder being divided among your family starting with your parents. If you have no surviving parents then your brothers and sisters will inherit – even if you no longer have or want any contact with them. This is why a will is important. Even if you wish your estate to be divided in the way it would should you die intestate a will enables you to make specific bequests (such as leaving a treasured possession to a particular friend or relative).

When you marry, any previous will you have made is nullified and your new spouse becomes your beneficiary. When you divorce it is vital to make a new will, particularly in Scotland as it remains valid, which could also cause complications.

The Law Society recommends that you use a solicitor to make a will. If you write it yourself, any small mistake (or illegible handwriting) may render it invalid. It costs around £60 for a single will or £100 for a couple. By getting professional advice you can also address such issues as what if one of the beneficiaries that you intend to receive a gift, dies before you. Also a solicitor will ensure that the will is correctly witnessed – your signature must be witnessed by two competent and independent people, present at the same time. Witnesses and their husbands or wives must not benefit from the will, so it is obviously important to select the witnesses from people who will not benefit.

A will is particularly important for those who are unmarried and cohabiting as the partner has no legal rights to inherit property, even if they have shared that person's home and life for many years.

A will should not be altered. Any changes should not be made to the original document but must be either made in a codicil (a supplement to a will) or a new will should be drawn up. Wills should be stored in a safe place – either with your solicitor or bank, but there will be a charge – or at the probate office.

(See also **Inheritance Tax**.)

WINDFALLS

This is the term given to free shares or cash payments paid to investors, savers, borrowers and policyholders with building societies or life companies that were formerly mutual (owned by their members) but have demutualized and either been taken over or listed on the stock market. The windfall is either paid out of reserves in the life fund (if it is a mutual life company) or from the surpluses built up by the building society.

To deter members from forcing a mutual to pay a windfall, many have now set up schemes to deter potential windfall seekers who are also known as carpetbaggers. Most are charitable assignment schemes which require all new investors to sign away any windfall payments to charity for so many years (five or ten years after opening an account) in the event of a merger or conversion to a plc.

(See also **Building Societies** and **Mutuals**.)

WITH-PROFITS

With-profits investments are run by life insurance companies and – as their name implies – investors literally share in the profits of the fund. Hence the term, with-profits. Endowment policies, personal pensions and life insurance bonds can all be of the with-profits variety.

Instead of the value of each investor's investment rising and falling in line with rises and falls in the underlying value of the shares and other investments held by the fund, rises and falls in the stock markets are smoothed out by a system of bonuses.

In return for a commitment to save a regular amount over a set period of time, the life insurance company offers a sum assured – the minimum the policyholder would receive if they continued to pay the regular premiums until maturity if they were to die before the maturity date. To this sum assured the company adds bonuses – the investor's share of the profits of the fund. These are known as annual or reversionary bonuses. There may also be a final or terminal bonus when the investment or policy matures. Once added the annual bonuses cannot be taken away. However, the terminal bonus which can account for as much as half of the total pay-out is not guaranteed. When looking at past performance and selecting an investment, investors should therefore be wary of companies that rely too heavily on terminal bonuses to boost performance as these may not be maintained in future.

The theory of with-profits investments is that when stock markets perform well investors do not receive the full benefit of this investment performance. However, in years when investments perform less well the 'reserves' built up in the fund can ensure that investment returns are maintained. As a result, sharp rises and falls are ironed out. So with-profits funds are considered safer than less traditional types of life insurance investment.

The other types of investment fund offered by life insurance companies are unit-linked and unitized with-profits. These newer types of investment fund are now far more popular than the traditional with-profits investments. This is because investors benefit from the full growth in the stock market. Unit-linked funds rise and fall with the underlying movements in the life insurance investment fund with investors owning units in this fund. They do not have to wait until the end of the year for their share of the growth of the fund. The price of units rises and falls daily in line with movements in the stock market and other investments held by the fund.

Unitized with-profits are similar in that investors own units in a fund but they also benefit from bonuses. These latest versions of with-profits policies are designed to be easier for investors to understand. Rather than declaring a sum assured investors purchase units in a with-profits fund. Rather than adding bonuses to a sum assured, the life company increases the fund's unit price to reflect, over a whole year, an increase equivalent to the declared bonus rate.

At the time of writing, average unit-linked ten-year

savings plans were outperforming the average ten-year with-profits saving plans.

Investors who take out long-term with-profits investments such as endowment policies or pensions should be aware that they are committing to invest a certain amount of money over a specific period. If they break this contract by demanding their money back before the end of the term they will receive a surrender value. In the early years of a with-profits investment these surrender values may be less than has been paid into the investment. As years go on, surrender values will remain less than their investment would be worth if it were left alone.

WITH-PROFITS BONDS

These are usually single premium investments in a life insurance with-profits fund. They are riskier than building society savings accounts but tend to pay a higher rate of return. They are not as risky as most stock-market based investments and as such tend to appeal to older and more cautious investors looking for a relatively secure home for their money with a better rate of return than a savings account. Current compound average returns per year are running at between 5 and 10 per cent depending on the bond and the length of time it has been running.

As with all with-profits plans, bonds offer two types of bonuses – annual and terminal. Annual bonuses once earned and added to the policy cannot be withdrawn even if the stock market crashes. So an element of the policy is guaranteed. Investors will not see their money fall to below that amount; however, there may be a market value adjuster (MVA) – a deduction to take account of recent market falls. The MVA is designed to protect the insurance company from using its reserves to pay out to investors who want to cash in following a severe market fall.

Terminal bonuses may be earned after the bond has been held for a minimum length of time, usually five years. This can be thought of as a loyalty bonus. But if the stock market has fallen or been volatile you may find that this terminal bonus is small or non-existent. Watch out for penalties for cashing in your bond before five years are up. Investors are usually subject to early encashment charges. This will be shown as a surrender value.

Also note that the charges for with-profits bonds tend to be higher than for unit-linked investments such as unit trusts. Those who invest £20,000 can find that the value of their investment falls to nearer £19,000 on day one as a result of initial charges and that total charges over ten years add up to more than £3,500. Typically the initial charge is 5 per cent. However, there is also an allocation rate – how much of your investment before the initial charge is taken into account. Allocation rates can vary from 97 per cent to 102 per cent with companies often applying higher allocation rates for larger investments. The combined effect of these two factors determines how much of your capital is invested on day one. This is known as the effective allocation rate and is the percentage of your initial capital invested after the application of both the initial charge and the allocation rate.

All proceeds from a with-profits bond are deemed to have had basic rate tax deducted at source. This is similar to building society or bank interest; however, non-taxpayers cannot reclaim the tax paid. Higher rate taxpayers, on the other hand, still have to suffer a further tax liability. However, higher rate taxpayers can offset part, or even all, of this potential extra tax as the first 5 per cent of any withdrawal each year, for up to twenty years, is treated as being a return of capital and as such does not suffer the potential further income tax charge. There is no personal liability to capital gains tax on a with-profits bond investment.

WORKING FAMILIES TAX CREDIT

The working families tax credit (WFTC) was introduced in October 1999 and replaced the Family Credit. Administered by the Inland Revenue (from April 2000 the credit was payable through the pay packet), the tax credit is means tested and is aimed at parents who have one or more children and work at least 16 hours a week. There is a basic tax credit plus additional tax credits for each child. In addition, parents can claim a childcare tax credit which pays up to 70 per cent of the eligible costs of childcare up to a maximum cost of £100 for one child and £150 for two or more children. The WFTC is calculated by adding all the credits together. If the income of the family (after tax and national insurance contributions) is above a set threshold, then the credit is reduced. As from April 2001 the WFTC will provide families with a minimum income guarantee of £214 a week for a family with one child and from October 2001 to £225 per week.

Families also benefit from the Children's Tax Credit, introduced in April 2001, a non-means tested tax credit of £10.00 a week from April 2001. The tax allowance is £5,200. However, tax relief is restricted to 10 per cent tax relief giving a total tax saving of £520. The Children's Tax Credit replaces the married couple's allowance which was scrapped in April 2000.

In the first year of a child's life the credit rises to £20 a week from April 2002.

The Children's Tax Credit is reduced where the main earner is a higher rate taxpayer.

X

EX AND CUM PRICES

These terms refer to shares or bonds and relate to the rights associated with those securities – normally dividend payments or extra share issues. If a share price published in the newspaper has xd next to it, this stands for ex-dividend. Investors who buy shares xd will not be entitled to the next dividend payment. This is a stock-market settlement detail. Once a company announces it is to pay a dividend and the date of that payment, then the Stock Exchange selects a cut-off point after which new shareholders will not earn the dividend. The cut-off point is known as the xd date. Once the dividend is paid the xd period finishes. In the same way, when a company announces it is to issue new shares through a rights issue there is a cut-off date after which new shareholders will not qualify. This is the ex-rights date shown as xr next to a share price.

The opposite of xd and xr are cum dealings. Cum means including any rights. As most shares on the stock market are cum dividend or cum rights the term is not usually printed next to a share price. It is assumed a share or bond is dealing cum rights unless otherwise stated.

Y

YIELD

This is the technical term for the income people earn from their investments. Yields are applied to shares, bonds – both fixed interest and variable rate – and bank and building society deposits.

Yield is always expressed as a percentage. To calculate a yield, take the amount of gross income earned and divide it by the market price of the share or bond and multiply by 100. Market price and yield have an inverse relationship. As the price of a bond or share rises, the yield from the interest or dividend falls and vice versa. A yield from a deposit account is simply the amount of interest paid.

The City also talks about yield curves. The big commercial banks pay different rates of interest depending on the length of large deposits made with them by other financial institutions. They pay low rates on deposits held in overnight accounts and steadily higher ones on deposits held for one month, three months, six months and so on. This reflects the money market's belief that interest rates are likely to rise over time. This series of rising rates is the yield curve. If the money markets believe interest rates are going to fall in the long term, the yield curve will turn negative, with rates for long-term deposits lower than shorter-term deposits.

Z

ZEROS

Zeros is the name given to zero dividend preference shares, which although they are a class of share are more like bonds although they do not pay interest in the normal way. Zeros are a class of share issued by investment trusts.

When a zero is taken out, no interest is paid to the investor until the end of its life. The advantage is that when interest is paid, it is generally at a higher rate than with many other sorts of bonds. This rate of interest, known as the gross redemption yield, is set at the beginning so investors know what their return will be.

Another advantage is that during the life of the zero there is no tax to pay as no interest is being earned. As investors know what and when the return will be, they can plan ahead for capital gains tax. They are also flexible as they can be sold at any point during their lifespan.

The best way to buy a zero is at its launch. This way you can buy direct, avoiding dealers' charges and the zero will be cheaper. However, you can buy a zero at any time with some representing good value with only four or five years to run.

There are no guarantees with zeros but they are more secure than some other forms of investments. One thing to check before buying is the hurdle rate. This indicates the rate of growth the zero must achieve each year by the wind-up date to repay the promised gross redemption yield. A negative hurdle is good news, it means that the asset value of the fund can fall and still be high enough to repay at the end.

Useful Addresses

'Age Concern Guide to Raising
  Capital From Your Home'
Age Concern
Astral House, 1268 London Road
London SW16 4ER
Telephone 020 8765 7200
Web site www.ace.org.uk

Association of British Insurers
51 Gresham Street
London EC2V 7HQ
Telephone 020 7600 3333
Web site www.abi.org.uk

Association of Consulting Actuaries
1 Wardrobe Place
London EC4V 5AH
Telephone 020 7248 3163
Web site www.aca.org.uk

Association of Friendly Societies
Royex House
Aldermanbury Square
London EC2V 7HR
Telephone 020 7397 9550

Association of Investment Trust
  Companies (AITC)
Durrant House
8–13 Chiswell Street
London EC1Y 4YY
Telephone 020 7431 5222
Web site www.its.co.uk

Association of Policy Market
  Makers
Telephone 020 7739 3949

Association of Residential Letting
  Agents (ARLA)
Telephone 01494 431 680

Association of Unit Trust and
  Investment Funds (AUTIF)
65 Kingsway, London WC2B 6TD
Telephone 020 8207 1361
  (9 a.m. to 9 p.m., 7 days a week)
Web site www.investmentfunds.
  org.uk

British Insurance and Investment
  Brokers Association (BIIBA)
Biiba House, 14 Bevis Marks,
  London EC3A 7NT
Telephone 020 7623 9043
Web site www.biiba.org.uk

Charities Aid Foundation
25 Kings Hill Avenue, West
  Malling
Kent ME19 4TA
Telephone 01732 520 000
Web site www.cafonline.org

Council of Mortgage Lenders
3 Savile Row, London W1X 1AF
Telephone 020 7437 0075
Web site www.cml.org.uk

Ethical Investment Research
  Information Service (EIRIS)
Telephone 020 7840 5700

Equifax
Dept 1E, PO Box 3001, Glasgow
  G81 2DT

Experian Ltd
Consumer Help Service, PO Box
  8000, Nottingham NG1 5GX

The Financial Ombudsman Service
South Quay Plaza, 183 Marsh Wall
London E14 9SR
Telephone 020 7676 1000
Web site www.financial-
  ombudsman.org.uk

Financial Services Authority
25 The North Colonnade, Canary
  Wharf, London E14 5HS
Telephone 020 7676 1000
Web site www.fsa.gov.uk

Financial Services Compensation
  Scheme
Cotton's Centre, Cottons Lane
  London SE1 2QB
Telephone 020 7367 6000
Web site www.the-ics.org.uk

Institute of Actuaries
Staple Inn Hall, High Holborn
London WC1V 7QJ
Telephone 020 7632 2100
Web site www.actuaries.org.uk

IFA Promotion (for details of
  independent financial advisers in
  your area)
Telephone 0117 971 1177

Law Society
Telephone 0207 242 1222
Web site www.make-a-will.org.uk
For Scotland, call 0131 226 7411 or
  www.scotlaw.org.uk

National Association of Citizens'
  Advice Bureaux
115–123 Pentonville Rd
London N1 9LZ
Telephone 020 7833 2181

National Debtline
Telephone 0121 359 8501

National Savings
Telephone 0645 645 000
  (8.30 a.m. to 8 p.m. Mon–Fri, and
  9 a.m. to 1 p.m. Saturday)
Web site
  www.nationalsavings.co.uk

Occupational Pensions Advisory
  Service (OPAS)
Telephone 020 7233 8080

The Pensions Tracing Service
Telephone 0191 225 6316

ProShare
Telephone 0207 220 1730
Web site www.proshare.org.uk

Register of fee-based advisers
Telephone 0870 01 31 925

Registry of Friendly Societies
Victory House, 30–24 Kingsway
London WC2B 6ES
Telephone 020 7663 5025

Safe Home Income Plans
374–378 Ewell Rd, Surbiton
Surrey KT6 7BB
Telephone 020 8390 8166

Society of Practitioners of
  Insolvency
4th Floor, Halton House, 20–23
  Holborn, London EC2N 2JE
Telephone 020 7831 6563

Subsidence Claims Advisory
  Bureau
Telephone 01424 733 727
Web site www.bureauinsure.co.uk

UK Social Investment Forum
Web site www.uksif.org

extracts reading groups

competitions books new

discounts extracts extracts

competitions extracts

books new discounts events

events books extracts

reading groups

new extracts reading groups

new titles reading groups

interviews events new

reading groups books events extracts

books discounts

new books events interviews

events new events new books extracts

discounts extracts discounts books

www.panmacmillan.com

extracts events reading groups

competitions books extracts new